Animal Rights
and
Human Obligations

EDITED
BY

TOM REGAN
North Carolina State University

PETER SINGER
La Trobe University

PRENTICE-HALL, INC., ENGLEWOOD CLIFFS, NEW JERSEY

Library of Congress Cataloging in Publication Data
Main entry under title:

Animal rights and human obligations.

Bibliography: p. 246
1. Animals, Treatment of—Addresses, essays,
lectures. 2. Animals, Treatment of—Moral and
religious aspects—Addresses, essays, lectures.
I. Regan, Tom II. Singer, Peter.
HV4711.A56   179'.3   75–29432
ISBN 0–13–037531–4
ISBN 0–13–037523–3 pbk.

© 1976 by PRENTICE-HALL, INC., Englewood Cliffs, N.J.

10 9 8 7 6 5 4 3 2 1

Printed in the United States of America

PRENTICE-HALL INTERNATIONAL, INC., London
PRENTICE-HALL OF AUSTRALIA, PTY. LTD., Sydney
PRENTICE-HALL OF CANADA, LTD., Toronto
PRENTICE-HALL OF INDIA PRIVATE LIMITED, New Delhi
PRENTICE-HALL OF JAPAN, INC., Tokyo
PRENTICE-HALL OF SOUTHEAST ASIA (PTE.), Singapore

PREFACE

Although human beings eat other animals, experiment upon them, and destroy their habitats, we rarely pause to consider whether our practices toward them are ethically defensible.

Now there are signs of a reconsideration of our usual attitude to animals. The environmental movement has made millions aware of what we have done to wild animals. When whole species disappear forever, we can hardly fail to think about what we have done. New discoveries about the abilities of nonhuman animals, including the ability of chimpanzees to learn a complex sign language, have made us realize how closely related we are to the other animals. The threat of global famine has led to a spate of articles pointing out that modern methods of rearing animals for food waste more protein than they produce, and this in turn leads some people to ask, If the mass rearing and slaughter of animals does not help to keep us fed, how is this practice to be justified? Meanwhile the long-simmering issue of vivesection periodically flashes into prominence in a manner that shows that it is by no means dead. When details of a U.S. Air Force proposal to use 200 beagles to test poisonous gases became public in 1973, the Defense Department received more letters of protest than it had received about the bombing of North Vietnam.

Is this concern for animals sloppy sentimentalism or an awakening of the conscience of the tyrant species to the nature of the tyranny we exercise over other species? To foster serious discussion of this question, we have brought together in this volume some of the most important writings, ancient and modern, on our relations with nonhuman animals. We have selected articles that contain *argument*, whether for or against existing practices, rather than those that are mainly rhetoric or appeals to emotion. In this way we hope that our collection will contribute to a clearer and more rational debate about the rights of animals and our obligations to them.

T.R. / P.S.

CONTENTS

III
DO HUMANS HAVE OBLIGATIONS TO OTHER ANIMALS?

INTRODUCTION

The remains of animals are very much a part of our day-to-day life. Their pelts and skins are used in our dress in such articles as shoes, belts, vests, gloves, skirts, and watchbands; in sporting goods such as baseballs, footballs, and gloves of "genuine cowhide"; in home furnishings like rugs, chairs, sofas, and hassocks; in the chamois cloth used for polishing, and in countless other items. Animal waste products are also used extensively. The feces of chickens, cows, and other animals go into fertilizers, while animal urine finds its way into perfumes and body lotions. Even animal fats make contact with us; these are used in soap, lipstick, and chewing gum, to mention just a few of their many uses.

The use of animal remains in these and other ways is so routine that few people are concerned or even think about it at all. Many are unaware of the widespread use of animal remains. As an interesting experiment we might draw up a personal inventory of goods and possessions (including items we hope eventually to own), and then determine how many of these contain something of animal origin. The results of this experiment are usually surprising—and sometimes also disturbing.

Lack of knowledge or concern also characterizes our most intimate contact with animals—namely, our eating of them. To eat the flesh of another animal is so much a part of everyday life, at least in the developed countries of the world, that most people fail to make any firm association between the meat they eat and the animal from which it comes. If we do think of domestic animals, we visualize cows serenely grazing in green meadows, or chickens scurrying about a pleasant farmyard. Many of us, imbued from childhood on with images of "Old MacDonald's Farm," prefer to go on thinking that the animals we eat have been raised in such idyllic surroundings. The truth, however, is a different story.

For the fact is that in ever-increasing numbers farm animals are being raised in incredibly crowded, unnatural environments according to what are called "intensive rearing methods." Some of the details and consequences of these methods are presented in Peter Singer's essay, "Down on the Factory Farm." He reveals that animals raised by these methods often lead lives characterized by extreme deprivation, pain, and frustration.

Why are intensive rearing methods widely used today? The answer is simple: Animals are raised this way because this is the only economically feasible way the farmer can meet the public's demand for meat. In other words, the farmer is not entirely responsible for forcing animals to live the lives they do; we consumers, too, must take a large share of the responsibility. And the fact that we may be ignorant of how animals live does not lessen our responsibility, since such ignorance is inexcusable.

Less obvious but no less real is the responsibility we must accept for another major cause of animal suffering—namely, the use of animals in scientific research. Once, again, our grasp of this issue often is shrouded in ignorance and misunderstanding. But two things are clear. First, most laboratory animals are forced to lead lives that are alien to their natures; and second, the lives of these animals, like those of animals raised for slaughter, are characterized in many cases by deprivation and pain.

If these facts were true of just a few animals, the question of how they are treated might be considered of small consequence. In reality, however, vast numbers of animals are confined in laboratories. In the United States alone, for example, a study conducted by Rutgers University's College of Agriculture and Environmental Sciences for the year 1971 revealed that American researchers used 45 million rodents, 700,000 rabbits, 200,000 cats, 85,283 primates, 46,264 swine, 22,961 sheep, 1,724,279 birds, 15 to 20 million frogs, 190,415 turtles, 61,176 snakes, 51,005 lizards, and about 500,000 dogs.[1] In short, the use of animals as subjects in research is as commonplace in the scientific community as is the use of animal flesh for food in the world at large.

Two questions naturally arise here. How are animals actually being used in research? And is this use of animals morally justified? Richard Ryder's essay "Experiments on Animals" describes a number of experiments involving animals as subjects, and clearly implies that he thinks this use of animals is not morally justified. The research practices Ryder

---

[1]As reported in *Science Digest*, November 1973, p. 32.

describes should be kept in mind in reading the other essays in this book, and in trying to assess our responsibility.

Our responsibility becomes clearer when we learn that a major portion of experimental research is conducted in university and other laboratories subsidized by public funds—that is, by taxpayers' money. The sums run into high figures. In the United States alone, federal support of research involving animals for 1972 has been estimated at over $1.5 billion,[2] not including the amounts allocated for psychological experimentation. Individuals whose tax dollars are being spent to maintain these laboratories must share at least part of the responsibility for research programs that condemn vast numbers of animals to a life of suffering and often a cruel death.

Concern over the treatment accorded to animals is not an abstract, theoretical matter. How we treat animals affects us as humans; the quality of animal life affects the quality of human life. Thus the need to understand and to evaluate various philosophical positions becomes a matter of practical significance.

In this anthology we focus on three fundamental questions. The first concerns the concept of human and animal nature; the second deals with whether humans have moral obligations to nonhuman animals; and the third asks whether those animals have rights. In the rest of this introduction we will highlight how the authors included in this book think these questions should be answered.

ANIMAL AND HUMAN NATURE

There is considerable disagreement among the thinkers represented in Section II as to the difference between animal nature and human nature. Aristotle, writing in the fourth century B.C., stated that some of the so-called "lower (that is, nonhuman) animals" share many capacities in common with human beings, including (1) the capacity to gain nourishment; (2) the capacity to reproduce; (3) the capacity to be aware of the world through sensory apparatus; and (4) the capacity to desire, feel, remember, and imagine. Capacities (1) and (2), Aristotle points out, are shared by plants and animals—both human and nonhuman, but plants do not have capacities (3) and (4). In his view man alone possesses the capacity to reason, and so man can be defined as "a rational animal."

Historically, there have been two major challenges to Aristotle's views. The first, which we will review later, argues that man is not the

---

[2]According to "Animal Agony and Heat Stroke Research," a report prepared by United Action for Animals, as a part of its "Secrecy in Government Series."

only animal having the capacity to reason. The second, to which we now direct our attention, denies that animals have *any* of the mental capacities Aristotle attributes to them. This view received its classic expression in the work of the seventeenth-century French philosopher René Descartes.

In Descartes' view, animals are *automata*—"machines." Like man-made machines, animals are not conscious beings; they are "thought-less." They cannot be said to have a mind or soul, concepts which Descartes uses interchangeably. True, they may act *as if* they desire some things rather than others; and they may behave *as if* they feel pain when they are, say, kicked or stabbed. But these appearances should not deceive us, Descartes believes, as they evidently deceived Aristotle. For these aspects of animal behavior can be explained without assuming that animals really are conscious of either desires or pain. Indeed, they can be explained without assuming that animals are conscious of anything.

Descartes sets forth various reasons for his views on animals. Four should be mentioned here. First, Descartes believes that the whole of the corporeal (or material) world can be explained by the laws of physics; and since the bodies of animals are part of the material world, their behavior can be explained in this fashion. Second, whatever can be explained by the laws of physics can be explained without having recourse to minds or consciousness; accordingly, the behavior of animals can be explained without recourse to their "minds" or their "consciousness." Third, there are theological objections to supposing that animals are conscious beings. For if they are conscious, then—given Descartes' categories of thought—animals would have to have minds or souls; and if they have souls, then their souls might be immortal as are the souls of men. But this would be at odds with official Church doctrine that only the souls of human beings are immortal. Fourth, Descartes claims that animals fail to pass the decisive test for possessing thought or con-sciousness: they are *unable to speak* or in other ways *to use a language.* True, some animals such as parrots can be taught to utter certain words; and true, too, animals do "converse" with one another by singing, grunting, and the like. But these and other alleged evidences of the capacity to speak fall short of establishing that animals are capable of grasping even the most basic rudiments of a language. In Descartes' opinion animals cannot speak, and because they cannot speak we have every reason to deny that they can think; they are mere "thoughtless brutes," altogether devoid of a mind and, therefore, of consciousness.

Critical response to Descartes' views was not long in coming, as may be inferred from the contents of his two letters reproduced in Section

II. In these selections Descartes softens his earlier view that animals do not think, and now says that they *probably* do not. But even this modification would fail to satisfy some of the other contributors in this volume. Both Voltaire and David Hume, for example, submit that there is as much reason to believe that animals other than man think as there is for believing that man is able to do so. We will have more to say on this topic shortly.

As for Descartes' argument that animals cannot think because they are unable to speak, what we must ask is (1) is it true that animals actually do lack a language, and (2) do animals actually lack the ability to learn to use one? Both questions have given rise to much lively debate. Montaigne, for example, argues that animals are able to speak to one another, though people may not be able to understand them. More recently there has been a good deal of discussion about chimps who "talk." Some aspects of this area of inquiry are covered in the selection by Peter Jenkins. There we learn that, although no one has ever been able to teach a chimpanzee to speak a language such as English, a number of researchers have been successful in teaching chimpanzees to communicate by nonverbal means—for example, the American Sign Language used by the deaf. Whether the mastery of such means of communications represents the mastery of a *language* is still a controversial issue, as Jenkins observes. In any event, the experiments and results Jenkins reports clearly must be taken into account when assessing Descartes' claim that animals have no thoughts because they have no language.

Descartes, then, represents one challenge to the Aristotelian conception of the lower animals. A second challenge disputes Aristotle's claim that man is the *only* rational animal. This challenge is made by several authors in this volume, including Voltaire and Hume.

To dispute whether man is the only rational animal presupposes that we agree on what is meant by rationality. This is an area where agreement is not always easy to secure, but perhaps the following explanation may be helpful. To be able to reason involves being able to recognize that certain things support or necessitate certain other things. For example, we can demonstrate our ability to reason *deductively* if we can recognize what follows necessarily from the premises (1) "All men are mortal" and (2) "Socrates is a man." What follows is the conclusion, (3) "Socrates is mortal." To be able to reason *inductively*, on the other hand, requires that we have the capacity to see how some things make other things more likely or more probable. The child who reasons that fire burns reasons in this way. Thus, if we were to assume that all reasoning is either deductive or inductive (which is, in fact, disputable), then the question "Are any of the lower animals rational?" could be understood as asking "Can any of the lower animals reason inductively or deductively?"

How might we go about trying to answer this question? In the case of human beings, of course, we can test for the presence or absence of reason by putting premises into words and asking people what they think follows from what has been said; and the people we are testing can respond by using words also. In the case of animals, however, this kind of testing procedure does not seem to be available. Animals seem to be constitutionally incapable of speaking a language such as English. Thus, if this is the *only* way of testing for a being's capacity to reason, it would seem that we must conclude that the lower animals cannot reason (although even here we would have to reach this conclusion in the light of the continuing progress being made in teaching animals to communicate by *other* means, like those described in the selection by Jenkins).

What we need to ask, however, is whether this is the only kind of test that can reasonably be devised. In particular, we need to ask whether or not we can infer that a creature is capable of reasoning by carefully observing its *nonverbal* behavior. It seems that most of those who think that some lower animals are rational rest their case largely on just such a basis. Certainly Hume and Voltaire do. And so, too, it is clear, does the renowned biologist Charles Darwin. For example, in discussing the behavior of certain monkeys, Darwin states that a single painful or disagreeable experience is sometimes sufficient for these animals to stop doing what led to the unwanted experience. Now, the question is, does this represent a creative, noninstinctive use of intelligence? Does it or does it not demonstrate that the monkey has the capacity to "figure things out" for himself, reasoning that he must not do such and such if he is to avoid so and so? Granted, the monkey does not verbalize such a train of thought. But is this a sufficient reason for denying that he has the capacity for thinking it? To make this clearer, suppose that a human being lacks the capacity to speak or write a language such as English. And suppose that he behaves in a manner analogous to the monkey. Would we say that *he* lacks the ability to reason because *he* is unable to speak or write? Questions of these kinds must be considered if we are to generate light and not just heat in discussing whether or not the lower animals can reason.

But there is another idea that looms very large in the present context. This is the idea of *instinct*. Animals (including humans) sometimes are said to have various instincts or to do various things instinctively. Just what is an instinct, and how are we supposed to be able to determine that a certain way of behaving is or is not a matter of instinct?

These are difficult, important questions. They form part of the subject matter of the essay by Mary Midgley. Of particular interest is the distinction between what are termed *closed instincts,* or "behavior patterns fixed genetically in every detail" and *open instincts,* or "general tendencies to certain *kinds* of behavior, such as hunting, tree-climbing, washing, singing or the care of the young." These concepts help us, Midgley thinks, to understand in what sense, and to what extent, it is or is not true to say that humans and other animals do (or do not) have instincts. One question we might take to Midgley's essay is whether the presence of instincts of either kind necessarily excludes the presence of reason.

As we have seen, then, among the questions that arise in discussing the nature of the lower animals are (1) Are they conscious beings, that is, do they experience such things as desire and pain? and (2) Are they rational—can they reason? Some philosophers give negative answers to these questions, Descartes to both, Aristotle and Aquinas to the second. The controversy has been sparked over the years by various interpretations of the Bible which stress the unique nature of man and his dominion over other animals. These opinions are often based on the belief that the lives of lower animals are characterized by ruthlessness and violence and by preoccupation with sex. These beliefs are built into the concept of bestiality, which explains why we commonly refer to persons who are especially ruthless or sex-possessed as "beasts." Indeed, as Mary Midgley points out in "The Concept of Beastliness," there is a long tradition in philosophy according to which man is thought of as having "a beast within," a "lower self," so to speak, constantly tempting him to act in a beastly rather than a humane manner. In other words, to act violently or to give free rein to one's sexual impulses is to act "like an animal."

Should we put any credence in the dogma of "the beast within"? Midgley argues that we should not, because the basic presuppositions of this dogma—namely, that the so-called lower animals are ruthlessly violent and sex-possessed—are unsupported by what contemporary ethologists (those who study the behavior of animals) have discovered. If Midgley is right, we have to revise not only our conception of the lower animals but also our conception of man.

Finally, we need to ask whether, in the light of the generally accepted tenets of evolutionary theory, it is tenable to suppose, as does Descartes, for example, that there is an enormous gulf that separates man from the lower animals. This question was much debated in the nineteenth century upon the publication of Darwin's major works. For that there is *not* an "enormous gulf" is one of Darwin's principal themes. "My object," he writes in the selection included, "is to show that there is no fundamental difference between man and the higher mammals in their mental faculties." Whether or not Darwin is correct here is a matter of interest not only to the biologist; it has an important bearing on the question considered in Section III: "Do humans have obligations to other animals?"

DO HUMANS HAVE OBLIGATIONS TO OTHER ANIMALS?

Whether humans have obligations to other (lower) animals is intimately connected with our inquiry into the nature of these other animals. The connection between these two questions can be explained as follows. In general, in order for us to have a duty to a being, that being must satisfy certain conditions; in particular, the being must have certain capacities. For example, we do not ordinarily think we have duties to such beings as clouds or rocks, whereas we do normally think we have duties to fellow humans. Presumably we think so because human beings have certain capacities which clouds and rocks lack. Thus, to answer the question whether humans have duties to lower animals we must ask two further questions: (1) What capacities must a being have if we are to have any duties to it? And (2) which lower animals, if any, have these capacities? Now, question (1) raises a matter we have yet to consider. But the answer to question (2) will depend upon how we answer the question, What is the nature of the lower animals? In this way, the question about the nature of the lower animals and the one about our duties to them are related. This is a relation that will become clearer as we highlight some of the answers given to question (1).

There are three capacities that have been thought by different thinkers to be such that, if a being lacked them, it would follow that we would not have any duties to it. The three are (1) *sentience*, or the capacity to experience pleasure and pain; (2) *rationality*, or the capacity to reason; and (3) *autonomy*, or the capacity to make free choices. Let us review the grounds and implications of each of these, beginning with rationality: A being must have the capacity to reason if we are to have any duties to it. This idea goes back to Aristotle, but was formulated more forcefully in the thirteenth century by the philosopher-theologian St. Thomas Aquinas.

First, Aquinas regards rationality (or intellect) as a capacity that makes beings more or less perfect: the greater a being's rationality or intellect, the more perfect it is. Man, who has some degree of rationality, is more perfect than other animals, who lack this capacity; while angels, who are more rational than man, also are more perfect. Likewise, God, who is an absolutely perfect being, is a "pure intellect." Second, Aquinas thinks that, at least so far as the terrestrial world is concerned, the less perfect beings can be rightfully subordinated to, and were intended by God to be subordinated by, the more perfect. Thus, plants, which are less perfect than either man or animals, can be treated as both see fit; while man, a more perfect being than the lower animals, may use the lower animals as he desires, but not vice versa. It follows that man, according to Aquinas, need have no moral qualms about eating the lower animals—it is not a "savage" thing to do; it is not contrary to nature. What is both savage and contrary to nature is when a lower animal eats a man.

In regard to animal sentience—their capacity to feel pain or pleasure —Aquinas, like Aristotle and unlike Descartes, believes that animals are sentient, and that because they have the capacity to feel pain it is possible to treat them cruelly—that is, to cause them unnecessary pain. Although Aquinas thinks it is *wrong* to treat them in this way, he does not think we have a *duty* to the lower animals to abstain from treating them cruelly. To understand this apparent contradiction requires some explanation.

The key to Aquinas's position is the idea that we can have duties only to those beings who have the capacity to reason. These include (a) ourselves, (b) our fellow man, and (c) God. Thus, anytime it happens to be true that we have done something wrong, it will also be true that we have failed to fulfill a duty we have to ourselves, our neighbor, or God. Now, because lower animals cannot reason, according to Aquinas, we can no more have any duties *to them* than we can have duties *to things.* The only way we can do something wrong that involves doing something to lower animals is if our treatment of them leads us to sin against some *rational* being—either ourselves, our fellow man, or God. In fact, Aquinas thinks this is just what happens; he thinks that people who treat animals cruelly are naturally inclined to treat rational beings in a similar way, while those who extend their kindness to animals are disposed to extend their kindness to rational beings as well. Thus, we have no *direct* duties to the lower animals.

Now, one thing that needs to be asked here is whether or not cruelty to animals usually does lead to cruelty to humans. Aquinas and others certainly think so. But the question that we must ask is: Where is the evidence, and how good is it, that is supposed to support this belief? This is a crucial question. For if the evidence is weak, then, given Aquinas's views, there would *not* be anything wrong with treating animals cruelly. And this certainly seems to be a questionable idea. One needs to ask, therefore, how well Aquinas and others manage to defend this belief.

This question aside, Aquinas's views might be challenged in more fundamental ways. First, a critic could agree with Aquinas that a being must be rational if we are to have duties to it, and still disagree with him over whether we have duties to animals. For a critic might believe that at least *some* of the lower animals have the capacity to reason, a claim which, coupled with Aquinas's other beliefs, would yield the conclusion that we do have duties to these animals. Plutarch, for one, would accept a position like this. Second, some of Aquinas's critics would dispute his views in an even more fundamental way. They would dispute the very basis which he proposes for determining those beings to whom we have duties. Aquinas says this is to be determined by asking, "What beings are rational?" These critics would demur and say we need to ask, instead, "What beings are sentient?" According to this way of thinking, in other words, it is enough that a being can experience pleasure and pain, for us to have duties to it—for example, the duty not to cause it unnecessary pain. And what these thinkers would insist upon is that we really have this duty *directly* to those animals who are sentient. We have this duty to them, in other words, quite independently of how those who treat animals cruelly are disposed, on that account, to treat human beings. Both Jeremy Bentham and John Stuart Mill would seem to hold this position, as do Plutarch and Peter Singer. But perhaps the fullest statement of this position, in the present collection, is the one given in the selection by Albert Schweitzer.

Does this mean, according to these thinkers, that it is always wrong to kill an animal as a source of food or to inflict pain on it in the course of doing scientific research? The answer here would seem to be no. Mill and Bentham, for example, would argue that this treatment of animals would be wrong only if the animals suffered more pain than the amount of pleasure humans secured; and Schweitzer, for one, makes it clear that he is not opposed in principle to using animals as subjects in scientific research. What he is in principle opposed to is using them in *needless* research. And Plutarch and Singer, finally, would seem to allow that it is not wrong to, say, kill and eat an animal, if doing so is necessary to save a human life.

This idea comes through especially clearly in the selection by Plutarch. What he maintains is, first, that it is not necessary to eat meat to survive or attain sound health (a fact well-attested by the hundreds of millions of vegetarians in the world) and second, that more often than not, people who eat meat think of ways to raise and slaughter animals that are not dictated by considerations of health but by palate. Now, because these particular pleasures are unnecessary, Plutarch argues, it follows that the pain caused these animals is unnecessary, as well; and because the pain is unnecessary, it is wrong to treat them in this fashion. Thus, though there may be special circumstances in which slaughtering and eating animals is not wrong, it usually is so, according to Plutarch. Henry S. Salt's essay on vegetarianism, in which he endeavors to explain what a vegetarian believes and how vegetarianism can be defended against a number of common objections, is particularly relevant in this context.

But there is a third way in which we might conceive of animals that seems to lead to conclusions more like those of Aquinas than those of Plutarch. This is after the fashion of the eighteenth-century German philosopher Immanuel Kant. Kant reasons that man but not an animal exists as "an end in himself"—that, in other words, the very existence of man, but not the very existence of a lower animal, is intrinsically worthwhile or has value in itself. Of course, this difference in the intrinsic worth of man and animal must be due to something that makes the two different, and Kant is aware of this requirement. And what he seems to believe (interpreting Kant is a hazardous occupation) is that men are, but animals are not, autonomous beings—beings who have free will.

When Kant says that man has free will or is autonomous, he means that man has the capacity to act according to the conception of laws, instead of merely acting in accordance with laws. To make this clearer, consider an event such as a stone falling. A stone falls according to some law—in this case, the law of gravity. The stone does not ask itself, "Should I fall?" or "Could I consistently will that every stone placed in circumstances like my own fall?" The stone merely falls. Similarly, Kant seems to suppose, when an animal behaves in a certain way—for example, a dog barks when it hears a noise outside—it doesn't ask these or similar questions; it simply barks. Indeed, like the stone, it has no alternative but to bark. For, given that certain conditions have been fulfilled, there is a natural law which guarantees that the dog will bark. So reasons Kant. In fact, contrary to some other thinkers, one of the reasons Kant thinks animals lack the ability to choose between alternatives is because they have no ego—no self-consciousness. Thus, lacking an ego, they cannot conceive of how they ought to act. Lacking an ego, they cannot conceive of any "I".

In the case of man or, more generally, of what Kant calls "rational beings," however, the situation is different. For man can choose to act according to those natural laws which apply to his behavior—for example, various psychological or sociological laws—or according to his conception of how he thinks he *ought* to act. And this ability to frame judgments about how he ought to act and, in turn, to choose to act as he thinks he ought, even if the laws of psychology or sociology might incline him to act otherwise, is, Kant thinks, capacity that separates man, as an autonomous animal, from all those other animals that happen to exist on the face of the earth. Thus what Kant seems to believe is that it is because man has this capacity that he exists as an end in himself, while it is because the other animals lack this capacity that their existence is not intrinsically worthwhile. And he also seems to think that it is because of this difference that an individual human being does have direct duties to all other human beings but does not have any direct duties to other animals. Accordingly, when Kant turns to articulate what he thinks is the supreme principle of morality, he does so in such a way that it stipulates how we are to treat *human* beings but not how we are to treat other animals. "We are always to act," he writes, "so as to treat humanity, both in our own person and in the person of every other, always as an end, never as a means merely."

Of course, Kant does not think, any more than Aquinas, that cruelty to animals is good. But, like Aquinas, the reason he feels it is not good is because of the effects this kind of treatment has on *men*, not because of the needless pain the animals themselves suffer. As Kant writes, "he who is cruel to animals becomes hard also in his dealings with men." Like Aquinas, therefore, Kant believes that there is nothing directly wrong with causing animals to suffer unnecessarily. What makes this wrong, when and if it is wrong, are the consequences this leads to in our treatment of beings who exist as "ends in themselves"—human (rational) beings.

How might we respond to Kant? A number of different questions naturally arise. First, we might ask if it is true that man exists as an "end in himself." Indeed, we might ask whether this idea makes any sense at all. These are two of the questions taken up in the selection by Kant's fellow German philosopher, Arthur Schopenhauer. Schopenhauer's view is that Kant's idea of an "end in itself" fails to make any sense at all, a criticism which, if true, certainly would have fatal consequences for Kant's ethical theory. Schopenhauer's criticism, therefore, should be considered very carefully.

Also deserving of careful attention is Schopenhauer's response to another question—that of whether or not it is true that man has, while other animals lack, self-consciousness. Schopenhauer thinks animals do possess self-consciousness, and some of the most interesting things he has to say revolve around this question. For example, he points out how it is that languages, including English, have a vocabulary for talking about animals that implies their lack of ego. (In English, for example, Schopenhauer points out that animals are referred to by the impersonal pronoun "it"; he might also have noted, as Salt does, that, despite the fact that man is an animal, the word "animal" normally is used in such a way as to refer to creatures other than man.)

Schopenhauer also discusses the degree to which man resembles other animals. He concludes that there are more similarities than dissimilarities. This resemblence is present, he thinks, not only when we consider the physical constitution of each; it is present, besides, when we consider the fact that both have a *will*.

A final question that needs to be asked in our response to Kant is whether he is right in believing that we can have a duty to a being only if that being has free will and exists as an end in itself. In particular, we need to ask here, as we did in the case of Aquinas, whether it is not enough that a being can feel pain or pleasure for us to have at least one direct duty to it—namely, to see that it not suffer needlessly.

There are, then at least these three different views that should be examined when we ask the question "Do humans have duties to other animals?" As to which one is the most reasonable, that is a matter for decision only after informed reflection. But two of them—the ones held by Aquinas and Kant—are examples of what Peter Singer refers to as "speciesist" ways of thinking. A speciesist, Singer says, is a person who "allows the interests of his species to override the greater interests of members of other species." As such, speciesism has many of the same features as racism, according to Singer. In particular, both involve a systematic refusal to apply principles of justice in an equitable fashion. The routine use of animals as a source of food and as subjects in scientific research is the fruit of widespread speciesist thinking, Singer implies. It is Singer's belief that speciesism is as much an expression of unreasoned prejudice and bigotry as is racism and that, compassionate men having acted to eliminate the one, they must now begin a concerted effort to eliminate the other.

Questions about the existence and grounds of our duties to animals, as we have seen, are difficult, and have led to a variety of answers. One final one that ought to be mentioned is the position of the noted American neurosurgeon Robert J. White. Although his essay addresses itself to the question of vivisection (or the use of animals in research), the position he sets forth has wider implications. "I believe," he writes, "that the inclusion of lower animals in our ethical system is philosophically meaningless and operationally impossible and that, consequently, antivivisection theory and practice have no moral or ethical basis." In reading White's essay we need to ask what grounds he offers for the elimination of animals from "our ethical system," and how good these grounds are. It is important to ask, too, whether White's position is distinct from or consistent with those who, like Aquinas and Kant, maintain that we have no direct duties to animals.

DO ANIMALS HAVE RIGHTS?

Our final question, Do animals have rights? is central to the essays in Section IV. This question is intimately related to the debates over the nature of animals and our obligations to them. One way to begin reflection here is to see how the question about animal rights has been thought to be related to the question about our duties to them.

Let us suppose that we do have obligations to animals—for example, the obligation not to treat them cruelly. Would it follow from this that animals have the *right* not to be treated cruelly? Some thinkers believe this would follow, because they accept the thesis that whenever one being has an obligation to another, that other being has a corresponding right, and vice versa. This is known as the *correlativity thesis.* If this thesis is accepted, then obviously if it is true that we have duties to animals, it must also be true that animals have corresponding rights.

But is the correlativity thesis true? Some philosophers think not. Some argue, for example, that it might be plausibly maintained that we have a duty to preserve great works of art, like the Pietà, as well as natural resources, such as the oceans or our woodlands. Yet these same thinkers contend that we do not suppose that the Pietà, the Atlantic Ocean, or our forests have rights. Thus, they think the correlativity thesis is false.

Proponents of the thesis, however, think this objection misses the mark. For they think the thesis applies only to cases of *direct* duty, while this objection appeals to cases in which our duties are indirect. To make this clearer, consider our supposed duty to take care of the Pietà. Now, preserving the Pietà is not something we owe *it*; it is not something that is *its* due. Rather, preserving it is something we owe to future generations of *human beings*, because the loss of the Pietà would bring about a loss in *their* enjoyment of beauty. Thus, to speak of our "duty to the Pietà" turns out to be an elliptical way of speaking about our direct duty to future generations of human beings. And since it is to them we have a direct duty, it is they, not the Pietà, who have the right that the Pietà be preserved. The same kind of analysis can be given of our beliefs that oceans, woodlands, and so on ought to be preserved. These beliefs present no exceptions to the correlativity thesis, since, on reflection, our duties here, as in the case of the Pietà, can be seen to be indirect ones. So, at least, reason defenders of the correlativity thesis.

But is this defense of the correlativity thesis sound? This question plays a prominent role in the selections in Section IV. For example, an affirmative answer seems to be implied by Joel Feinberg, who claims that animals do have rights because we do have direct duties to them. A negative answer appears to be implied by the nineteenth-century English Thomist, Father Joseph Rickaby, who denies that animals have rights.

Two other questions must be addressed, before one can reasonably affirm or deny that animals have rights. What is a right? And what kinds of rights are there? Concerning the first question, some thinkers, including Feinberg and D. G. Ritchie, contend that to have a right is to have *a claim* to something or against others. Thus, to have the right to life, for example, is to have a claim against others not to take one's life; and to have a right to one's property is to have a claim against others not to take one's property. Other thinkers have maintained that a right is *an entitlement*.[3] Thus, for example, to have the right to marry whomever one pleases is to be *entitled* to marry whomever one wishes; and to have such an entitlement is not necessarily to make any claims against others, although having such a right can be a basis for making such claims. Clearly, to determine which one, if either, of these two analyses of rights is correct requires careful reflection. Given either analysis, however, it would seem that animals *could* have rights. For though they lack a language to *articulate* their claims or entitlements, this lack would not seem to rule out the possibility that they have rights. Very young children, the aged, and the mentally feeble of all ages lack the verbal capacity to articulate their claims or entitlements, yet we nonetheless recognize the rights of each. Then again, perhaps animals do lack these claims or entitlements. Indeed, the fact that proposed analyses of rights often leave unanswered the substantive questions one wants to answer—in particular, whether or not animals have rights—may be one of the reasons why Salt in his essay "Animal Rights" minimizes the importance of such endeavors and characterizes "the controversy concerning 'rights' [as] little else than an academic battle over words."

As for what *kinds* of rights there are, this, too, is a controversial matter. At least two kinds of rights should be distinguished: (1) rights we acquire because of something that we or somebody else has done, which we might call *special rights*; and (2) rights a being has just because of the kind of being it is, which we might refer to as *natural rights*. As an example of a special right, one might cite the legal right of the beneficiary to an inheritance, if he or she is so designated in the will of a deceased person. To have such a right is to have a claim (or entitlement) because of a past action of another human being. It is not a right which the beneficiary has just because of the kind of being he or she is. On the other hand, if we consider the alleged rights to life, liberty, and the pursuit of happiness, these do not seem to be rights which we could acquire because of anything that we have done. They are, it seems, rights which, if we have them, are possessed just *because* of the kind of being we are.

---

[3]See H. J. McCloskey: "Rights," *Philosophical Quarterly*, vol. 15 (1965), pp. 115–27.

Now, the question, Do animals have rights? can be understood as asking whether animals have special rights, or natural rights, or both. Salt, for example, seems to think that animals have special rights because they have legal rights—for example, as the beneficiary in a will. Ritchie disputes this, arguing that works of art might be protected by laws and yet not be said, on that account alone, to have legal rights. Whether or not animals have legal rights, then, is a controversial matter. A patient exploration of some aspects of this question can be found in the selection by Feinberg.

Even more controversial is the question whether animals have *natural* rights. This is not surprising, since a natural right is a right which a being has because of its nature, and the nature of the lower animals is itself a highly controversial issue. But before we can say whether animals have natural rights—or any rights—we must ask a more fundamental question; What kinds of beings *can* have rights? The answer may tell us whether animals are that kind of being. So let us describe some of the ways thinkers have answered this question.

First, there is the view that a being must be *rational* if it is to be capable of having rights. This is the view we find set forth in the selection by Joseph Rickaby, who argues, following Aristotle and Aquinas, that animals lack the capacity to reason. From this it follows, he thinks, that we have no direct duties to them nor do they have any rights against us. Animals are, Rickaby says, "of the number of *things*," and so we can never be accused of violating any rights of theirs in using them—for example, by eating them or by using them as subjects in scientific research.

Many objections have been raised against this view. Some of these are developed by Feinberg, who points out that infants and the mentally feeble may not demonstrate any ability to reason, and yet we still are reluctant to deny that they have rights. Of course, in the case of infants, we might say that they are potentially able to reason. However, in the case of mental defectives, it is unlikely that we would deny that they had rights, even if it is true that they not only are not rational but also lack any potential for becoming so. Thus, the price one seems to pay for making rationality a requirement for a being's having rights is that at least some *human* beings could not have them. What we need to ask, therefore, is whether or not this is too great a price to pay.

A similar question awaits those who, following Kant, would make *free will* a requirement for the possession of rights. Rickaby, once again, seems to believe something like this, as witness his claim that humans are, but animals are not, "autocentric." But what needs to be asked is whether we would be prepared to deny that infants and the severely mentally enfeebled lack rights. That they lack free will, given their station in life, is, it would seem, a fact that would be admitted by all parties to the dispute. Thus, though it is true that by making either rationality or free will requirements for the possession of rights we might thereby exclude animals from possessing them, it also seems clear that we would exclude some human beings as well. And Feinberg, for one, is not willing to accept such a consequence, which is why he rejects both rationality and free will (or "moral agency") as requirements that must be met if a being is to possess any rights.

A third view is that a being must have *interests* if it is to have any rights—it must be the kind of being that can care, or be concerned, about what happens to it.[4] Given this view, then, if one were to think that animals did not care about what happened to them, it would follow that they could not have any rights, natural or otherwise. And there have been some thinkers who have explicitly maintained or implied just this. Descartes' views on the nature of animals, for example, would seem to imply that animals cannot have rights because they do not have interests.

Not surprisingly, this position has not been free of its critics—Feinberg, in particular. But Feinberg is critical without disputing the correctness of the requirement that a being must have interests if it can possibly have rights. Indeed, Feinberg thinks this requirement contains "an important insight." Where he disagrees is over the question of whether or not animals do have interests. He thinks they do, whereas things, such as rocks and clouds, do not; animals have, he thinks, a "conative life"—conscious wishes, hopes, urges, impulses, etc. Thus, there can be such a thing as "the good" of an individual animal, though not of an individual thing. Animals, therefore, or at least the "higher" ones, are the types of being who *can* have rights, according to Feinberg.

A fourth possible requirement is *sentience*—the capacity to experience pleasure and pain. The adequacy of this view is disputed in the selection by Ritchie, in which he enumerates a number of "difficulties" he thinks would follow if animals, because of their sentience, were accorded equal rights with man. For example, if the rights of animals were to mean anything at all, then no animal could be put to death without first having a fair trial. And would it not be our duty, Ritchie asks, to protect weak animals from the attacks of the strong? But this, he implies, is absurd—a consequence which he thinks shows that we

---

[4]See Leonard Nelson: *A System of Ethics*, trans. N. Gutermann (New Haven: Yale University Press, 1956). Reprinted in *Animals, Men and Morals*, ed. S. and R. Godlovitch and John Harris (New York: Taplinger, 1972). See also the McCloskey essay, "*Rights*," cited above. Nelson thinks animals do have interests and, therefore, that they do satisfy the condition necessary for having rights. McCloskey thinks animals fail to satisfy this condition.

cannot mean that animals have rights in any *strict* sense. But if, on the other hand, animals are supposed to have rights in some weaker sense —rights that are not equal to human rights—then this will be a mere license to permit human interest, not the interests of animals, to be the ultimate test of how animals should be treated. In either case, therefore, Ritchie thinks no persuasive account of the rights of animals can be given based on the mere fact of their sentience. Indeed, he seems to think that it is in the self-interest of animals that they not have rights, because if they did, and men became, out of deference to them, vegetarians, then very few animals would exist in the first place. Ritchie seems to think that an animal is better off having lived and been eaten than never to have lived at all. This is a thesis that comes in for some critical attention in Salt's "Logic of the Larder."

Now, one thing we should realize is that no answer to the question, What kind of being *can* have rights? will tell us what rights, if any, animals actually *do* possess. Answers to this question can merely tell us what a being must be like *if* it can possibly possess rights. And even if it is true that animals are the kind of beings that can possess rights, it would not follow from this that they actually do possess them or that they actually do possess a particular right—say, the right to life. Yet another dimension to the debate about animal rights, accordingly, is the debate between those who think that animals *do* have rights but disagree (or at least appear to) over the questions of what rights they have and on what basis it can be shown that they have the rights they do. Feinberg, for example, thinks that animals have a right not to be treated cruelly; Salt thinks they have a right to exercise their emotional and cognitive capacities "in so far as surrounding circumstances permit"; and Tom Regan argues that they have a natural right to life, if it supposed that all humans do. Yet another thinker, James Rachels, argues that at least some animals have the rights to property and to liberty. It is this latter right to which Rachels devotes most of his attention, arguing that the concept of liberty (or absence from external constraint) can be applied to animals in the same sense in which it can be applied to human beings. Moreover, Rachels thinks that there is just as much reason for believing that animals have this right as for believing that people do. Even when the concept of liberty is understood to mean *moral freedom*, it applies to some animals, he thinks, because experiments have shown that chimpanzees, for example, have the capacity to exhibit compassion, a trait which, in human beings, we judge to be morally admirable. Rachels's arguments are examined critically by Donald VanDeVeer. Allowing that Rachels is "on the side of the angels" in his attitudes toward and beliefs about animals, VanDeVeer submits that Rachels's arguments for ascribing rights to animals are inadequate as they stand. In VanDeVeer's view, Rachels may be right, but not for the right reasons. Rachels, however, in his reply, argues that VanDeVeer's criticisms miss the mark. Which view is correct can only be determined by a careful examination of each.

To recapitulate: There are several distinct but related questions that come up within the debate about the rights of animals. Some appear to be factual—for example, Do animals have interests? Others are conceptual, inquiring into the meaning of certain ideas—for example, What is a right? And perhaps some, like Do animals have a self? are not easily classifiable, let alone answerable. What is clear is that none of these questions is easy to answer and none is frivolous. For each one of them, either directly or indirectly, bears on how we should understand our relationship to our fellow animals and how, as a consequence of this understanding, we should treat them. And these are matters that can have significance in our everyday life, whenever, for instance, we sit down to eat a meal or go out to buy a pair of shoes.

FURTHER QUESTIONS

The questions considered by the authors in this anthology do not exhaust those that need to be asked when we reflect on how animals are, and ought to be treated. Other factual, conceptual, and moral questions also need to be examined. For example, consider how we should understand the concept of duty. This is a concept that plays an important role in many of the debates covered in the readings in this book. But what does it mean to say that we "have a duty" to do something? And how, if at all, does the meaning of this expression resemble or differ from what it means when we say that we "have a desire" or "an inclination" to do it? These are vitally important, basic questions that must be answered correctly if we are to fully understand the debate about whether or not we have duties to animals. Yet they are questions which are rarely, if ever, touched in the selections in this anthology.

On the factual side, there are as many questions as there are ways in which animals are used or forced to live and die. For example: How are those animals raised whose fluids are used by the cosmetic industry in such goods as perfumes? How are those animals slaughtered whose skins and pelts are used in coats and other wearing apparel? And how, exactly, are animals hunted by trappers? Zoos, too, need to be examined carefully, and the charge that they often serve as a place for grossly inhumane reasearch is itself in need of research. And what of those sports whose primary purpose is to hunt and kill animals? How many animals' lives are claimed in this way? Even the pet industry should fall within the scope of our inquiry. The so-called "puppy mills," for example, which are in the business of mass-producing pets as fast as they can (at the rate of $200 million worth per year in the United States alone[5]) should be more closely investigated. The fact is that we need to educate ourselves about the many ways animals are raised and used. And the first thing we need to realize is that there is much more to be learned than we might suppose.

From the moral point of view, the facts we discover need to be evaluated, and the concepts we clarify, applied. This means that we must ask how the practices we gather information about—for example, the slaughter of baby seals or mink farming—do or do not show that mankind is failing to fullfill its duties to, or to respect the rights of, animals. And this we must do, even while we continue to think about whether or not we have duties to animals or they rights against us.

THE CONTRIBUTIONS OF LITERATURE

The anthology concludes with two selections that are literary rather than philosophical. Jonathan Swift's famous satiric essay was intended to draw attention to the plight of the Irish poor; in the context of this volume, however, it suggests a rather different question: if it is all right to rear and kill animals for food, what objection can be made to Swift's proposal? As for Desmond Stewart's short story, the reader may safely be left to his or her own reflections.

TOM REGAN

[5]As reported by Jack Anderson: "Study Hits 'Puppy Mill' Operations," in his "Washington Merry-Go-Round" column, February 9, 1974, *The Raleigh News and Observer.*

1

Contemporary Realities

PETER SINGER

Down on the Factory Farm

For most humans, especially those in modern urban and suburban communities, the most direct form of contact with non-human animals is at meal time: we eat them. This simple fact is the key to our attitudes to other animals, and also the key to what each one of us can do about changing these attitudes. The use and abuse of animals raised for food far exceeds, in sheer numbers of animals affected, any other kind of mistreatment. Hundreds of millions of cattle, pigs, and sheep are raised and slaughtered in the United States alone each year; and for poultry the figure is a staggering 3 *billion*. (That means that about 5,000 birds —mostly chickens—will have been slaughtered in the time it takes you to read this page.) It is here, on our dinner table and in our neighborhood supermarket or butcher's shop, that we are brought into direct touch with the most extensive exploitation of other species that has ever existed.

In general, we are ignorant of the abuse of living creatures that lies behind the food we eat. Consider the images conjured up by the word "farm": a house, a barn, a flock of hens, overseen by a strutting rooster, scratching around the farmyard, a herd of cows being brought in from the fields for milking, and perhaps a sow rooting around in the orchard with a litter of squealing piglets running excitedly behind her.

Very few farms were ever as idyllic as that traditional image would have us believe. Yet we still think of a farm as a pleasant place, far removed from our own industrial, profit-conscious city life. Of those few who think about the lives of animals on farms, not many know

From Peter Singer, *Animal Liberation*. © New York Review of Books, 1975, and distributed through Random House, New York.

much of modern methods of animal raising. Some people wonder whether animals are slaughtered painlessly, and anyone who has followed a truckload of cattle must know that farm animals are transported in very crowded conditions; but few suspect that transportation and slaughter are anything more than the brief and inevitable conclusion of a life of ease and contentment, a life that contains the natural pleasures of animal existence without the hardships that wild animals must endure in the struggle for survival.

These comfortable assumptions bear little relation to the realities of modern farming. For a start, farming is no longer controlled by simple country folk. It is a business, and big business at that. In the last thirty years the entry of large corporations and assembly-line methods of production have turned farming into "agribusiness." . . .

The first animal to be removed from the relatively natural conditions of the traditional farms and subjected to the full stress of modern intensive farming was the chicken. Chickens have the misfortune of being useful to humans in two ways: for their flesh and for their eggs. There are now standard mass-production techniques for obtaining both these products.

Agribusiness enthusiasts consider the rise of the chicken industry to be one of the great success stories of farming. At the end of World War II chicken for the table was still relatively rare. It came mainly from small independent farmers or from the unwanted males produced by egg-laying flocks. Today "broilers"—as table chickens are now usually called—are produced literally by the million from the highly automated factory-like plants of the large corporations that own or control 98 percent of all broiler production in the United States.[1]

The essential step in turning the chicken from a farmyard bird into a manufactured item was confining them indoors. A broiler producer today gets a load of 10,000, 50,000, or even more day-old chicks from the hatcheries, and puts them straight into a long, windowless shed—usually on the floor, although some producers use tiers of cages in order to get more birds into the same size shed. Inside the shed, every aspect of the birds' environment is controlled to make them grow faster on less feed. Food and water are fed automatically from hoppers suspended from the roof. The lighting is adjusted according to advice from agricultural researchers: for instance, there may be bright light 24 hours a day for the first week or two, to encourage the chicks to gain quickly; then the lights may be dimmed slightly and made to go off and on every two hours, in the belief that the chickens are readier to eat

[1]Harrison Wellford, Sowing the Wind: The Politics of Food, Safety and Agribusiness (New York: Grossman Press, 1971), p. 104.

after a period of sleep; finally there comes a point, around six weeks of age, when the birds have grown so much that they are becoming crowded, and the lights will then be made very dim at all times. The point of this dim lighting is to reduce the effects of crowding. Toward the end of the eight- or nine-week life of the chicken, there may be as little as half a square foot of space per chicken—or less than the area of a sheet of quarto paper for a 3½ lb. bird. Under these conditions with normal lighting the stress of crowding and the absence of natural outlets for the bird's energies lead to outbreaks of fighting, with birds pecking at each other's feathers and sometimes killing and eating one another. Very dim lighting has been found to reduce this and so the birds are likely to live out their last weeks in near-darkness.

Feather-pecking and cannibalism are, in the broiler producer's language, "vices." They are not natural vices, however—they are the result of the stress and crowding to which the modern broilerman subjects his birds. Chickens are highly social animals, and in the farmyard they develop a hierarchy, sometimes called a "pecking order." Every bird yields, at the food trough or elsewhere, to those above it in rank, and takes precedence over those below. There may be a few confrontations before the order is firmly established but more often than not a show of force, rather than actual physical contact, is enough to put a chicken in its place. As Konrad Lorenz, a renowned figure in the field of animal behavior, wrote in the days when flocks were still small:

> Do animals thus know each other among themselves? They certainly do.... Every poultry farmer knows that ... there exists a very definite order, in which each bird is afraid of those that are above her in rank. After some few disputes, which need not necessarily come to blows, each bird knows which of the others she has to fear and which must show respect to her. Not only physical strength, but also personal courage, energy, and even the self-assurance of every individual bird are decisive in the maintenance of the pecking order.[2]

Other studies have shown that a flock of up to 90 chickens can maintain a stable social order, each bird knowing its place; but 10,000 birds crowded together in a single shed is obviously a different matter.[3] The birds cannot establish a social order, and as a result they fight frequently with each other. Quite apart from the inability of the individual bird to recognize so many other birds, the mere fact of extreme crowding probably contributes to irritability and excitability in chickens, as it

---

[2]K. Lorenz, *King Solomon's Ring* (London: Methuen and Co., 1964), p. 147.
[3]Ian Duncan, "Can the Psychologist Measure Stress?" *New Scientist*, October 18, 1973.

does in humans and other animals. This is something farming magazines are aware of, and they frequently warn their readers:

> Feather-pecking and cannibalism have increased to a formidable extent
> of late years, due, no doubt, to the changes in technique and the swing
> towards completely intensive management of laying flocks and table
> poultry.... The most common faults in management which may lead
> to vice are boredom, overcrowding in badly ventilated houses ... lack of
> feeding space, unbalanced food or shortage of water, and heavy infesta-
> tion with insect pests.[4]

Clearly the farmer must stop "vices," because they cost him money;
but although he may know that overcrowding is the root cause, he cannot do anything about this, since in the competitive state of the industry,
eliminating overcrowding could mean eliminating his profit margin at
the same time. He would have fewer birds to sell, but would have had
to pay the same outlay for his building, for the automatic feeding
equipment, for the fuel used to heat and ventilate the building, and
for labor. So the farmer limits his efforts to reducing the consequences
of the stress that costs him money. The unnatural way in which he
keeps his birds causes the vices; but to control them the poultryman
must make the conditions still more unnatural. Very dim lighting is one
way of doing this. A more drastic step, though one now almost universally used in the industry, is "de-beaking." This involves inserting the
chick's head in a guillotine-like device which cuts off part of its beak.
Alternatively the operation may be done with a hot knife. Some poultrymen claim that this operation is painless, but an expert British Government committee under zoologist Professor F. W. Rogers Brambell appointed to look into aspects of intensive farming found otherwise:

> ... between the horn and the bone is a thin layer of highly sensitive
> soft tissue, resembling the "quick" of the human nail. The hot knife
> used in de-beaking cuts through this complex of horn, bone and sensi-
> tive tissue, causing severe pain.[5]

De-beaking, which is routinely performed in anticipation of cannibalism by most poultrymen, does greatly reduce the amount of damage
a chicken can do to other chickens. It also, in the words of the Brambell
Committee, "deprives the bird of what is in effect its most versatile

[4]The Smallholder, January 6, 1962; quoted by Ruth Harrison, Animal Machines
(London: Vincent Stuart, 1964), p. 18.
[5]Report of the Technical Committee to Enquire into the Welfare of Animals
Kept under Intensive Livestock Husbandry Systems (London: Her Majesty's Stationery Office, 1965), para. 97.

member" while it obviously does nothing to reduce the stress and over-crowding that lead to this unnatural cannibalism in the first place. . . .

"A hen," Samuel Butler once wrote, "is only an egg's way of making another egg." Butler, no doubt, was being humorous; but when Fred. C. Haley, President of a Georgia poultry firm that controls the lives of 225,000 laying hens, describes the hen as "an egg producing machine" his words have more serious implications. To emphasize his business-like attitude Haley adds: "The object of producing eggs is to make money. When we forget this objective, we have forgotten what it is all about."[6]

Nor is this only an American attitude. A British farming magazine has told its readers:

> The modern layer is, after all, only a very efficient converting machine, changing the raw material—feedingstuffs—into the finished product—the egg—less, of course, maintenance requirements.[7]

Remarks of this kind can regularly be found in the egg industry trade journals throughout the United States and Europe, and they express an attitude that is common in the industry. As may be anticipated, their consequences for the laying hens are not good.

Laying hens go through many of the same procedures as broilers, but there are some differences. Like broilers, layers have to be de-beaked, to prevent the cannibalism that would otherwise occur in their crowded conditions; but because they live much longer than broilers, they often go through this operation twice. So we find a poultry specialist at the New Jersey College of Agriculture advising poultrymen to de-beak their chicks when they are between one and two weeks old because there is, he says, less stress on the chicks at this time than if the opera-tion is done earlier, and in addition "there are fewer culls in the laying flock as a result of improper de-beaking." In either case, the article continues, the birds must be de-beaked again when they are ready to begin laying, at around twenty weeks of age.[8]

Laying hens get no more individual attention than broilers. Alan Hainsworth, owner of a poultry farm in upstate New York, told an in-quiring local reporter that four hours a day is all he needs for the care of his 36,000 laying hens, while his wife looks after the 20,000 pullets (as the younger birds not yet ready to lay are called): "It takes her

[6]*Poultry Tribune*, January 1974.
[7]*Farmer and Stockbreeder*, January 30, 1962; quoted by Ruth Harrison, *Animal Machines*, p. 50.
[8]*American Agriculturist*, July 1966.

about 15 minutes a day. All she checks is their automatic feeders, water cups and any deaths during the night."

This kind of care does not make for a happy flock, as the reporter's description shows:

> Walk into the pullet house and the reaction is immediate—complete pandemonium. The squawking is loud and intense as some 20,000 birds shove to the farthest side of their cages in fear of the human intruders.[9]

Julius Goldman's Egg City, 50 miles northwest of Los Angeles, is one of the world's largest egg producing units, consisting of 2 million hens divided into block long buildings containing 90,000 hens each, five birds to a 16 by 18 inch cage. When the *National Geographic Magazine* did an enthusiastic survey of new farming methods, Ben Shames, Egg City's executive Vice-President, explained to its reporter the methods used to look after so many birds:

> We keep track of the food eaten and the eggs collected in 2 rows of cages among the 110 rows in each building. When production drops to the uneconomic point, all 90,000 birds are sold to processors for pot-pies or chicken soup. It doesn't pay to keep track of every row in the house, let alone indivdual hens; with 2 million birds on hand you have to rely on statistical samplings.[10]

Nearly all the big egg producers now keep their laying hens in cages. Originally there was only one bird to a cage; and the idea was that the farmer could then tell which birds were not laying enough eggs to give an economic return on their food. Those birds were then killed. Then it was found that more birds could be housed and costs per bird reduced if two birds were put in each cage. That was only the first step, and as we have seen, there is no longer any question of keeping a tally of each bird's eggs. The advantages of cages for the egg producer now consist in the greater number of birds that can be housed, warmed, fed, and watered in one building, and in the greater use that can be made of labor-saving automatic equipment.

The cages are stacked in tiers, with food and water troughs running along the rows, filled automatically from a central supply. They have sloping wire floors. The slope—usually a gradient of 1 in 5—makes it more difficult for the birds to stand comfortably, but it causes the eggs to roll to the front of the cage where they can easily be collected by hand or, in the more modern plants, carried by conveyor belt to a packing plant.

[9]*Upstate*, August 5, 1973, report by Mary Rita Kiereck.
[10]*National Geographic Magazine*, February 1970.

When a reporter from the New York *Daily News* wanted to see a typical modern egg farm, he visited Frenchtown Poultry Farm, in New Jersey, where he found that

> Each 18 by 24 inch cage on the Frenchtown farm contains nine hens who seemed jammed into them by some unseen hand. They barely have enough room to turn around in the cages.
> "Really, you should have no more than eight birds in a cage that size," conceded Oscar Grossman, the farm's lessor. "But sometimes you have to do things to get the most out of your stock."[11]

Actually, if Mr. Grossman had put only eight birds in his cages they would still have been grossly overcrowded; at nine to a cage they have only ⅓ square foot per bird.

In 1968 the farm magazine *American Agriculturalist* advised its readers in an article headed "Bird Squeezing" that it had been found possible to stock at ⅓ square foot per bird by putting four birds in a 12 by 16 inch cage. This was apparently a novel step at the time; the steady increase in densities over the years is indicated by the fact that a 1974 issue of the same magazine describing the Lannsdale Poultry Farm, near Rochester, New York, mentions the same housing density without any suggestion that it is unusual.[12] In reading egg industry magazines I have found numerous reports of similar high densities, and scarcely any that are substantially lower. My own visits to poultry farms in the United States have shown the same pattern. The highest reported density that I have read about is at the Hainsworth farm in Mt. Morris, New York, where four hens are squeezed into cages 12 inches by 12 inches, or just one square foot—and the reporter adds: "Some hold five birds when Hainsworth has more birds than room".[13] This means ¼ and sometimes ⅕ square foot per bird. At this stocking rate a *single sheet of quarto paper represents the living area of two to three hens.*

Under the conditions standard on modern egg farms in the United States and other "developed nations" every natural instinct the birds have is frustrated. They cannot walk around, scratch the ground, dustbathe, build a nest, or stretch their wings. They are not part of a flock. They cannot keep out of each other's way and weaker birds have no escape from the attacks of stronger ones, already maddened by the unnatural conditions. . . .

Intensive production of pigs and cattle is now also common; but of all the forms of intensive farming now practiced, the quality veal industry ranks as the most morally repugnant, comparable only with bar-

[11]*Daily News*, September 1, 1971.
[12]*American Agriculturist*, August 1968, April 1974.
[13]*Upstate*, August 5, 1973.

barities like the force-feeding of geese through a funnel that produces the deformed livers made into *pâté de foie gras*. The essence of veal raising is the feeding of a high-protein food (that should be used to reduce malnutrition in poorer parts of the world) to confined, anemic calves in a manner that will produce a tender, pale-colored flesh that will be served to gourmets in expensive restaurants. Fortunately this industry does not compare in size with poultry, beef, or pig production; nevertheless it is worth our attention because it represents an extreme, both in the degree of exploitation to which it subjects its animals and in its absurd inefficiency as a method of providing people with nourishment.

Veal is the flesh of a young calf, and the term was originally reserved for calves killed before they had been weaned from their mothers. The flesh of these very young animals was paler and more tender than that of a calf that had begun to eat grass; but there was not much of it, since calves begin to eat grass when they are a few weeks old and still very small. So there was little money in veal, and the small amount available came from the unwanted male calves produced by the dairy industry. These males were a nuisance to the dairy farmers, since the dairy breeds do not make good beef cattle. Therefore they were sold as quickly as possible. A day or two after being born they were trucked to market where, hungry and frightened by the strange surroundings and the absence of their mothers, they were sold for immediate delivery to the slaughterhouse.

Once this was the main source of veal in the United States. Now, using methods first developed in Holland, farmers have found a way to keep the calf longer without the flesh becoming darker in color or less tender. This means that the veal calf, when sold, may weigh as much as 325 lbs., instead of the 90-odd lbs. that newborn calves weigh. Because veal fetches a premium price, this has made rearing veal calves a profitable occupation.

The trick depends on keeping the calf in highly unnatural conditions. If the calf were left to grow up outside, its playful nature would lead it to romp around the fields. Soon it would begin to develop muscles, which would make its flesh tough. At the same time it would eat grass and its flesh would lose the pale color that the flesh of newborn calves has. So the specialist veal producer takes his calves straight from the auction ring to a confinement unit. Here, in a converted barn or purpose-built shed, he will have rows of wooden stalls. Each stall will be 1 foot 10 inches wide and 4 feet 6 inches long. It will have a slatted wooden floor, raised above the concrete floor of the shed. The calves will be tethered by a chain around the neck to prevent them from turning around in their stalls. (The chain may be removed when the calves grow too big to turn around in such narrow stalls.) The stall will have no straw or other bedding, since the calf might eat it, spoiling the paleness of his flesh.

Here the calves will live for the next thirteen to fifteen weeks. They will leave their stalls only to be taken out to slaughter. They are fed a totally liquid diet, based on non-fat milk powder with added vitamins, minerals, and growth-promoting drugs. . . .

The narrow stalls and their slatted wooden floors are a serious source of discomfort for the calves. The inability to turn around is frustrating. When he lies down, the calf must lie hunched up, sitting almost on top of his legs rather than having them out to one side as he would do if he had more room. A stall too narrow to turn around in is also too narrow to groom comfortably in; and calves have an innate desire to twist their heads around and groom themselves with their tongues. A wooden floor without any bedding is hard and uncomfortable; it is rough on the calves' knees as they get up and lie down. In addition, animals with hooves are uncomfortable on slatted floors. A slatted floor is like a cattle grid, which cattle will always avoid, except that the slats are closer together. The spaces, however, must still be large enough to allow manure to fall or be washed through, and this means that they are large enough to make the calves uncomfortable.[14]

The special nature of the veal calf has other implications that show the industry's lack of genuine concern for the animals' welfare. Obviously the calves sorely miss their mothers. They also miss something to suck on. The urge to suck is strong in a baby calf, as it is in a baby human. These calves have no teat to suck on, nor do they have any substitute. From their first day in confinement—which may well be only the third or fourth day of their lives—they drink from a plastic bucket. Attempts have been made to feed calves through artificial teats, but the problems of keeping the teats clean and sterile are apparently too great for the farmer to try to overcome. It is common to see calves frantically trying to suck some part of their stalls, although there is usually nothing suitable; and if you offer a veal calf your finger he will immediately begin to suck on it, as a human baby sucks its thumb.

Later on the calf develops a desire to ruminate—that is, to take in roughage and chew the cud. But roughage is strictly forbidden and so, again, the calf may resort to vain attempts to chew the sides of its stall. Digestive disorders, including stomach ulcers, are common in veal calves, as are chronically loose bowel movements.

As if this were not enough, there is the fact that the calf is deliberately kept anemic. As one veal producers' journal has said,

[14]Ruth Harrison, *Animal Machines*, p. 72.

Color of veal is one of the primary factors involved in obtaining "top-dollar" returns from the fancy veal market . . . "light color" veal is a premium item much in demand at better clubs, hotels and restaurants. "Light color" or pink veal is partly associated with the amount of iron in the muscle of the calves.[15]

So veal feeds are deliberately kept low in iron. A normal calf would obtain iron from grass or other forms of roughage, but since a veal calf is not allowed this he becomes anemic. Pale pink flesh is in fact anemic flesh. The demand for flesh of this color is a matter of snob appeal. The color does not affect the taste and it certainly does not make the flesh more nourishing—rather the opposite.

Calves kept in this manner are unhappy and unhealthy animals. Despite the fact that the veal producer selects only the strongest, healthiest calves to begin with, uses a medicated feed as a routine measure, and gives additional injections at the slightest sign of illness, digestive, respiratory and infectious diseases are widespread. It is common for a veal producer to find that one in ten of a batch of calves do not survive the fifteen weeks of confinement. Ten percent mortality over such a short period would be disastrous for anyone raising calves for beef, but the veal producer can tolerate this loss because of the high price restaurants are prepared to pay for his product. If the reader will recall that this whole laborious, wasteful, and painful process exists for the sole purpose of pandering to would-be gourmets who insist on pale, soft veal, no further comment should be needed.

[15]The Stall Street Journal, published by Provimi, Inc., Watertown, Wisconsin, November 1973.

RICHARD RYDER

Experiments on Animals

... most experiments are not worth doing and the data obtained are
not worth publishing.
—Prof. H. F. Harlow (*Journal of Comparative and Physiological Psychology*, 1962.)

In August 1970 Her Majesty's Stationery Office printed the Home
Office "Return of Experiments performed under the Cruelty to Animals Act 1876 during 1969." It was recorded that 5,418,929 experiments were performed in that year. Of these, 4,743,609 were carried
out without anaesthesia. Of the experiments performed with anaesthesia,
500,335 allowed recovery from the influence of the anaesthetic. There
were 14,684 experiments performed on cats, and 17,160 on dogs. These
experiments were performed by 9,252 out of a total of 13,791 licenses.

Over 900,000 experiments were performed on behalf of Government
bodies, such as the Medical Research Council and the Ministry of Defence. Nearly a million and a half experiments were mandatory tests
of drugs under the Diseases of Animals Act 1950 and the Therapeutic
Substances Act 1956.

There are 605 places registered in Britain for the performance of experiments on living animals, calculated to cause pain. Registered laboratories were visited 2,850 times during the year by thirteen Home
Office Inspectors. Twenty-three irregularities were reported.

In practice the Home Office considers the number of animals used
may reasonably be assumed to be no more than the number of experiments returned. There is however no absolute rule on this issue.

From Richard Ryder, "Experiments on Animals" in *Animals, Men and Morals*, ed.
S. and R. Godlovitch and J. Harris (New York: Taplinger), 1972. © Richard Ryder.

The table below shows the rapid growth in the numbers of experiments performed since 1885.

Year	Total Experiments	Number of Inspectors
1885	797	1
1910	95,731	2
1920	70,367	3
1930	450,822	2
1939	954,691	3
1950	1,779,215	4
1960	3,701,184	5
1963	4,196,566	6
1967	4,755,680	8
1968	5,212,215	10
1969	5,418,929	13

Note:

It can be seen from figures that the Cruelty to Animals Act of 1876 was framed to control fewer than 800 experiments in a year, and the same unaltered Act is intended to control nearly 7,000 times that number of experiments today. Over the two years, 1967–1969, the number of experiments has increased at the average rate of 331,624 experiments per year.

In 1885 the ratio of Inspectors to the number of experiments was approximately 1 to 800. In 1969 the ratio was 1 to 416,000. The ratio of Inspectors' visits to the number of experiments performed is approximately 1 to 2,000.

These figures for the United Kingdom are given in detail because of their alleged accuracy. Few other countries publish official statistics on this issue. Estimates of the number of animal lives sacrificed annually in the laboratories of the USA range widely between 20,000,000 and 200,000,000. A report published in the *Journal of Surgical Research* (June, 1967) estimated an annual turnover for American laboratories of approximately 250,000 monkeys, 100,000 cats and 250,000 dogs. (If, therefore, the ratio of dogs used to the total number of experiments is similar in the USA to that in the UK, then the American total for all animals used annually would be in the region of 80,000,000.)

The number of primates used is increasing so rapidly that at least nine Asian and eight African primate species are considered to be threatened with extinction (International Union for the Conservation of Nature Bulletin Vol. XII, p. 120). It is estimated that between four and nine chimpanzees are killed for every individual captured for research (*New Scientist*, April 23, 1970, p. 167). The Board of Trade reports that in 1966, 22,308 licences were issued for the importation of primates into the UK for experimental purposes (House of Commons, May 31, 1967) and it is recorded that the USA imported 1,500,000 rhesus monkeys in a period of only six years. It is calculated, therefore, that as men use not less than 250,000 monkeys and apes annually for biomedical research, a threat exists for the rarer species (*Biologist,* Vol. XVII, Jan. 1970).

Only approximately one quarter of active licensees publish the results of their experiments. The majority of experiments are unpublished apparently because the results are "inconclusive" or "insufficiently important." (Littlewood Report, p. 53, p. 166.)

Of those experiments performed by Government Departments in 1969, 148,848 were carried out at the Microbiological Research and Chemical Defence Establishment at Porton, Wiltshire, under the control of the Ministry of Defence.

Behind the Statistics

Although purely academic establishments probably do not account for as many experiments as do commercial enterprises, there is a tendency for an increasing number of different university departments to incorporate research on animals. Not only may there be animals kept in departments of Anatomy, Pathology, Pharmacology, Biochemistry, Physiology, Medicine and Veterinary Studies, but also, nowadays, in departments of Psychology, Zoology, Ecology, Forestry, and Agriculture.

In the field of Psychology the number of experiments is very large and many of these are of a disturbing sort. For example the papers published dealing with experiments on the brains of living animals (including cutting, coagulating, vacuum removal of brain tissue, electrical and chemical stimulation) reported in the international journal, *Psychological Abstracts,* now numbers about 700 in one year. As very few of these papers report on the use of less than ten animals and as it is known (in the UK) that only about one experiment in four is published it can be seen that the number of psychological experiments involving living brain operations is now very many each year.

Although an increasing number of monkeys are being used, it is the unfortunate and friendless laboratory rat which has been the psychologist's main victim. Professor P. L. Broadhurst illustrates this when he reports that psychologists have blinded rats, then deafened them and finally eliminated their sense of smell in order to observe how they learn in a maze; "it was found that rats deprived in this way showed very little ability to learn." Broadhurst also reports that male rats were forced into homosexual behaviour with other rats "by keeping them on an electric grid and shocking them through the feet." (P. L. Broadhurst, *The Science of Animal Behaviour*, Penguin, 1963.)

Very many psychological experiments involve "punishment" of animals. As Dr. Keller Breland describes it, "the typical laboratory experiment involving punishment or threat of punishment is conducted in a very restricted area—a closed box or small pen. Sometimes the animal is even strapped down. A light or buzzer signals the onset of a shock—the most common 'punishment' in such experiments. When the shock is applied, the animal tries to escape, but if he is boxed in or tied down, he cannot do so." (Breland and Breland, *Animal Behaviour*, p. 63.)

In the majority of accounts there is no report of what happened to the animals after the experimental procedures were completed. Some papers use the word "sacrificed" sanctimoniously, others optimistically say "killed painlessly"—but just how painless is it to receive three or four blows of the head on the edge of a workbench, or an injection into the heart? (An eyewitness recently told me that in one Oxford laboratory rats were killed "humanely" by being swiftly disembowelled.)

Similarly misleading may be the claims that procedures are carried out under anaesthesia. Restraining devices and paralysing drugs can today be so effective that an anaesthetic is often unnecessary from the purely practical point of view. The risk of giving a dose too large and thereby losing an expensive chimpanzee, for example, may often tempt a scientist or technician, inexperienced with sophisticated anaesthetic techniques, to give a dose too small, from which the animal quickly recovers—but not of course until after it has been strapped securely to the operating table. Recent research suggests that human surgical patients, even when apparently completely anaesthetised, have power to recall some of the events during anaesthesia (Hetherington, B.P.S. Conference, 1970) and it is hard to believe that anaesthesia in animal experiments, only rarely expertly induced, is always entirely successful in maintaining levels of total unconsciousness.

It can be seen from the Home Office returns that only 15 per cent of British experiments involve anaesthesia. It should not be imagined that all the remaining procedures involve drastic operations causing intense pain. They do, however, include practically all tests of poisons, chemical and biological weapons, the use of electric shock in behavioural studies, the cultivation of tumours and the deliberate infection with diseases; these experiments often involve considerable suffering which is rarely, if ever, mitigated by analgesia or anaesthesia.

Over 25 per cent of all British experiments are *mandatory* tests of drugs (such as ordinary cold pills, sedatives, sleeping tablets, laxatives etc.) under the Therapeutic Substances Act of 1956 and the Diseases of Animals Act 1950. This figure does not include the testing of new foodstuffs and food additives, which are extensively tested on a voluntary basis in order to ensure that they contain "nothing injurious to health" as laid down under the Food and Drugs Act 1955. Cosmetics and toiletries may also be tested for toxicity, and the Medicines Act 1968 gives the government the power to actually require such testing. Indeed this Act (when finally implemented) may have the effect of greatly increasing the already very considerable amount of mandatory testing with animals.

The classical toxicity test for all such substances has been the LD_{50}. This crude and cruel procedure consists in determining the dosage level at which 50 per cent of the test animals survive and 50 per cent die. Almost by definition one is establishing a level of dosage at which the animals will be made ill, most of them lingering near death before succumbing or surviving. Where not very poisonous substances are tested, enormous dosages are forced into the animals so that as Professor A. C. Frazer points out:

> In some cases death in animals was caused merely by the physical properties (osmotic and pH effects, for example) of the large volumes or high concentrations that were given to them; these properties had no relevance to the low concentrations used in food technology.

It takes little imagination to see that suffering must be involved in, for example, the mandatory forced feeding of dogs with huge and lethal quantities of new medicinal stomach powders or breath sweeteners.

Differences in reaction to toxic substances vary considerably between species so that the value of these tests remains doubtful. Although thalidomide was extensively tested on animals in several countries, its terrible properties were not discovered. Conversely, penicillin, the greatest medical discovery of the century, was not extensively tested on animals before its miraculous therapeutic qualities were demonstrated in human patients. If it had been fully tested on animals its high toxicity for guinea pigs would have almost certainly prevented its clinical use.

The LD_{50} is carried out upon several different species at a time. The traditional choice of species is the rat, mouse, rabbit, dog (usually beagles) and the monkey. Prolonged toxicity studies consist of multiple doses spread over weeks or years. As Dr. S. B. Baker has written—"these from time immemorial have been the mainstay of the pharmacologists' studies of toxicity. In practice, they are of little use and are expensive in animals."

Substances intended for export are often tested in Britain in order to conform with the laws of the importing country, which are sometimes even more stringent and comprehensive (and cruel) than the British law.

So many experiments are performed that only a small percentage of them need to be cruel for the numbers to still remain very considerable.

If, for instance, only one per cent of British experiments every year (and this must be far short of the actual number) intentionally cause pain, then that means that 50,000 animals suffer. Furthermore it seems likely that there are just as many cases where suffering is caused accidentally, through carelessness or lack of sensitivity on the part of the technician or experimenter.

However, let us proceed with some examples of experiments, not chosen for their exceptional cruelty, but for the representative nature of the various ways in which suffering can occur in a laboratory.

Examples of Experiments on Animals

1. Despite the fact that it is well known that seat belts cause foetal deaths in pregnant women it is reported that tests will be undertaken at the University of Oklahoma Medical Centre using pregnant baboons. Dr. Warren M. Crosby has received $103,800 under contract from the US Dept of Transportation for this project. These animals, in the third trimester of pregnancy will be placed on impact sleds and subjected to crash experiments at Holloman Air Force Base, New Mexico. (*Med. Trib.*, September 5, 1968.)

2. Researchers for Technology Inc., San Antonio, Texas constructed a pneumatically driven piston to impact an anvil attached to a special helmet called HAD I producing impact to the heads of 13 monkeys. But they found the blows were insufficient to cause concussion, so they made a more powerful device called HAD II which they used on the same 13 monkeys and found that it caused cardiac damage, haemorrhages and brain damage from protrusion of plastic rings which they had implanted under the monkeys' skulls.

Monkey number 49-2 was again subjected to HAD II six days later, then 38 days later was struck multiple blows until she died.

Some of the animals who temporarily survived suffered subsequent fits and the researchers were impressed to find that after the experiments the monkeys' behaviour "was distinctly abnormal. The usual post-acceleration behaviour in the cage was that of hanging upside down cowering in a corner."

3. Dr. L. M. Potash of the Department of Psychology, University of Alberta, Edmonton, Canada, elicited vocalisation from 16 Japanese quails by gradually lowering a concentric stainless steel electrode into their brains in 0.3 to 0.4 mm steps and electrically stimulating with an amperage of 300 μ. He notes that "electrical brain stimulation has elicited vocalisation in a number of avian species (crow, Adams 1965; parrot, Adams 1965; pigeon, Akerman, 1965; chicken, Adams, 1965;

Murphay and Phillips, 1967; Putkommen, 1966, 1967; von Holst and St. Paul, 1963)." (*Behaviour*, 36, 1970.)

4. K. H. Kurtz and J. Pearl of the University of Buffalo report that: "recent studies (Baron, Brookshire and Littman, 1957, Levine, Chevalier and Korchin, 1956) have obtained results suggesting that experiences of intense fear predispose an organism to react with increased fear in subsequent situations employing aversive stimulation, i.e. to be generally more fearful."

In their own study they subjected 30 female hooded rats to intense electric shocks at irregular intervals without warning. They note that such treatment "evoked squealing, defecation and vigorous attempts to jump out of the compartment." (*Journal of Comparative and Physiological Psychology*, 1960.)

R. W. Sperry of the California Institute of Technology is well-known for his "split-brain" experiments in which he divided the brains of living animals into two entirely separate yet functioning pieces.

In one such experiment he "split" brains of seven rhesus monkeys and confirmed R. E. Myer's finding with chimpanzees that there is no transfer of skills from one hand to the other. It is rather as if there were two animals with the same body. (*Journal of Comparative and Physiological Psychology*, 1960.)

6. N. J. Carlson gave electric shocks to sixteen dogs and found that his "high-shock group" acquired "anxiety" faster. (*Journal of Comparative and Physiological Psychology*, 1960.)

7. J. S. Schwartzbaum from Hartford, Connecticut, points out that monkeys which have had a part of their brain cut out (which is called the amygdola) will sometimes eat faeces. In this study he used eight pre-adolescent rhesus monkeys. After opening their skulls under anaesthesia he removed their amygdolas "using a small-gauge sucker" in order to observe "these dietary changes." (*Journal of Comparative and Physiological Psychology*, 1960.)

8. H. F. and Margaret Harlow of the University of Wisconsin separated sixty-three rhesus monkeys from their mothers five to nine hours after birth and housed them in individual wire-mesh cages measuring fifteen inches by eighteen inches by twenty-four inches. (*Journal of Comparative and Physiological Psychology*, 1960.)

This is part of a long term study of the effects of maternal deprivation in rhesus monkeys.

9. K. R. Henry of Wisconsin University placed 571 hybrid mice in a large chromatography jar and sounded a five inch electric bell generat-

ing 102 decibels of noise for 90 seconds. "Records were made of the incidence of wild running, tonic, clonic and lethal seizures." 181 of the mice died. (*Journal of Comparative and Physiological Psychology*, 1969.)

10. O. S. Ray and R. J. Barrett of Pittsburgh gave electric shocks to the feet of 1,042 mice. They then caused convulsions by giving more intense shocks through cup-shaped electrodes applied to the animals' eyes or through pressure spring clips attached to their ears. Unfortunately some of the mice who "successfully completed Day One training were found sick or dead prior to testing on Day Two." (*Journal of Comparative and Physiological Psychology*, 1969.)

11. A. R. Caggiula and R. Eiberger of the universities of Pittsburgh and Michigan describe the "Copulation of Virgin Male Rats Evoked by Painful Peripheral Stimulation."
They prevented the animals from biting at the electrodes delivering the shock by surrounding them by other electrified wires—"several contacts with the protective wire were sufficient to discourage future attempts." (*Journal of Comparative and Physiological Psychology*, 1969.)

12. Mrs P. Y. Berry of Kuala Lumpur killed 91 toads and examined stomach contents demonstrating that the "Bufo asper species feeds exclusively on the ground and that its feeding, like that of many amphibians, seems to depend on the abundance and availability of food." (*Zoological Journal of the Linnean Society*, 49, 1970.)

13. E. H. Stidier, J. W. Procter and D. J. Howell starved bats to death and concluded that "the tolerance of these species of Myosis are not remarkable in respect to weight-loss tolerance of other mammals." (*Journal of Mammalogy*, 51, 1970.)

14. Researchers sponsored by the National Institute of Health report on the experimental induction of heart attacks in dogs. (*Medical Tribune*, 1968.)

15. Other NIH workers have given thalidomide to monkeys, rabbits and rats producing deformed offspring. (*J. Pharmacol. Exper. Therapeut.*, 160, 1968.) (This research was performed after, not before, it had been discovered that thalidomide caused deformities in human babies.)

16. J. V. Brady placed monkeys in restraining devices and gave them electric shocks every twenty seconds during six hour experimental periods. After twenty-three days monkeys began to die suddenly of stomach ulcers. (*Scientific American*, 1958.)

17. R. G. Braun of Holloman Air Force Base noted that "six monkeys in restraint chairs for thirty days developed oedema and psoriasis of the

feet and legs, and decubital ulcers in and around their ischial callosites."
Nevertheless he concluded that "long-term behavioural studies requir-
ing continuously restrained primates are feasible." (*Journal of Experimental Animal Behaviour*, 1968, 11, (I).)

18. I. T. Kurtsin of Leningrad reports that "healing of burns on the
skin proceeded substantially more slowly in dogs with experimental
neurosis (106 to 133 days after the burn)." Similarly, healing of lacera-
tions took forty to sixty days—"the process of healing in the neurotic
subjects was protracted, as bleeding and granulation developed followed
by slow epithelialisation." He has also exposed neurotic dogs to high
levels of radiation. He found that 70% of dogs "with a weak nervous
system" died as a result of radiation sickness. (M. W. Fox and W. B.
Sauders, eds., *Abnormal Behaviour in Animals*, 1968, Chapter 6).

19. At the Tasman Vaccine Laboratory, New Zealand, cats were
killed by infection. "On arrival, the cats were identified, bled by cardiac
puncture and immediately force-fed with 15 ml of a 20% suspension
of virulent paneucopenia virus-infected kitten intestine. These animals
were observed several times daily and post-mortem examinations were
made on those found dead or destroyed in extremis." (*Veterinary, Record*, December 1968.)

20. Indian scientists paralysed monkeys by giving lumbar injections
of pure OX-Dapro—"the three monkeys with flaccid areflexic paraplegia
showed no response to either stamping on the tail or pin-prick applied
to the lower-limbs." (*Nature*, May 6, 1967.)

21. K. M. Bykov and I. T. Kurtsin of Leningrad using dogs observed
the "effects of various pathological processes such as experimental gas-
tritis and gastric ulcer, luteritis and proctitis, cystitis, and cholecystitis,
fractures of the long bones, injuries to the soft tissues, experimental
osseous tuberculosis and application of a tourniquet to a limb." (*Medzig*,
Moscow, 1960.)

22. A. N. Worden reports on an experiment performed by G. Pam-
piglione on fifty-seven puppies born of starved mothers. Twenty-eight
of those pups died soon after birth and the survivors showed abnormali-
ties such as "atheroid movements of the head and neck and ataxic gait
... one animal died during an epileptiform fit and two others were
found dead or injured in circumstances also suggestive of fits." Others
"often ran in narrow circles." (M. W. Fox, W. B. Saunders, *op. cit.*
Chapter 16.)

23. Dr. R. White of Case Western Reserve School of Medicine re-

ports that he has transplanted the brains of small dogs into the necks of large dogs.

24. On July 1, 1946 the world's fourth atomic bomb was dropped on a target of seventy-five ships containing 4,500 experimental animals. (*The Star*, July 3, 1946.)

25. W. R. Adey of the University of California prepared monkeys caught in the jungles of Thailand by placing them in neck restraint devices, cutting off their tails and extracting their canine teeth. Electrodes were implanted deep in their brains. Catheters were inplanted in bladders for urine collection into main blood vessels and into the heart. After behavioural training some of these monkeys were fired into space. (*New York Post*, July 8, 1969.) One of these monkeys, Bonny, died unexpectedly after an eight and a half day flight.

26. W. R. Thompson and R. Melzak kept puppies isolated individually in small boxes for nine months and thus "denied them any experience with the outside world." Tubes were placed on their limbs and a collar around their neck to prevent tactile contact with their own body. The effects of this deprivation were studied. (*Scientific American*, 1956.)

27. Licklider kept animals awake by placing them in rotating drums. Those animals which survived were highly irritable and aggressive after thirty days without sleep. (*Journal of Comparative and Physiological Psychology*, 1950.)

28. Curt P. Richter of John Hopkins Medical School, Baltimore, investigated the phenomenon of sudden death in animals and men. He did this by dropping rats into specially designed cylindrical tanks filled with water and noting how long it took them to drown. The rats either died promptly from "hopelessness"—"they seem literally to 'give up' " —or swam for up to sixty hours before finally drowning. Among the variables tested, it was concluded that trimming their whiskers, "destroying possibly their most important means of contact with the outside world," resulted in more sudden deaths. (Chapter 16 in *Psychopathology*, ed. Reed, Alexander & Tomkins, 1958.)

Some British Experiments

1. D. I. H. Simpson, I. Zlotnik, D. A. Rutter, researchers at the Microbiological Research Establishment, Porton, Salisbury, injected guineapigs, rhesus and vervet monkeys with Vervet Monkey Disease.

The animals developed a febrile illness lasting six-days—"during this period the animals ate and drank very little, lost weight and remained hunched up and immobile in their cages." In the monkeys "the febrile stage continued until immediately before death which occurred six to nine days after infection."

Those animals surviving the illness were killed with ether or injections of nembutal into the heart.

Pathological study revealed the spleen of the guinea pigs was "sometimes three times its normal size" and "brains were congested." (*British Journal of Experimental Pathology*, 1968.)

2. R. Kumar at University College, London studied the "effects of fear on exploratory behaviour in rats" and concluded that "inescapable aversive stimulation, in this case electric shocks to rats' feet, consistently resulted in subsequent avoidance of the environment in which the shocks had been given." (*Quarterly Journal of Experimental Psychology*, 1970.)

3. Researchers fed 113 puppies on excessive doses of irradiated ergosterol—"Pup No. 1 suffered rapid loss of weight, vomiting, diarrhoea, conjunctivitis which kept the lids almost completely closed, until death occurred on the eleventh day." (*British Journal of Experimental Pathology*, 1932.)

4. Ophthalmologists at Oxford studied the effect of ten eye irritants on unanaesthetised rabbits—"the oedema of the cornea may assume fantastic proportions, the cornea being sometimes swollen to nearly twenty times the normal thickness." In some cases the eyes "disintegrate and deliquesce within a few days." (*British Journal of Ophthalmology*, 1948 Monograph.)

5. E. Weston Hurst and J. L. Pawan of the Lister Institute in London injected substances into the brain of monkeys and observed that "violent muscular spasms, occasionally sufficient to throw the animal bodily across cage occurred, and gradually passed into a state of general weakness ending in death." Some animals "bit themselves severely, two chewing off the end of a finger, and one, the whole skin of the forearm, exposing the muscles from the elbow to the wrist." (*The Lancet*, September 19, 1931.)

6. N. K. Humphrey and L. Weiskrantz at Cambridge made surgical lesions on the brains of monkeys and observed that subsequently the animals "stumbled around their cages, bumping into the walls and hitting their heads on protruding objects. If they had to steady themselves by catching hold of the wire, they reached too short, too far, or in the wrong direction, missed their target and fell; they appeared quite insensitive to hard pinches on one or both sides of their bodies and often let their limbs droop lifeless; they made no attempt to reach for food and showed no interest in it if it was put into their hands, although

they took it greedily if it was pressed against their lips." (*Quarterly Journal of Experimental Psychology*, 1969.)

7. R. J. Neale and G. Wiseman at Sheffield University studied some of the effects of "semi-starvation and complete starvation" of rats. (*Journal of Physiology*, October, 1968.)

8. D. Lamb and L. Reid exposed rats to tobacco smoke over a period of six weeks. The animals were placed in aluminium cabinets fed with smoke by a Wright Auto-Smoker set to smoke one cigarette in six to ten minutes. (*British Medical Journal*, January 4, 1969.)

9. At the National Institute for Medical Research, Mill Hill, London, W. Feldberg and S. L. Sherwood injected chemicals into the brains of cats—"with a number of widely different substances, recurrent patterns of reaction were obtained. Retching, vomiting, defaecation, increased salivation and greatly accelerated respiration leading to panting were common features." They report that an injection of acetylcholine either "produces a peculiar high-pitched cry or the cat retches a few times or does both." They found that "the intraventricular injection of banthine in the unanaesthetised cat causes profound motor impairment." The injection into the brain of a large dose of Tubocurarine caused the cat to jump "from the table to the floor and then straight into its cage, where it started calling more and more noisily whilst moving about restlessly and jerkily . . . during the next four minutes the movements became wilder . . . finally the cat fell with legs and neck flexed, jerking in rapid clonic movements, the condition being that of a major (epileptic) convulsion . . . within a few seconds the cat got up, ran for a few yards at high speed and fell in another fit. The whole process was repeated several times within the next ten minutes, during which the cat lost faeces and foamed at the mouth." This animal finally died thirty-five minutes after the brain injection. (*Journal of Physiology*, 1954, 123.)

10. At the Royal College of Surgeons, London, albino guinea-pigs were fed a scorbutogenic diet so that after six weeks they "developed overt scurvy with typical loss of hair and petechial haemorrhages on pressure points." The typical symptoms of scurvy include bleeding from the mucous membranes of noses, eyes and alimentary or respiratory tracts, and extensive ulceration. (*The Lancet*, March 4, 1967.)

11. Recordings were made by T. Biscoe and M. Purves from the stripped sinus nerves of "anaesthetised" cats whose hindlegs were strapped to a bicycle pedal and rotated at up to 100 revs per minute. However it was noted that "the anaesthesia was not deep enough to abolish the reflexes and, in the experiments, the movements imposed on the hind limbs met with some resistance." (*Journal of Physiology*, 1967.)

12. At the Department of Human Anatomy at Oxford mice had their thymus glands removed, were given total body irradiation, and then infected with leprosy. These experiments were performed by R. Rees, A. G. Weddell, M. F. Walters and E. Palmer. (*Nature*, August 5, 1967.)

13. S. Zuckerman (formerly Chief Scientific Adviser to HM Government) studied the effects of high explosive blast on monkeys, cats, rabbits, guinea-pigs, rats, mice and pigeons. (*Lancet*, August 24, 1940.)

14. G. Duncan and A. Blalock anaesthetised dogs and then experimentally crushed their legs for five hours. Only one dog survived this treatment—the rest died of shock. (*Lancet*, October 10, 1942.)

15. G. R. Hervey, a Medical Research Council scientist at Cambridge, surgically joined rats together in pairs of artificial Siamese twins and found that 33 per cent died either during operation or shortly afterwards. Those which survived underwent brain surgery. (*Journal of Physiology*, March 1959.)

16. A pathologist in Glasgow infected kittens with lung-worm. Experimental forms of treatment killed the majority of animals—"and death was preceded by excessive salivation, impairment of locomotion and vision, muscular twitchings, panting, respiratory distress and convulsions." (*The Veterinary Record*, December 28, 1968.)

17. J. Hopewell and E. A. Wright of St. Mary's Hospital Medical School, London, had the left halves of the brains of seven-day-old rats irradiated with X-rays, whilst they were breathing varying concentrations of oxygen. After a few weeks the animals were killed and the irradiated and non-irradiated halves of their brains were compared in weight. The authors say that "compared with the adult rat [the brain] of the young nestling rat is very sensitive to radiation damage." (*International Journal of Radiation Biology*, 1909.)

18. E. G. Jones and T. P. S. Powell of the Department of Human Anatomy in Oxford in a series of experiments using more than twenty animals at a time, made lesions in the brains of Rhesus Monkeys as part of an anatomical study of sensory pathways in the brain. (*Brain*, Vol. 93, 1970.)

19. T. Adamson, R. Boyd, J. Hill, I. Normand, E. Reynolds and L. Strang of University College Hospital Medical School, London, asphyxiated foetal lambs, which had been removed by caesarian section from their mothers. (*Journal of Physiology*, April 1970.)

20. L. W. Duchen and Sabina Strich of the Institute of Psychiatry, De Crespigny Park, and the Maudsley Hospital, London, injected botul-

inus toxin into the legs of mice, causing local paralysis and atrophy. (*Quarterly Journal of Experimental Physiology*, January 1968.)

21. D. P. Cuthbertson and W. J. Tilstone of the University of Glasgow and Glasgow Royal Infirmary broke the limbs of rats to find the effect this had on mineral metabolism. (*Quarterly Journal of Experimental Physiology*, October 1968.)

22. M. Malik of Queens University in Belfast devised a "new 'burning iron' device for the experimental production of contact burns on laboratory animals' skin." This, he suggests, might be used to replace old methods, which include "use of naked flame, dipping the animal into hot water, contact with hot plates and irradiation and flash burns." (*Laboratory Animals*, October 1970.)

Life in the Laboratory

This sample of experiments gives some idea of the sorts of procedures used daily in laboratories throughout the world. Often before and occasionally after these experiences (if they survive them, that is to say) the research animals are kept in the laboratories for months and even years. Sometimes captured from the great arboreal freedom of their jungle homes, monkeys are closely confined in cages only three or four feet square. Usually they receive no variety of diet but only approved proprietary pellets. They may see no other living creatures except a white-coated technician on a brief daily visit. Very often the animal-room is without windows, being artificially ventilated by a machine which produces a constant unvarying drone. In order to facilitate cleaning, the animals live upon wire-mesh. They can never sit or lie down on a flat, soft or yielding surface. Little wonder that by the time they are needed for the knife or the needle they are so crazed or inert that they are no longer representative examples of animal life. Psychologists who study the behaviour of thousands of such creatures annually, rarely make allowances for the fact that their pathetic subjects have been so deprived that they have become more like monsters than animals. Many people who have experienced close affectionate relationships with individuals of other species testify to the considerable potential for emotional and intellectual development that animals have. When properly cared for a pet dog or cat can develop great subtleties of behaviour that the laboratory animal never shows. Those who have been fortunate enough to closely observe unfrightened animals living in the wild are often struck by the complexity and richness of the life they lead. These positive pleasures the laboratory animal never knows; for him the same four white walls and the smell of disinfectant. As Professor Broadhurst enthusiastically describes it—"It is now possible to rear and breed many smaller laboratory animals solely on a diet of tap-water and compressed food, not unlike dog biscuits or cattle cake. Some laboratories have automatic devices for delivering this food and water to the animals in their cages; sanitary arrangements may also be automatic. The animals have suitably sized wire-mesh floors in their cages so that droppings and urine pass straight through and are washed away from time to time. . . . And so the laboratory animal is raised in these optimum conditions until it is needed for experimental puposes." (*The Science of Animal Behaviour*, pp. 49, 50.)

Such "optimum conditions" are reminiscent of factory farms and seem to inspire similar arguments in support of them. Referring to the size of the cage the animals are kept in, Broadhurst comments, "It is often thought to be too small, but with nocturnal animals such as the rat or mouse, which spend most of the day asleep—since it is their 'night'—the size of the cage is immaterial after a certain point." (ibid., p. 48.)

These excerpts from a laboratory manual published by a well-known American university give some idea what day to day life is like for many laboratory animals:

> There are two ways a frightened cat can be removed from a cage. One is with a snare. Hold the snare in your right hand and pull the cord tight. There will be coughing and fierce struggling. Try to keep the cat from choking to death as you pull the cat out by a snare. Always keep a safe distance between it and yourself.

The manual further advises, with complete composure:

> After feeding all the dogs in your area remove any dead dogs from the cages. Put the carcasses in the cold room then wash your hands.

This bland callousness is one of the most disturbing qualities of some experimenters. They accept, almost without thought, that their murderous activities are perfectly ordinary. In the statistical sense they are unfortunately correct, for as we know, over 5 million laboratory animals are used every year in just one country.

II

Animal and Human Nature

THE BIBLE

God Created Man
in His Own Image

CHAPTER ONE

20 And God said, Let the waters bring forth swarms of living creatures, and let birds fly above the earth across the firmament of the
heavens." ²¹So God created the great sea monsters and every living
creature that moves, with which the waters swarm, according to their
kinds, and every winged bird according to its kind. And God saw that
it was good. ²²And God blessed them, saying, "Be fruitful and multiply
and fill the waters in the seas, and let birds multiply on the earth."
²³And there was evening and there was morning, a fifth day.

24 And God said, "Let the earth bring forth living creatures according to their kinds: cattle and creeping things and beasts of the earth
according to their kinds." And it was so. ²⁵And God made the beasts of
the earth according to their kinds and the cattle according to their kinds,
and everything that creeps upon the ground according to its kind. And
God saw that it was good.

26 Then God said, "Let us make man in our image, after our likeness;
and let them have dominion over the fish of the sea, and over the
birds of the air, and over the cattle, and over all the earth, and over
every creeping thing that creeps upon the earth." ²⁷So God created
man in his own image, in the image of God he created him; male and
female he created them. ²⁸And God blessed them, and God said to them,
"Be fruitful and multiply, and fill the earth and subdue it; and have
dominion over the fish of the sea and over the birds of the air and over

From *Genesis*, Chapter 1, verses 20–31 and Chapter 9, verses 1–3.

every living thing that moves upon the earth." [29]And God said, "Behold, I have given you every plant yielding seed which is upon the face of all the earth, and every tree with seed in its fruit; you shall have them for food. [30]And to every beast of the earth, and to every bird of the air, and to everything that creeps on the earth, everything that has the breath of life, I have given every green plant for food." And it was so. [31]And God saw everything that he had made, and behold, it was very good. And there was evening and there was morning, a sixth day.

CHAPTER NINE

And God blessed Noah and his sons, and said to them, "Be fruitful and multiply, and fill the earth. [2]The fear of you and the dread of you shall be upon every beast of the earth, and upon every bird of the air, upon everything that creeps on the ground and all the fish of the sea; into your hand they are delivered. [3]Every moving thing that lives shall be food for you; and as I gave you the green plants, I give you everything."

ARISTOTLE

How Humans Differ
from Other Creatures

I

Of the psychic powers above enumerated some kinds of living things, as we have said, possess all, some less than all, others one only. Those we have mentioned are the nutritive, the appetitive, the sensory, the locomotive, and the power of thinking. Plants have none but the first, the nutritive, while another order of living things has this *plus* the sensory. If any order of living things has the sensory, it must also have the appetitive; for appetite is the genus of which desire, passion, and wish are the species; now all animals have one sense at least, viz. touch, and whatever has a sense has the capacity for pleasure and pain and therefore has pleasant and painful objects present to it, and wherever these are present, there is desire, for desire is just appetition of what is pleasant. Further, all animals have the sense for food (for touch is the sense for food); the food of all living things consists of what is dry, moist, hot, cold, and these are the qualities apprehended by touch; all other sensible qualities are apprehended by touch only indirectly. Sounds, colours, and odours contribute nothing to nutriment; flavours fall within the field of tangible qualities. Hunger and thirst are forms of desire, hunger a desire for what is dry and hot, thirst a desire for what is cold and moist, flavour is a sort of seasoning added to both. We must later clear up these points, but at present it may be enough to say that all

Selection I is from Aristotle; *On the Soul*, Book II, Chapter 3, 414a (28)–415a (10).
Selection II is from Aristotle, *The Parts of Animals*, Book I, Chapter I, 641a (35)–641b (10).

animals that possess the sense of touch have also appetition. The case of imagination is obscure; we must examine it later. Certain kinds of animals possess in addition the power of locomotion, and still another order of animate beings, i.e. man and possibly another order like man or superior to him, the power of thinking, i.e. mind. It is now evident that a single definition can be given of soul only in the same sense as one can be given of figure. For, as in that case there is no figure distinguishable and apart from triangle, etc., so here there is no soul apart from the forms of soul just enumerated. It is true that a highly general definition can be given for figure which will fit all figures without expressing the peculiar nature of any figure. So here in the case of soul and its specific forms. Hence it is absurd in this and similar cases to demand an absolutely general definition, which will fail to express the peculiar nature of anything that *is*, or again, omitting this, to look for separate definitions corresponding to each *infima species*. The cases of figure and soul are exactly parallel; for the particulars subsumed under the common name in both cases—figures and living beings—constitute a series, each successive term of which potentially contains its predecessor, e.g. the square the triangle, the sensory power the self-nutritive. Hence we must ask in the case of each order of living things, What is its soul, i.e. What is the soul of plant, animal, man? Why the terms are related in this serial way must form the subject of later examination. But the facts are that the power of perception is never found apart from the power of self-nutrition, while—in plants—the latter is found isolated from the former. Again, no sense is found apart from that of touch, while touch is found by itself; many animals have neither sight, hearing, nor smell. Again, among living things that possess sense some have the power of locomotion, some not. Lastly, certain living beings—a small minority—possess calculation and thought, for (among mortal beings) those which possess calculation have all the other powers above mentioned, while the converse does not hold—indeed some live by imagination alone, while others have not even imagination. The mind that knows with immediate intuition presents a different problem.

It is evident that the way to give the most adequate definition of soul is to seek in the case of *each* of its forms for the most appropriate definition.

II

What has been said suggests the question, whether it is the whole soul or only some part of it, the consideration of which comes within the province of natural science. Now if it be of the whole soul that this should treat, then there is no place for any other philosophy beside it.

For as it belongs in all cases to one and the same science to deal with correlated subjects—one and the same science, for instance, deals with sensation and with the objects of sense—and as therefore the intelligent soul and the objects of intellect, being correlated, must belong to one and the same science, it follows that natural science will have to include the whole universe in its province. But perhaps it is not the whole soul, nor all its parts collectively, that constitutes the source of motion; but there may be one part, identical with that in plants, which is the source of growth, another, namely the sensory part, which is the source of change of quality, while still another, and this not the intellectual part, is the source of locomotion. I say not the intellectual part; for other animals than man have the power of locomotion, but in none but him is there intellect.

SAINT THOMAS AQUINAS
Differences between Rational and Other Creatures

In the first place then, the very condition of the rational creature, in that it has dominion over its actions, requires that the care of providence should be bestowed on it for its own sake: whereas the condition of other things that have not dominion over their actions shows that they are cared for, not for their own sake, but as being directed to other things. Because that which acts only when moved by another, is like an instrument; whereas that which acts by itself, is like a principal agent. Now an instrument is required, not for its own sake, but that the principal agent may use it. Hence whatever is done for the care of the instruments must be referred to the principal agent as its end: whereas any such action directed to the principal agent as such, either by the agent itself or by another, is for the sake of the same principal agent. Accordingly intellectual creatures are ruled by God, as though He cared for them for their own sake, while other creatures are ruled as being directed to rational creatures.

Again. That which has dominion over its own act, is free in its action, because *he is free who is cause of himself*: whereas that which by some kind of necessity is moved by another to act, is subject to slavery. Therefore every other creature is naturally under slavery; the intellectual nature alone is free. Now, in every government provision is made for the free for their own sake; but for slaves that they may be useful to

From Saint Thomas Aquinas, *Summa Contra Gentiles*, literally translated by the English Dominican Fathers (Benziger Brothers, 1928), Third Book, Part II, Chap. CXII.

the free. Accordingly divine providence makes provision for the intellectual creature for its own sake, but for other creatures for the sake of the intellectual creature.

Moreover. Whenever certain things are directed to a certain end, if any of them are unable of themselves to attain to the end, they must needs be directed to those that attain to the end, which are directed to the end for their own sake. Thus the end of the army is victory, which the soldiers obtain by their own action in fighting, and they alone in the army are required for their own sake; whereas all others, to whom other duties are assigned, such as the care of horses, the preparing of arms, are requisite for the sake of the soldiers of the army. Now, it is clear from what has been said, that God is the last end of the universe, whom the intellectual nature alone obtains in Himself, namely by knowing and loving Him, as was proved above. Therefore the intellectual nature alone is requisite for its own sake in the universe, and all others for its sake.

Further. In every whole, the principal parts are requisite on their own account for the completion of the whole, while others are required for the preservation or betterment of the former. Now, of all the parts of the universe, intellectual creatures hold the highest place, because they approach nearest to the divine likeness. Therefore divine providence provides for the intellectual nature for its own sake, and for all others for its sake.

Besides. It is clear that all the parts are directed to the perfection of the whole: since the whole is not on account of the parts, but the parts on account of the whole. Now, intellectual natures are more akin to the whole than other natures: because, in a sense, the intellectual substance is all things, inasmuch as by its intellect it is able to comprehend all things; whereas every other substance has only a particular participation of being. Consequently God cares for other things for the sake of intellectual substances.

Besides. Whatever happens to a thing in the course of nature happens to it naturally. Now, we see that in the course of nature the intellectual substance uses all others for its own sake; either for the perfection of the intellect, which sees the truth in them as in a mirror; or for the execution of its power and development of its knowledge, in the same way as a craftsman develops the conception of his art in corporeal matter; or again to sustain the body that is united to an intellectual soul, as is the case in man. It is clear, therefore, that God cares for all things for the sake of intellectual substances.

Moreover. If a man seek something for its own sake, he seeks it always, because *what is per se, is always:* whereas if he seek a thing on account of something ese, he does not of necessity seek it always but only in reference to that for the sake of which he seeks it. Now, as we proved above, things derive their being from the divine will. Therefore whatever is always is willed by God for its own sake; and what is not always is willed by God, not for its own sake, but for another's. Now, intellectual substances approach nearest to being always, since they are incorruptible. They are, moreover, unchangeable, except in their choice. Therefore intellectual substances are governed for their own sake, as it were; and others for the sake of intellectual substances.

The fact that all the parts of the universe are directed to the perfection of the whole is not in contradiction with the foregoing conclusion: since all the parts are directed to the perfection of the whole, in so far as one part serves another. Thus in the human body it is clear that the lungs belong to the body's perfection, in that they serve the heart: wherefore there is no contradiction in the lungs being for the sake of the heart, and for the sake of the whole animal. In like manner that other natures are on account of the intellectual is not contrary to their being for the perfection of the universe: for without the things required for the perfection of the intellectual substance, the universe would not be complete.

Nor again does the fact that individuals are for the sake of the species militate against what has been said. Because through being directed to their species, they are directed also to the intellectual nature. For a corruptible thing is directed to man, not on account of only one individual man, but on account of the whole human species. Yet a corruptible thing could not serve the whole human species, except as regards its own entire species. Hence the order whereby corruptible things are directed to man, requires that individuals be directed to the species.

When we assert that intellectual substances are directed by divine providence for their own sake, we do not mean that they are not also referred by God and for the perfection of the universe. Accordingly they are said to be provided for on their own account, and others on account of them, because the goods bestowed on them by divine providence are not given them for another's profit: whereas those bestowed on others are in the divine plan intended for the use of intellectual substances. Hence it is said (Deut. iv. 19): *Lest thou see the sun and the moon and the other stars, and being deceived by error, thou adore and serve them, which the Lord thy God created for the service of all the nations that are under heaven:* and (Ps. viii. 8): *Thou hast subjected all things under his feet, all sheep and oxen: moreover, the beasts also of the field: and* (Wis. xii. 18): *Thou, being master of power, judgest with tranquillity, and with great favour disposest of us.*

Hereby is refuted the error of those who said it is sinful for a man to kill dumb animals: for by divine providence they are intended for man's use in the natural order. Hence it is no wrong for man to make use of them, either by killing or in any other way whatever. For this reason the Lord said to Noe (Gen. ix. 3): *As the green herbs I have delivered all flesh to you.*

And if any passages of Holy Writ seem to forbid us to be cruel to dumb animals, for instance to kill a bird with its young: this is either to remove man's thoughts from being cruel to other men, and lest through being cruel to animals one become cruel to human beings: or because injury to an animal leads to the temporal hurt of man, either of the doer of the deed, or of another: or on account of some signification: thus the Apostle expounds the prohibition against *muzzling the ox that treadeth the corn.*

RENÉ DESCARTES

Animals Are Machines

I

I had explained all these matters in some detail in the Treatise which I formerly intended to publish. And afterwards I had shown there, what must be the fabric of the nerves and muscles of the human body in order that the animal spirits therein contained should have the power to move the members, just as the heads of animals, a little while after decapitation, are still observed to move and bite the earth, notwithstanding that they are no longer animate; what changes are necessary in the brain to cause wakefulness, sleep and dreams; how light, sounds, smells, tastes, heat and all other qualities pertaining to external objects are able to imprint on it various ideas by the intervention of the senses; how hunger, thirst and other internal affections can also convey their impressions upon it; what should be regarded as the "common sense" by which these ideas are received, and what is meant by the memory which retains them, by the fancy which can change them in diverse ways and out of them constitute new ideas, and which, by the same means, distributing the animal spirits through the muscles, can cause the members of such a body to move in as many diverse ways, and in a manner as suitable to the objects which present themselves to its senses and to its internal passions, as can happen in our own case apart from the direc-

Selection I is from Descartes, *Discourse on Method* in *Philosophical Works of Descartes*, trans. E. S. Haldane and G. R. T. Ross (London: Cambridge University Press), vol. I, pp. 115–18. Selections II and III are from two letters by Descartes, to the Marquess of Newcastle (November 23, 1646) and to Henry More (February 5, 1649), in *Descartes: Philosophical Letters*, trans. and ed. Anthony Kenny. © 1970, Oxford University Press. Reprinted by permission of The Clarendon Press, Oxford.

tion of our free will. And this will not seem strange to those, who, knowing how many different *automata* or moving machines can be made by the industry of man, without employing in so doing more than a very few parts in comparison with the great multitude of bones, muscles, nerves, arteries, veins, or other parts that are found in the body of each animal. From this aspect the body is regarded as a machine which, having been made by the hands of God, is incomparably better arranged, and possesses in itself movements which are much more admirable, than any of those which can be invented by man. Here I specially stopped to show that if there had been such machines, possessing the organs and outward form of a monkey or some other animal without reason, we should not have had any means of ascertaining that they were not of the same nature as those animals. On the other hand, if there were machines which bore a resemblance to our body and imitated our actions as far as it was morally possible to do so, we should always have two very certain tests by which to recognise that, for all that, they were not real men. The first is, that they could never use speech or other signs as we do when placing our thoughts on record for the benefit of others. For we can easily understand a machine's being constituted so that it can utter words, and even emit some responses to action on it of a corporeal kind, which brings about a change in its organs; for instance, if it is touched in a particular part it may ask what we wish to say to it; if in another part it may exclaim that it is being hurt, and so on. But it never happens that it arranges its speech in various ways, in order to reply appropriately to everything that may be said in its presence, as even the lowest type of man can do. And the second difference is, that although machines can perform certain things as well as or perhaps better than any of us can do, they infallibly fall short in others, by the which means we may discover that they did not act from knowledge, but only from the disposition of their organs. For while reason is a universal instrument which can serve for all contingencies, these organs have need of some special adaptation for every particular action. From this it follows that it is morally impossible that there should be sufficient diversity in any machine to allow it to act in all the events of life in the same way as our reason causes us to act.

By these two methods we may also recognise the difference that exists between men and brutes. For it is a very remarkable fact that there are none so depraved and stupid, without even excepting idiots, that they cannot arrange different words together, forming of them a statement by which they make known their thoughts; while, on the other hand, there is no other animal, however perfect and fortunately circumstanced it may be, which can do the same. It is not the want of organs that brings this to pass, for it is evident that magpies and parrots are able to utter words just like ourselves, and yet they cannot speak as we do, that is, so as to give evidence that they think of what they say. On the other hand, men who, being born deaf and dumb, are in the same degree, or even more than the brutes, destitute of the organs which serve the others for talking, are in the habit of themselves inventing certain signs by which they make themselves understood by those who, being usually in their company, have leisure to learn their language. And this does not merely show that the brutes have less reason than men, but that they have none at all, since it is clear that very little is required in order to be able to talk. And when we notice the inequality that exists between animals of the same species, as well as between men, and observe that some are more capable of receiving instruction than others, it is not credible that a monkey or a parrot, selected as the most perfect of its species, should not in these matters equal the stupidest child to be found, or at least a child whose mind is clouded, unless in the case of the brute the soul were of an entirely different nature from ours. And we ought not to confound speech with natural movements which betray passions and may be imitated by machines as well as be manifested by animals; nor must we think, as did some of the ancients, that brutes talk, although we do not understand their language. For if this were true, since they have many organs which are allied to our own, they could communicate their thoughts to us just as easily as to those of their own race. It is also a very remarkable fact that although there are many animals which exhibit more dexterity than we do in some of their actions, we at the same time observe that they do not manifest any dexterity at all in many others. Hence the fact that they do better than we do, does not prove that they are endowed with mind, for in this case they would have more reason than any of us, and would surpass us in all other things. It rather shows that they have no reason at all, and that it is nature which acts in them according to the disposition of their organs, just as a clock, which is only composed of wheels and weights is able to tell the hours and measure the time more correctly than we can do with all our wisdom.

I had described after this the rational soul and shown that it could not be in any way derived from the power of matter, like the other things of which I had spoken, but that it must be expressly created. I showed, too, that it is not sufficient that it should be lodged in the human body like a pilot in his ship, unless perhaps for the moving of its members, but that it is necessary that it should also be joined and united more closely to the body in order to have sensations and appetites similar to our own, and thus to form a true man. In conclusion, I have here enlarged a little on the subject of the soul, because it is one of the greatest importance. For next to the error of those who deny God, which I think I have already sufficiently refuted, there is none which is more effectual in leading feeble spirits from the straight path of virtue, than to imagine that the soul of the brute is of the same nature as our own, and that in consequence, after this life we have nothing to fear or to hope for, any more than the flies and ants. As a matter of fact, when one comes to know how greatly they differ, we understand much better the reasons which go to prove that our soul is in its nature entirely independent of body, and in consequence that it is not liable to die with it. And then, inasmuch as we observe no other causes capable of destroying it, we are naturally inclined to judge that it is immortal.

II

I cannot share the opinion of Montaigne and others who attribute understanding or thought to animals. I am not worried that people say that men have an absolute empire over all the other animals; because I agree that some of them are stronger than us, and believe that there may also be some who have an instinctive cunning capable of deceiving the shrewdest human beings. But I observe that they only imitate or surpass us in those of our actions which are not guided by our thoughts. It often happens that we walk or eat without thinking at all about what we are doing; and similarly, without using our reason, we reject things which are harmful for us, and parry the blows aimed at us. Indeed, even if we expressly willed not to put our hands in front of our head when we fall, we could not prevent ourselves. I think also that if we had no thought we would eat, as the animals do, without having to learn to; and it is said that those who walk in their sleep sometimes swim across streams in which they would drown if they were awake. As for the movements of our passions, even though in us they are accompanied with thought because we have the faculty of thinking, it is none the less very clear that they do not depend on thought, because they often occur in spite of us. Consequently they can also occur in animals, even more violently than they do in human beings, without our being able to conclude from that that they have thoughts.

In fact, none of our external actions can show anyone who examines them that our body is not just a self-moving machine but contains a soul with thoughts, with the exception of words, or other signs that are relevant to particular topics without expressing any passion. I say words or other signs, because deaf-mutes use signs as we use spoken words; and I say that these signs must be relevant, to exclude the speech of parrots, without excluding the speech of madmen, which is relevant to particular topics even though it does not follow reason. I add also that these words or signs must not express any passion, to rule out not only cries of joy or sadness and the like, but also whatever can be taught by training to animals. If you teach a magpie to say good-day to its mistress, when it sees her approach, this can only be by making the utterance of this word the expression of one of its passions. For instance it will be an expression of the hope of eating, if it has always been given a titbit when it says it. Similarly, all the things which dogs, horses, and monkeys are taught to perform are only expressions of their fear, their hope, or their joy; and consequently they can be performed without any thought. Now it seems to me very striking that the use of words, so defined, is something peculiar to human beings. Montaigne and Charron may have said that there is more difference between one human being and another than between a human being and an animal; but there has never been known an animal so perfect as to use a sign to make other animals understand something which expressed no passion; and there is no human being so imperfect as not to do so, since even deaf-mutes invent special signs to express their thoughts. This seems to me a very strong argument to prove that the reason why animals do not speak as we do is not that they lack the organs but that they have no thoughts. It cannot be said that they speak to each other and that we cannot understand them; because since dogs and some other animals express their passions to us, they would express their thoughts also if they had any.

I know that animals do many things better than we do, but this does not surprise me. It can even be used to prove they act naturally and mechanically, like a clock which tells the time better than our judgement does. Doubtless when the swallows come in spring, they operate like clocks. The actions of honeybees are of the same nature, and the discipline of cranes in flight, and of apes in fighting, if it is true that they keep discipline. Their instinct to bury their dead is no stranger than that of dogs and cats who scratch the earth for the purpose of burying their excrement; they hardly ever actually bury it, which shows that they act only by instinct and without thinking. The most that one can say is that though the animals do not perform any action which shows us that they think, still, since the organs of their body are not very different from ours, it may be conjectured that there is attached to those organs some thoughts such as we experience in ourselves, but of a very much less perfect kind. To which I have nothing to reply except that if they thought as we do, they would have an immortal soul like us. This is unlikely, because there is no reason to believe it of some animals without believing it of all, and many of them such as oysters and sponges are too imperfect for this to be credible. But I am afraid of boring you with this discussion, and my only desire is to show you that I am, etc.

III

But there is no prejudice to which we are all more accustomed from our earliest years than the belief that dumb animals think. Our only reason for this belief is the fact that we see that many of the organs of animals are not very different from ours in shape and movement. Since we believe that there is a single principle within us which causes these motions—namely the soul, which both moves the body and thinks —we do not doubt that some such soul is to be found in animals also. I came to realize, however, that there are two different principles causing our motions: one is purely mechanical and corporeal and depends solely on the force of the spirits and the construction of our organs, and can be called the corporeal soul; the other is the incorporeal mind, the soul which I have defined as a thinking substance. Thereupon I investigated more carefully whether the motions of animals originated from both these principles or from one only. I soon saw clearly that they could all originate from the corporeal and mechanical principle, and I thenceforward regarded it as certain and established that we cannot at all prove the presence of a thinking soul in animals. I am not disturbed by the astuteness and cunning of dogs and foxes, or all the things which animals do for the sake of food, sex, and fear; I claim that I can easily explain the origin of all of them from the constitution of their organs.

But though I regard it as established that we cannot prove there is any thought in animals, I do not think it is thereby proved that there is not, since the human mind does not reach into their hearts. But when I investigate what is most probable in this matter, I see no argument for animals having thoughts except the fact that since they have eyes, ears, tongues, and other sense-organs like ours, it seems likely that they have sensation like us; and since thought is included in our mode of sensation, similar thought seems to be attributable to them. This argument, which is very obvious, has taken possession of the minds of all men from their earliest age. But there are other arguments, stronger and more numerous, but not so obvious to everyone, which strongly urge the opposite. One is that it is more probable that worms and flies and caterpillars move mechanically than that they all have immortal souls.

It is certain that in the bodies of animals, as in ours, there are bones, nerves, muscles, animal spirits, and other organs so disposed that they can by themselves, without any thought, give rise to all animals the motions we observe. This is very clear in convulsive movements when the machine of the body moves despite the soul, and sometimes more violently and in a more varied manner than when it is moved by the will.

Second, it seems reasonable, since art copies nature, and men can make various automata which move without thought, that nature should produce its own automata, much more splendid than artificial ones. These natural automata are the animals. This is especially likely since we have no reason to believe that thought always accompanies the disposition of organs which we find in animals. It is much more wonderful that a mind should be found in every human body than that one should be lacking in every animal.

But in my opinion the main reason which suggests that the beasts lack thought is the following. Within a single species some of them are more perfect than others, as men are too. This can be seen in horses and dogs, some of whom learn what they are taught much better than others. Yet, although all animals easily communicate to us, by voice or bodily movement, their natural impulses of anger, fear, hunger and so on, it has never yet been observed that any brute animal reached the stage of using real speech, that is to say, of indicating by word or sign something pertaining to pure thought and not to natural impulse. Such speech is the only certain sign of thought hidden in a body. All men use it, however stupid and insane they may be, and though they may lack tongue and organs of voice; but no animals do. Consequently it can be taken as a real specific difference between men and dumb animals.

For brevity's sake I here omit the other reasons for denying thought to animals. Please note that I am speaking of thought, and not of life or sensation. I do not deny life to animals, since I regard it as consisting simply in the heat of the heart; and I do not deny sensation, in so far as it depends on a bodily organ. Thus my opinion is not so much cruel to animals as indulgent to men—at least to those who are not given to the superstitions of Pythagoras—since it absolves them from the suspicion of crime when they eat or kill animals.

Perhaps I have written at too great length for the sharpness of your intelligence; but I wished to show you that very few people have yet sent me objections which were as agreeable as yours. Your kindness and candour has made you a friend of that most respectful admirer of all who seek true wisdom, etc.

VOLTAIRE

A Reply to Descartes

What a pitiful, what a sorry thing to have said that animals are machines bereft of understanding and feeling, which perform their operations always in the same way, which learn nothing, perfect nothing, etc.!

What! that bird which makes its nest in a semi-circle when it is attaching it to a wall, which builds it in a quarter circle when it is in an angle, in a circle upon a tree; that bird acts always in the same way? That hunting-dog which you have disclined for three months, does it not know more at the end of this time than it knew before your lessons? Does the canary to which you teach a tune repeat it at once? do you not spend a considerable time in teaching it? have you not seen that it has made a mistake and that it corrects itself?

Is it because I speak to you, that you judge that I have feeling, memory, ideas? Well, I do not speak to you; you see me going home looking disconsolate, seeking a paper anxiously, opening the desk where I remember having shut it, finding it, reading it joyfully. You judge that I have experienced the feeling of distress and that of pleasure, that I have memory and understanding.

Bring the same judgment to bear on this dog which has lost its master, which has sought him on every road with sorrowful cries, which enters the house agitated, uneasy, which goes down the stairs, up the stairs, from room to room, which at last finds in his study the master it loves, and which shows him its joy by its cries of delight, by its leaps, by its caresses.

Barbarians seize this dog, which in friendship surpasses man so prodigiously; they nail it on a table, and they dissect it alive in order

---

From Voltaire, *Philosophical Dictionary*, "Animals."

to show the mesenteric veins. You discover in it all the same organs of feeling that are in yourself. Answer me, machinist, has nature arranged all the means of feeling in this animal, so that it may not feel? has it nerves in order to be impassible? Do not suppose this impertinent contradiction in nature.

But the schoolmasters ask what the soul of animals is? I do not understand this question. A tree has the faculty of receiving in its fibres its sap which circulates, of unfolding the buds of its leaves and its fruit; will you ask what the soul of this tree is? it has received these gifts; the animal has received those of feeling, of memory, of a certain number of ideas. Who has bestowed these gifts? who has given these faculties? He who has made the grass of the fields to grow, and who makes the earth gravitate toward the sun.

"Animals' souls are substantial forms," said Aristotle, and after Aristotle, the Arab school, and after the Arab school, the angelical school, and after the angelical school, the Sorbonne, and after the Sorbonne, nobody at all.

"Animals' souls are material," cry other philosophers. These have not been in any better fortune than the others. In vain have they been asked what a material soul is; they have to admit that it is matter which has sensation: but what has given it this sensation? It is a material soul, that is to say that it is matter which gives sensation to matter; they cannot issue from this circle.

Listen to other brutes reasoning about the brutes; their soul is a spiritual soul which dies with the body; but what proof have you of it? what idea have you of this spiritual soul, which, in truth, has feeling, memory, and its measure of ideas and ingenuity; but which will never be able to know what a child of six knows? On what ground do you imagine that this being, which is not body, dies with the body? The greatest fools are those who have advanced that this soul is neither body nor spirit. There is a fine system. By spirit we can understand only some unknown thing which is not body. Thus these gentlemen's system comes back to this, that the animals' soul is a substance which is neither body nor something which is not body.

Whence can come so many contradictory errors? From the habit men have always had of examining what a thing is, before knowing if it exists. The clapper, the valve of a bellows, is called in French the "soul" of a bellows. What is this soul? It is a name that I have given to this valve which falls, lets air enter, rises again, and thrusts it through a pipe, when I make the bellows move.

There is not there a distinct soul in the machine: but what makes animals' bellows move? I have already told you, what makes the stars move. The philosopher who said, *"Deus est anima brutorium,"* was right; but he should go further.

DAVID HUME

Of the Reason of Animals

Next to the ridicule of denying an evident truth, is that of taking much pains to defend it; and no truth appears to me more evident, than that beasts are endow'd with thought and reason as well as men. The arguments are in this case so obvious, that they never escape the most stupid and ignorant.

We are conscious, that we ourselves, in adapting means to ends, are guided by reason and design, and that 'tis not ignorantly nor casually we perform those actions, which tend to self-preservation, to the obtaining pleasure, and avoiding pain. When therefore we see other creatures, in millions of instances, perform like actions, and direct them to like ends, all our principles of reason and probability carry us with an invincible force to believe the existence of a like cause. 'Tis needless in my opinion to illustrate this argument by the enumeration of particulars. The smallest attention will supply us with more than are requisite. The resemblance betwixt the actions of animals and those of men is so entire in this respect, that the very first action of the first animal we shall please to pitch on, will afford us an incontestable argument for the present doctrine.

This doctrine is as useful as it obvious, and furnishes us with a kind of touchstone, by which we may try every system in this species of philosophy. 'Tis from the resemblance of the external actions of animals to those we ourselves perform, that we judge their internal likewise to resemble ours; and the same principle of reasoning, carry'd one step farther, will make us conclude that since our internal actions resemble each other, the causes, from which they are deriv'd, must also be resembling. When any hypothesis, therefore, is advanc'd to explain a

From David Hume, *A Treatise of Human Nature*, Part III, Section xvi.

mental operation, which is common to men and beasts, we must apply the same hypothesis to both; and as every true hypothesis will abide this trial, so I may venture to affirm, that no false one will ever be able to endure it. The common defect of those systems, which philosophers have employ'd to account for the actions of the mind, is, that they suppose such a subtility and refinement of thought, as not only exceeds the capacity of mere animals, but even of children and the common people in our own species; who are notwithstanding susceptible of the same emotions and affections as persons of the most accomplish'd genius and understanding. Such a subtility is a clear proof of the falsehood, as the contrary simplicity of the truth, of any system.

Let us therefore put our present system concerning the nature of the understanding to this decisive trial, and see whether it will equally account for the reasonings of beasts as for these of the human species.

Here we must make a distinction betwixt those actions of animals, which are of a vulgar nature, and seem to be on a level with their common capacities, and those more extraordinary instances of sagacity, which they sometimes discover for their own preservation, and the propagation of their species. A dog, that avoids fire and precipices, that shuns strangers, and caresses his master, affords us an instance of the first kind. A bird, that chooses with such care and nicety the place and materials of her nest, and sits upon her eggs for a due time, and in a suitable season, with all the precaution that a chymist is capable of in the most delicate projection, furnishes us with a lively instance of the second.

As to the former actions, I assert they proceed from a reasoning, that is not in itself different, nor founded on different principles, from that which appears in human nature. 'Tis necessary in the first place, that there be some impression immediately present to their memory or senses, in order to be the foundation of their judgment. From the tone of voice the dog infers his master's anger, and foresees his own punishment. From a certain sensation affecting his smell, he judges his game not to be far distant from him.

Secondly, The inference he draws from the present impression is built on experience, and on his observation of the conjunction of objects in past instances. As you vary this experience, he varies his reasoning. Make a beating follow upon one sign or motion for some time, and afterwards upon another; and he will successively draw different conclusions according to his most recent experience.

Now let any philosopher make a trial, and endeavour to explain that act of the mind, which we call *belief*, and give an account of the principles, from which it is deriv'd, independent of the influence of custom on the imagination, and let his hypothesis be equally applicable to beasts as to the human species; and after he has done this, I promise to embrace his opinion. But at the same time I demand as an equitable condition, that if my system be the only one, which can answer to all these terms, it may be receiv'd as entirely satisfactory and convincing. And that 'tis the only one, is evident almost without any reasoning. Beasts certainly never perceive any real connexion among objects. 'Tis therefore by experience they infer one from another. They can never by any arguments form a general conclusion, that those objects, of which they have no experience, resemble those of which they have. 'Tis therefore by means of custom alone, that experience operates upon them. All this was sufficiently evident with respect to man. But with respect to beasts there cannot be the least suspicion of mistake; which must be own'd to be a strong confirmation, or rather an invincible proof of my system.

Nothing shews more the force of habit in reconciling us to any phaenomenon, than this, that men are not astonish'd at the operations of their own reason, at the same time, that they admire the *instinct* of animals, and find a difficulty in explaining it, merely because it cannot be reduc'd to the very same principles. To consider the matter aright, reason is nothing but a wonderful and unintelligible instinct in our souls, which carries us along a certain train of ideas, and endows them with particular qualities, according to their particular situations and relations. This instinct, 'tis true, arises from past observation and experience; but can any one give the ultimate reason, why past experience and observation produces such an effect, any more than why nature alone shou'd produce it? Nature may certainly produce whatever can arise from habit: Nay, habit is nothing but one of the principles of nature, and derives all its force from that origin.

CHARLES DARWIN

Comparison of
the Mental Powers of Man
and the Lower Animals

We have seen in the last two chapters that man bears in his bodily structure clear traces of his descent from some lower form; but it may be urged that, as man differs so greatly in his mental power from all other animals, there must be some error in this conclusion. . . .

My object in this chapter is to show that there is no fundamental difference between man and the higher mammals in their mental faculties. Each division of the subject might have been extended into a separate essay, but must here be treated briefly. As no classification of the mental powers has been universally accepted, I shall arrange my remarks in the order most convenient for my purpose; and will select those facts which have struck me most, with the hope that they may produce some effect on the reader. . . .

. . . The lower animals, like man, manifestly feel pleasure and pain, happiness and misery. Happiness is never better exhibited than by young animals, such as puppies, kittens, lambs, etc., when playing together, like our own children. Even insects play together, as has been described by that excellent observer, P. Huber, who saw ants chasing and pretending to bite each other, like so many puppies.

The fact that the lower animals are excited by the same emotions as ourselves is so well established, that it will not be necessary to weary the reader by many details. Terror acts in the same manner on them as

From Charles Darwin, *The Descent of Man*, Chapters III and IV.

on us, causing the muscles to tremble, the heart to palpitate, the sphincters to be relaxed, and the hair to stand on end. Suspicion, the offspring of fear, is eminently characteristic of most wild animals. It is, I think, impossible to read the account given by Sir E. Tennent, of the behaviour of the female elephants, used as decoys, without admitting that they intentionally practise deceit, and well know what they are about. Courage and timidity are extremely variable qualities in the individuals of the same species, as is plainly seen in our dogs. Some dogs and horses are ill-tempered, and easily turn sulky; others are good-tempered; and these qualities are certainly inherited. Every one knows how liable animals are to furious rage, and how plainly they show it. Many, and probably true, anecdotes have been published on the long-delayed and artful revenge of various animals. The accurate Rengger, and Brehm state the American and African monkeys which they kept tame, certainly revenged themselves. Sir Andrew Smith, a zoologist whose scrupulous accuracy was known to many persons, told me the following story of which he was himself an eye-witness; at the Cape of Good Hope an officer had often plagued a certain baboon, and the animal, seeing him approaching one Sunday for parade, poured water into a hole and hastily made some thick mud, which he skillfully dashed over the officer as he passed by, to the amusement of many bystanders. For long afterwards the baboon rejoiced and triumphed whenever he saw his victim.

The love of a dog for his master is notorious; as an old writer quaintly says, "A dog is the only thing on this earth that luvs you more than he luvs himself."

In the agony of death a dog has been known to caress his master, and every one has heard of the dog suffering under vivisection, who licked the hand of the operator; this man, unless the operation was fully justified by an increase of our knowledge, or unless he had a heart of stone, must have felt remorse to the last hour of his life.

As Whewell has well asked, "who that reads the touching instances of maternal affection, related so often of the women of all nations, and of the females of all animals, can doubt that the principle of action is the same in the two cases?" We see maternal affection exhibited in the most trifling details; thus Rengger observed an American monkey (a Cebus) carefully driving away the flies which plagued her infant; and Duvaucel saw a Hylobates washing the faces of her young ones in a stream. So intense is the grief of female monkeys for the loss of their young, that it invariably caused the death of certain kinds kept under confinement by Brehm in N. Africa. . . .

Most of the more complex emotions are common to the higher animals and ourselves. Everyone has seen how jealous a dog is of his master's affection, if lavished on any other creature; and I have observed the same fact with monkeys. This shows that animals not only love, but have desire to be loved. Animals manifestly feel emulation. They love approbation or praise; and a dog carrying a basket for his master exhibits in a high degree self-complacency or pride. There can, I think, be no doubt that a dog feels shame, as distinct from fear, and something very like modesty when begging too often for food. A great dog scorns the snarling of a little dog, and this may be called magnanimity. Several observers have stated that monkeys certainly dislike being laughed at; and they sometimes invent imaginary offences. In the Zoological Gardens I saw a baboon who always got into a furious rage when his keeper took out a letter or book and read it aloud to him; and his rage was so violent that, as I witnessed on one occasion, he bit his own leg till the blood flowed. Dogs show what may be fairly called a sense of humour, as distinct from mere play; if a bit of stick or other such object be thrown to one, he will often carry it away for a short distance; and then squatting down with it on the ground close before him, will wait until his master comes quite close to take it away. The dog will then seize it and rush away in triumph, repeating the same maneuvre, and evidently enjoying the practical joke.

We will now turn to the more intellectual emotions and faculties, which are very important, as forming the basis for the development of the higher mental powers. Animals manifestly enjoy excitement, and suffer from ennui, as may be seen with dogs, and, according to Rengger, with monkeys. All animals feel *Wonder*, and many exhibit *Curiosity*. They sometimes suffer from this latter quality, as when the hunter plays antics and thus attracts them; I have witnessed this with deer, and so it is with the wary chamois, and with some kinds of wild-ducks. . . .

Hardly any faculty is more important for the intellectual progress of man than *Attention*. Animals clearly manifest this power, as when a cat watches by a hole and prepares to spring on its prey. Wild animals sometimes become so absorbed when thus engaged that they may be easily approached. Mr. Bartlett has given me a curious proof how variable this faculty is in monkeys. A man who trains monkeys to act in plays used to purchase common kinds from the Zoological Society at the price of five pounds for each; but he offered to give double the price if he might keep three or four of them for a few days in order to select one. When asked how he could possibly learn so soon whether a particular monkey would turn out a good actor, he answered that it all depended on their power of attention. If when he was talking and explaining anything to a monkey its attention was easily distracted, as by a fly on the wall or other trifling object, the case was hopeless. If he tried by punishment to make an inattentive monkey act it turned sulky. On the other hand, a monkey which carefully attended to him could always be trained.

It is almost superfluous to state that animals have excellent *memories* for persons and places. A baboon at the Cape of Good Hope, as I have been informed by Sir Andrew Smith, recognized him with joy after an absence of nine months. I had a dog who was savage and averse to all strangers, and I purposely tried his memory after an absense of five years and two days. I went near the stable where he lived and shouted to him in my old manner; he showed no joy, but instantly followed me out walking, and obeyed me exactly as if I had parted with him only half an hour before. A train of old associations, dormant during five years, had thus been instantaneously awakened in his mind. Even ants, as P. Huber has clearly shown, recognized their fellow-ants belonging to the same community after a separation of four months. Animals can certainly by some means judge of the intervals of time between recurrent events.

The *Imagination* is one of the highest prerogatives of man. By this faculty he unites former images and ideas, independently of the will, and thus creates brilliant and novel results. A poet, as Jean Paul Richter remarks, "who must reflect whether he shall make a character say yes or no—to the devil with him; he is only a stupid corpse." Dreaming gives us the best notion of this power; as Jean Paul again says, "The dream is an involuntary art of poetry." The value of the products of our imagination depends of course on the number, accuracy, and clearness of our impressions, on our judgment and taste in selecting or rejecting the involuntary combinations, and to a certain extent on our power of voluntarily combining them. As dogs, cats, horses, and probably all the higher animals, even birds have vivid dreams, and this is shown by their movements and the sounds uttered, we must admit that they possess some power of imagination. There must be something special which causes dogs to howl in the night, and especially during moonlight, in that remarkable and melancholy manner called baying. All dogs do not do so; and, according to Houzeau, they do not then look at the moon, but at some fixed point near the horizon. Houzeau thinks that their imaginations are disturbed by the vague outlines of the surrounding objects, and conjure up before them fantastic images; if this be so, their feelings may almost be called superstitions.

Of all the faculties of the human mind, it will, I presume, be admitted that *Reason* stands at the summit. Only a few persons now dispute that animals possess some power of reasoning. Animals may constantly be seen to pause, deliberate, and resolve. It is a significant fact, that the more the habits of any particular animal are studied by a naturalist, the more he attributes to reason and the less to unlearnt instincts. In future chapters we shall see that some animals extremely low in the scale apparently display a certain amount of reason. . . .

We can only judge by the circumstances under which actions are performed, whether they are due to instinct, or to reason, or to the mere association of ideas: this latter principle, however, is intimately connected with reason. A curious case has been given by Prof. Möbius, of a pike, separated by a plate of glass from an adjoining aquarium stocked with fish, and who often dashed himself with such violence against the glass in trying to catch the other fishes, that he was sometimes completely stunned. The pike went on thus for three months, but at last learnt caution, and ceased to do so. The plate of glass was then removed, but the pike would not attack these particular fishes, though he would devour others which were afterwards introduced; so strongly was the idea of a violent shock associated in his feeble mind with the attempt on his former neighbours. If a savage, who had never seen a large plate-glass window, were to dash himself even once against it, he would for a long time afterwards associate a shock with a window-frame; but very differently from the pike, he would probably reflect on the nature of the impediment, and be cautious under analogous circumstances. Now with monkeys, as we shall presently see, a painful or merely a disagreeable impression, from an action once performed, is sometimes sufficient to prevent the animal from repeating it. If we attribute this difference between the monkey and the pike solely to the association of ideas being so much stronger and more persistent in the one than the other, though the pike often received much the more severe injury, can we maintain in the case of man that a similar difference implies the possession of a fundamentally different mind?. . .

I have seen, as I daresay have others, that when a small object is thrown on the ground beyond the reach of one of the elephants in the Zoological Gardens, he blows through his trunk on the ground beyond the object, so that the current reflected on all sides may drive the object within his reach. Again a well-known ethnologist, Mr. Westropp, informs me that he observed in Vienna a bear deliberately making with his paw a current in some water, which was close to the bars of his cage, so as to draw a piece of floating bread within his reach. These actions of the elephant and bear can hardly be attributed to instinct or inherited habit, as they would be of little use to an animal in a state of nature. Now, what is the difference between such actions, when performed by an uncultivated man, and by one of the higher animals? . . .

Abstraction, General Conceptions, Self-consciousness, Mental Individuality

It would be very difficult for any one with even much more knowledge than I possess, to determine how far animals exhibit any traces of these high mental powers. This difficulty arises from the impossibility of judging what passes through the mind of an animal; and again, the fact that writers differ to a great extent in the meaning which they attribute to the above terms, causes a further difficulty. If one may judge from various articles which have been published lately, the greatest stress seems to be laid on the supposed entire absence in animals of the power of abstraction, or of forming general concepts. But when a dog sees another dog at a distance, it is often clear that he perceives that it is a dog in the abstract; for when he gets nearer his whole manner suddenly changes, if the other dog be a friend. A recent writer remarks, that in all such cases it is a pure assumption to assert that the mental act is not essentially of the same nature in the animal as in man. If either refers what he perceives with his senses to a mental concept, then so do both. When I say to my terrier, in an eager voice (and I have made the trial many times), "Hi, hi, where is it?" she at once takes it as a sign that something is to be hunted, and generally first looks quickly all around, and then rushes into the nearest thicket, to scent for any game, but finding nothing, she looks up into any neighbouring tree for a squirrel. Now do not these actions clearly shew that some animal is to be discovered and hunted?

It may be freely admitted that no animal is self-conscious, if by this term it is implied, that he reflects on such points, as whence he comes or whither he will go, or what is life and death, and so forth. But how can we feel sure that an old dog with an excellent memory and some power of imagination, as shewn by his dreams, never reflects on his past pleasures or pains in the chase? And this would be a form of self-consciousness. On the other hand, as Büchner has remarked, how little can the hard-worked wife of a degraded Australian savage, who uses very few abstract words, and cannot count above four, exert her self-consciousness, or reflect on the nature of her own existence. It is generally admitted, that the higher animals possess memory, attention, association, and even some imagination and reason. If these powers, which differ much in different animals, are capable of improvement, there seems no great improbability in more complex faculties, such as the higher forms of abstraction, and self-consciousness, etc., having been evolved through the development and combination of the simpler ones. It has been urged against the views here maintained that it is impossible to say at what point in the ascending scale animals become capable of abstraction, etc.; but who can say at what age this occurs in our young children? We see at least that such powers are developed in children by imperceptible degrees. . . .

Sociability

Animals of many kinds are social; we find even distinct species living together; for example, some American monkeys; and united flocks of rooks, jackdaws, and starlings. Man shews the same feeling in his strong love for the dog, which the dog returns with interest. Every one must have noticed how miserable horses, dogs, sheep, etc., are when separated from their companions, and what strong mutual affection the two former kinds, at least, shew on their reunion. It is curious to speculate on the feelings of a dog, who will rest peacefully for hours in a room with his master or any of the family, without the least notice being taken of him; but if left for a short time by himself, barks or howls dismally. We will confine our attention to the higher social animals; and pass over insects, although some of these are social, and aid one another in many important ways. The most common mutual service in the higher animals is to warn one another of danger by means of the united senses of all. Every sportsman knows, as Dr. Jaeger remarks, how difficult it is to approach animals in a herd or troop. Wild horses and cattle do not, I believe, make any danger-signal; but the attitude of any one of them who first discovers an enemy, warns the others. Rabbits stamp loudly on the ground with their hind-feet as a signal: sheep and chamois do the same with their forefeet, uttering likewise a whistle. Many birds, and some mammals, post sentinels, which in the case of seals are said generally to be the females. The leader of a troop of monkeys acts as the sentinel, and utters cries expressive both of danger and of safety. Social animals perform many little services for each other: horses nibble, and cows lick each other, on any spot which itches: monkeys search each other for external parasites; and Brehm states that after a troop of the *Cercopithecus griseo-viridis* has rushed through a thorny brake, each monkey stretches itself on a branch, and another monkey sitting by, "conscientiously" examines its fur, and extracts every thorn or burr.

Animals also render more important services to one another: thus wolves and some other beasts of prey hunt in packs, and aid one another in attacking their victims. Pelicans fish in concert. The Hamadryas baboons turn over stones to find insects, etc.; and when they come to a large one, as many as can stand round, turn it over together and share the booty. Social animals mutually defend each other. Bull bisons in N. America, when there is danger, drive the cows and calves into the middle of the herd, whilst they defend the outside. . . .

It is certain that associated animals have a feeling of love for each other, which is not felt by non-social adult animals. How far in most cases they actually sympathise in the pains and pleasures of others, is more doubtful, especially with respect to pleasures. Mr Buxton, however, who had excellent means of observation, states that his macaws, which lived free in Norfolk, took "an extravagant interest" in a pair with a nest; and whenever the female left it, she was surrounded by a troop "screaming horrible acclamations in her honour." It is often difficult to judge whether animals have any feeling for the sufferings of others of their kind. Who can say what cows feel, when they surround and stare intently on a dying or dead companion; apparently, however, as Houzeau remarks, they feel no pity. That animals sometimes are far from feeling any sympathy is too certain; for they will expel a wounded animal from the herd, or gore or worry it to death. This is almost the blackest fact in natural history, unless, indeed, the explanation which has been suggested is true, that their instinct or reason leads them to expel an injured companion, lest beasts of prey, including man, should be tempted to follow the troop. In this case their conduct is not much worse than that of the North American Indians, who leave their feeble comrades to perish on the plains; or the Fijians, who, when their parents get old, or fall ill, bury them alive.

Many animals, however, certainly sympathise with each other's distress or danger. This is the case even with birds. Captain Stansbury found on a salt lake in Utah an old and completely blind pelican, which was very fat, and must have been well fed for a long time by his companions. Mr. Blyth, as he informs me, saw Indian crows feeding two or three of their companions which were blind; and I have heard of an analogous case with the domestic cock. We may, if we choose, call these actions instinctive; but such cases are much too rare for the development of any special instinct. I have myself seen a dog, who never passed a cat who lay sick in a basket, and was a great friend of his, without giving her a few licks with his tongue, the surest sign of kind feeling in a dog.

It must be called sympathy that leads a courageous dog to fly at any one who strikes his master, as he certainly will. I saw a person pretending to beat a lady, who had a very timid little dog on her lap, and the trial had never been made before; the little creature instantly jumped away, but after the pretended beating was over, it was really pathetic to see how perseveringly he tried to lick his mistress's face, and comfort her. Brehm states that when a baboon in confinement was pursued to be punished, the others tried to protect him. It must have been sympathy in the cases above given which led the baboons and Cercopitheci to defend their young comrades from the dogs and the eagle. I will give only one other instance of sympathetic and heroic conduct, in the case of a little American monkey. Several years ago a keeper at the Zoological Gardens showed me some deep and scarcely healed wounds on the nape of his own neck, inflicted on him, whilst kneeling on the floor, by a fierce baboon. The little American monkey, who was a warm friend of this keeper, lived in the same large compartment, and was dreadfully afraid of the great baboon. Nevertheless, as soon as he saw his friend in peril, he rushed to the rescue, and by screams and bites so distracted the baboon that the man was able to escape, after, as the surgeon thought, running great risk of his life.

Besides love and sympathy, animals exhibit other qualities connected with the social instincts, which in us would be called moral; and I agree with Agassiz that dogs possess something very like a conscience. . . .

Summary

There can be no doubt that the difference between the mind of the lowest man and that of the highest animal is immense. An anthropomorphous ape, if he could take a dispassionate view of his own case, would admit that though he could form an artful plan to plunder a garden—though he could use stones for fighting or for breaking open nuts, yet that the thought of fashioning a stone into a tool was quite beyond his scope. Still less, as he would admit, could he follow out a train of metaphysical reasoning, or solve a mathematical problem, or reflect on God, or admire a grand natural scene. Some apes, however, would probably declare that they could and did admire the beauty of the coloured skin and fur of their partners in marriage. They would admit, that though they could make other apes understand by cries some of their perceptions and simpler wants, the notion of expressing definite ideas by definite sounds had never crossed their minds. They might insist that they were ready to aid their fellow-apes of the same troop in many ways, to risk their lives for them, and to take charge of their orphans; but they would be forced to acknowledge that disinterested love for all living creatures, the most noble attribute of man, was quite beyond their comprehension.

Nevertheless the difference in mind between man and the higher animals, great as it is, certainly is one of degree and not of kind. We have seen that the senses and intuitions, the various emotions and faculties, such as love, memory, attention, curiosity, imitation, reason, etc., of which man boasts, may be found in an incipient, or even sometimes in a well-developed condition, in the lower animals. They are also capable of some inherited improvement, as we see in the domestic dog compared with the wolf or jackal. If it could be proved that certain high mental powers, such as the formation of general concepts, self-consciousness, etc., were absolutely peculiar to man, which seems extremely doubtful, it is not improbable that these qualities are merely the incidental results of other highly-advanced intellectual faculties; and these again mainly the result of the continued use of a perfect language. At what age does the new-born infant possess the power of abstraction, or become self-conscious, and reflect on its own existence? We cannot answer; nor can we answer in regard to the ascending organic scale. The half-art, half-instinct of language still bears the stamp of its gradual evolution. The ennobling belief in God is not universal with man; and the belief in spiritual agencies naturally follows from other mental powers. The moral sense perhaps affords the best and highest distinction between man and the lower animals; but I need say nothing on this head, as I have so lately endeavoured to shew that the social instincts—the prime principle of man's moral constitution—with the aid of active intellectual powers and the effects of habit, naturally lead to the golden rule, "As ye would that men should do to you, do ye to them likewise"; and this lies at the foundation of morality.

MICHEL DE MONTAIGNE

The Language of Animals

Presumption is our natural and original disease. The most wretched and frail of all creatures is man, and withal the proudest. He feels and sees himself lodged here in the dirt and filth of the world, nailed and rivetted to the worst and deadest part of the universe, in the lowest story of the house, the most remote from the heavenly arch, with animals of the worst condition of the three; and yet in his imagination will be placing himself above the circle of the moon, and bringing the heavens under his feet. 'Tis by the same vanity of imagination that he equals himself to God, attributes to himself divine qualities, withdraws and separates himself from the crowd of other creatures, cuts out the shares of the animals, his fellows and companions, and distributes to them portions of faculties and force, as himself thinks fit. How does he know, by the strength of his understanding, the secret and internal motions of animals?—from what comparison betwixt them and us does he conclude the stupidity he attributes to them? When I play with my cat, who knows whether I do not make her more sport than she makes me? We mutually divert one another with our play. If I have my hour to begin or to refuse, she also has hers. Plato, in his picture of the golden age under Saturn, reckons, among the chief advantages that a man then had, his communication with beasts, of whom, inquiring and informing himself, he knew the true qualities and differences of them all, by which he acquired a very perfect intelligence and prudence, and led his life more happily than we could do. Need we a better proof to condemn human impudence in the concern of beasts? This great

From Michel de Montaigne, "An Apology of Raymond Sebond," in *The Works of Michel de Montaigne*, trans. William Hazlitt (1865).

author was of opinion that nature, for the most part, in the corporal form she gave them, had only regard to the use of prognostics that were derived thence in his time. The defect that hinders communication betwixt them and us, why may it not be in our part as well as theirs? 'Tis yet to determine where the fault lies that we understand not one another—for we understand them no more than they do us; and by the same reason they may think us to be beasts as we think them. 'Tis no great wonder if we understand not them, when we do not understand a Basque or a Troglodyte. And yet some have boasted that they understood them, as Appollonius Tyanacus, Melampus, Tiresias, Thales, and others. And seeing, as cosmographers report, that there are nations that have a dog for their king, they must of necessity be able to interpret his voice and motions. We must observe the parity betwixt us: we have some tolerable apprehension of their meaning, and so have beasts of ours—much about the same. They caress us, threaten us, and beg of us, and we do the same to them.

As to the rest, we manifestly discover that they have a full and absolute communication amongst themselves, and that they perfectly understand one another, not only those of the same, but of divers kinds:

> The tamer herds, and wilder sort of brutes,
> Though we of higher race conclude them mutes,
> Yet after dissonant and various notes,
> From gentler lungs or more distended throats,
> As fear, or grief, or anger, do them move,
> Or as they do approach the joys of love.

In one kind of barking of a dog the horse knows there is anger, of another sort of bark he is not afraid. Even in the very beasts that have no voice at all, we easily conclude, from the society of offices we observe amongst them, some other sort of communication: their very motions discover it:

> As infants who, for want of words, devise
> Expressive motions with their hands and eyes.

And why not, as well as our dumb people, dispute, argue, and tell stories by signs? Of whom I have seen some, by practice, so clever and active that way that, in fact, they wanted nothing of the perfection of making themselves understood. Lovers are angry, reconciled, intreat, thank, appoint, and, in short, speak all things by their eyes.

> Even silence in a lover
> Love and passion can discover.

... As to speech, it is certain that if it be not natural it is not necessary. Nevertheless I believe that a child which had been brought up in an absolute solitude, remote from all society of men (which would be an experiment very hard to make), would have some kind of speech to express his meaning by. And 'tis not to be supposed that nature should have denied that to us which she has given to several other animals: for what is this faculty we observe in them, of complaining, rejoicing, calling to one another for succour, and inviting each other to love, which they do with the voice, other than speech? And why should they not speak to one another? They speak to us, and we to them. In how many several sorts of ways do we speak to our dogs, and they answer us? We converse with them in another sort of language, and use other appellations, than we do with birds, hogs, oxen, horses, and alter the idiom according to the kind:

> Thus from one swarm of ants some sally out,
> To spy another's stock or mark its rout.

Lectantius seems to attribute to beasts not only speech, but laughter also. And the difference of language which is seen amongst us, according to the difference of countries, is also observed in animals of the same kind. Aristotle, in proof of this, instances the various calls of partridges, according to the situation of places:

> And various birds do from their warbling throats,
> At various times, utter quite different notes,
> And some their hoarse songs with the seasons change.

PETER JENKINS

Teaching Chimpanzees to Communicate

I recently visited Oklahoma for the purpose of interviewing chimpanzees. This may sound like a fool's assignment of the "man bites dog" variety but in fact I was engaged in serious scientific inquiry. For the chimps in question were reputed to have broken through the language barrier which divides the realms of animals and men. A series of revolutionary experiments by behavioral psychologists in the United States, in which apes have been instructed in the rudiments of human language, are casting new doubt upon the exclusive claims of *homo sapiens*. The controversy which so fascinated the philosophers of the eighteenth century—and inspired Swift to reverse the rules between the language-using Houyhnhnmns and the Yahoos—is alive again within the scientific community, which is fiercely disputing whether the competence in nonverbal communication acquired by the chimps can properly or usefully be called language.

The most famous of these primate guinea pigs, Washoe, a female chimp aged around eight, now lives among her peers in captivity at the Institute of Primate Studies at the University of Oklahoma. But for four years, from 1966 to 1970, Washoe (named after a Nevada Indian tribe) was the first and most distinguished pupil of Professors Allen and Beatrice Gardner at the University of Nevada who revolutionized the whole study of nonverbal communication by teaching her to converse in American Sign Language.

Until that time much futile energy had been expended on trying to teach chimpanzees to speak. The most strenuous of these attempts was

From Peter Jenkins, "Ask No Questions," *The Guardian* (London) July 10, 1973.

made by the Hayes in the late forties with the chimpanzee Viki. Viki lived with them en famille and learnt to do many interesting things. For example, she could sort photographs into piles and would place a photo of her chimpanzee father in the animal pile with the cats and dogs, and her own picture in the human pile with Dr. and Mrs. Hayes. But the one thing Viki certainly couldn't do was talk. After six years of her specially devised head-start program, the best she achieved was four grunt-like sounds which roughly approximated human exclamation.

The Gardners were the first to perceive that inability to speak did not necessarily demonstrate in chimpanzees an incapacity for language. They tried again with a nonverbal language. American Sign Language (ASL) is a human language which serves among deaf people for normal communication and conversation. At Gallaudet College in Washington, D.C., it is used at the level of degree courses. It is not to be confused with the "deaf and dumb language" commonly used in England, which is a finger alphabet. ASL is a language of manually-produced signs and has its own grammar which is different from the grammar of English. Some of the signs in ASL are iconic but the majority are symbolic. Most linguists concede that ASL is a language; their dispute is over the degree of competence in chimpanzees to employ it syntactically in the way that humans command verbal language.

Washoe was born wild, but from the age of somewhere between 8 and 14 months she was brought up in a carefully controlled human environment. She lived in a two-and-a-half room caravan with all modern conveniences, where she was confined at night and took her meals separately, as in an old-fashioned nursery; otherwise, she was treated as far as possible like a human. She progressed through nappies to toilet training, from bottle and high chair to using utensils at table. She was given toys to play with and books to look at. She was taken on car trips and visits to other people's houses. Before bed she brushed her teeth in her own bathroom. But it was a laboratory upbringing, not a normal family environment. By day she was in the constant company of scientists working in shifts. They conversed with her and each other exclusively in sign language, although names were also permitted. Later it was discovered that exposure to human speech has no effect on a chimp's ability to learn ASL.

The results were remarkable. By the time she left Reno in 1970 Washoe had a vocabulary of around 140 signs. The Gardners observed her to use 294 two-sign combinations such as "more food," "give me drink" and "come open." It was discovered that in the vast majority of these combinations a small number (in fact a dozen) of "pivot" words was employed. These were "come gimme," "please," "you," "go," "me," "hurry," "more," "up," "open," "out," "in," and "food." The Gardners correlated these uses with the findings of child psychologist Roger Brown, and reported that 78 per cent of Washoe's two-sign combinations were the same as two-word combinations used by very young children.

Washoe picked up a few signs without being taught them, for example, "smoke"; the scientists were always asking each other for cigarettes. She invented her own sign for "bib" and it coincided with the approved ASL sign. She showed ability to use her vocabulary in context, for example, "sorry dirty" after wetting the carpet and "sorry hurt" after biting too hard. She put together a few more elaborate constructions such as "you me go out hurry." She used what seemed to be semantic constructions of the kind which in small children mark the early emergence of syntax, for example, distinguishing correctly between "me tickle you" and "you tickle me."

In 1970 Washoe moved to the University of Oklahoma with Dr. Roger Fouts, a research assistant of the Gardners. There for the first time since her early infancy she was put back among members of her own species. One day on the island where the chimps run loose and swing in the trees, a gopher snake appeared. Three of the chimps fled but one very young one remained. Washoe was observed to sign "come hurry hurry." The baby chimp did not understand and Washoe dragged him by the arm to safety. Her use of language to communicate with a member of her own species in a stress situation was considered significant.

I interviewed Washoe through the bars of her cage in distracting circumstances. The chimps were filling their mouths with water, blowing out their cheeks and ejecting it with considerable force, range, and accuracy at their human visitors. Washoe asked me for a cigarette, always the first request on prison visits. She made the sign "smoke" which is two fingers held to the mouth. She moved away and lay down on her back to puff at the cigarette and twice again, talking to herself, made the sign.

I was making notes of our interview and Washoe was interested in my pen. I asked her in sign language "what's that?" She gave the correct answer. The sign for pen is the first finger of one hand drawn along the open palm of the other. She correctly identified my shoes and my glasses. I showed her a flower and she signed "flower gimmee." I showed her an open pot of the oil which is used for lubricating chimps' feet. The sign for oil is within her vocabulary but after sniffing the pot she signed "smell, smell food" and repeated the remark three times rapidly. By this time she wanted another cigarette. I insisted she should say please. The sign for please is literally "ask like a lady." After some reluctance she signed "please Washoe smoke." She studied the cigarette and made the sign for "pencil." When she had finished her second cigarette I showed her my pen again and she signed "pencil please." That was the extent of our conversation.

Unlike Washoe, Lucy was reared like a human child from the day of her birth. Her language instruction did not begin until Dr. Fouts came to the University of Oklahoma, by which time she was five. His work with Lucy has confirmed the Gardners' experiment, and her language ability now approaches Washoe's. Lucy is part of another experiment, nothing to do with language, conducted by Dr. William Lemmon, the director of the Institute of Primate Studies. Dr. Lemmon is a clinical psychologist who lives in his ape colony and gives the impression of regarding all primates, human and ape, with the same detached curiosity.

Dr. Lemmon has boarded out four female and two male chimps in species isolation. The idea is to study the effects of human environment upon them. Lucy, when she is old enough (that will be between the ages 8 and 12) will be artificially impregnated, if that can be done for the first time with a chimpanzee, and Dr. Lemmon after long years of waiting will observe how her maternal behavior is affected by her human upbringing.

Lucy's "mother" is Mrs. Jane Temerlin, wife of Dr. Maury Temerlin who is also a psychologist and who keeps a house full of exotic birds. Unlike Washoe, Lucy was brought up to understand spoken English, and Mrs. Temerlin says that she and her husband sometimes have to spell words if they don't want Lucy to understand, for example, if they are discussing a trip in the car the mention of which would overexcite her. Lucy sleeps in her own bed in the Temerlin's bedroom. According to Mrs. Temerlin she seldom wets it. She shares their bathroom. She eats with the family at table. Only when mother and father are out at work is Lucy confined to a 600 square foot duplex cage built onto the side and roof of the Temerlin's house. Apparently she regards it not as a place of confinement, but as her own playroom where she can do as she likes.

Until quite recently the use of tools was considered another uniquely human attribute. Dr. Jane van Lawick-Goodall exploded that theory with her observations of wild apes in Africa. Lucy certainly has no difficulty with tools. If she can lay her hands on a screwdriver she will dismantle the electric plugs around the house. She was once caught having half removed a wheel from the Temerlin's car. But in her quieter moments she plays with toys, which have to be specially strong, looks at books and pictures, does drawings and abstract paintings using colours, which she can identify, or amuses herself in such childlike ways as scribbling on mummy's cheque book or ringing up on the telephone to listen to the recorded announcements.

However, life with Lucy isn't exactly a bowl of bananas. Mrs. Temerlin, who has a grown-up human son, evidently loves Lucy like a child and winced when Dr. Lemmon described her as like "a hyperactive retarded infant." Nevertheless she admitted that rearing a chimp was a long, long business and explained: "It means changing your way of life in all sorts of ways that you don't immediately realize when you start with that extremely appealing infant in your arms. For the first two years the only way to treat them is like a human infant, but by the time they are three they're too strong and impulsive."

Dr. Fouts took me along with him to Lucy's regular morning lesson which took place in the Temerlin's living room. The only unusual feature of the room was that the windows had no curtains; there were pictures on the wall and plants around the place. He went to fetch Lucy and carried her in like a very large child. She had her arms around his neck and was giving him big wet kisses on the mouth. Lucy was inordinately interested in me, which meant that what I observed was not her typical classroom behavior. She put her face very close to mine and stared at me in the manner of a rude child. She felt me up and down, frisking my pockets, exploring the buttons on my suit and shirt. She appeared to be about four feet tall in a standing crouch; according to Dr. Fouts she weighs 80 pounds. I was a little scared of her; what are intended by chimps to be playful bites can be extremely painful for humans; chimps themselves have very thick skins and, for the purpose of administering the equivalent of a disciplinary slap, the Temerlin's keep an electric cow prod.

Lucy was unpredictably boisterous. Suddenly she would vault over the sofa. She disappeared into the kitchen, reentered flying through the air, and did triple somersaults on the carpet to finish at my feet. She was too excited for much serious conversation. She and Dr. Fouts exchanged some signs, but many of hers were meaningless chimpanzee gestures. They were hard to distinguish. "What's she saying now?" I asked. "She's just picking her nose," he said. She was very interested in my shoes and when I asked her what they were signed "shoe" clearly enough.

Dr. Fouts took her to the bathroom where she sat on the lavatory and on instruction flushed it when she was done. Lucy's toilet training, I learned, was still somewhat unreliable, but chimps are naturally clean. Dr. Goodall observed them in their wild state wiping their bottoms with leaves. While Dr. Fouts was filling in his data sheets (Lucy's every authentic sign is recorded) she was off into the kitchen and came back with a bottle of pickle which she spilt on the carpet. In response to his chidings she signed "Dirty me" and "Sorry me dirty Lucy." He wrote that down. Then she curled up for a snooze on the sofa and he told me that her use of the word dirty was interesting. It had been taught to her to mean feces or as a noun for anything dirty such as dirty clothes. But she had adapted the sign for herself as an adjective and for example when cross with him for refusing to take her out might sign "dirty Roger." He compared this with the colloquial English usage of the word shit.

Lucy was soon on the go again, wanting to be tickled. According to Dr. Fouts she is capable of simple transformations such as "you tickle me" and "me tickle you." But she preferred to be tickled. One of the limitations of chimps seems to be that their interest in language is largely instrumental and inordinately concerned with food. Lucy will oblige by answering "what's that?" questions but has not been observed to display the curiosity found in small children who incessantly ask "what's that?" Lucy found his comb. "What's that?" he asked, and she signed correctly. She indicated, without signing, that he should comb his hair. "Whose?" he asked. "Roger," she replied.

I did not see Lucy at her linguistic best for, according to Dr. Fouts, she has invented some interesting constructions. When tasting a radish for the first time and not liking it she called it a "cry hurt food." She called a watermelon a "sweet drink food." She christened a stick of celery "pipe food." There appeared to be some logic or application of rule in her usages of the generics "food" or "fruit" and specifics within her vocabulary such as "banana." One day when watching at the window as her mother drove away to work she was observed to sign to herself "cry me" and "me cry." Dr. Fouts says cautiously: "She does seem to follow rules. She uses the word 'you' before verbs or the pronoun 'me' in a way which at least looks like syntax."

Dr. Fouts has succeeded in teaching very young chimpanzees, both home-reared and wild, to use ASL and there is no longer serious doubt that language ability, if that is what it is, up to Washoe's and Lucy's levels can be imparted relatively quickly and easily. The findings of the Gardners, confirmed and supplemented by Fouts, have also been reinforced by another experimenter using an entirely different method. Professor David Premack of the University of California constructed a synthetic written language consisting of colored metal-backed plastic shapes which his chimpanzees manipulate on a magnetic slate. The shapes are abstract; for example "banana" is neither yellow-colored nor banana-shaped. Premack's chimp Sarah has performed some remarkable feats on her slate. He claims that she can cope with plurals, the interrogative, and the logical connective "if . . . then." She can answer yes or no questions such as "? X same X" and solve problems such as "? banana name of apple" by choosing between the symbols for "yes" and "no" and substituting them on the slate for the interrogative symbol. Premack also reports that Sarah can do conditional constructions such as "Sarah take apple then Mary give Sarah chocolate" and make very simple transformations of such constructions.

The use of this synthetic language, not unlike symbolic logic, although intellectually more demanding than the rudiments of ASL, is at the same time creatively more restrictive: Sarah can only manipulate the pieces she is given. It has the advantage of enabling performance to be scored with great exactness, but is open to suspicion that the chimpanzee can manipulate the symbols according to rules without comprehending the linguistic meaning of the manipulations. Premack has done his best to isolate external stimuli, but discovered that Sarah's scores are consistently lower when a stranger acts as teacher, and her interest in her slate dwindles dramatically when no human is present at all.

Premack's experiments might be open to all sorts of objections were not his findings upholding those of Gardner and Fouts using a more natural form of language. His work reveals a remarkable level of cognitive ability in Sarah and, whether or not she is using language with purpose or understanding cognitive ability, could in large part (we do not know) determine capacity to master syntax. And if syntactical skill, whether innate or acquired, is the secret of what we call human language ability, then Sarah stands somewhere near the threshold. One school of behaviorist thinking on the subject believes that the structure of language, like any other form of learning, is acquired through cognitive ability. If so, the limit upon the linguistic development of the chimpanzees would be the limit set by their intelligence rather than any innate inability of the Chomskyian kind. It may be a coincidence, but the brain size of the chimpanzee correlates neatly with the brain size found in primitive man, *homo erectus*.

The answer to the question "Can apes use language?" depends, as Dr. Joad would have said, on what you mean by language. On this none of the experts can agree. As Dr. Fouts pointed out while we were in the company of Lucy: "If you really want to exclude chimpanzees you could define language as 'the mode of communication used by *homo sapiens.*' Until the scientific community agrees on a definition of language we are just floundering around."

Definitions available range from one low enough to include Washoe, Lucy, and Sarah to Professor Noam Chomsky's high concept of language, which has led him to assert that "human language appears to be a unique phenomenon, without significant analogue in the animal world." In Chomsky's view man's creative command of transformational grammar derives from his innate (genetically acquired) knowledge of the properties of all human language. He sees more linguistic ability in a human imbecile than in any superior problem-solving ape. At the other end of the scale the psychologists Hebb and Thompson define language merely as putting two or more noises or gestures together on purpose for a single effect and using the same noises or gestures in different combinations for different effects. This minimal definition clearly embraces our chimpanzees and admits a good many birds also into the exclusive circle of *homo sapiens.*

Among themselves the linguists differ on the origins of language but for the most part, behaviorists and Chomskyians alike set a standard too high for the chimpanzees. There is virtually no evidence to support an evolutionary theory of language, and therefore no reason to suppose that chimpanzees will acquire the language ability of man simply with the passage of millennia. Some biologists, notably F. H. Lennenberg, contend that language derives from physiological properties unique to man.

We might speculate on the strength of the experiments with the chimpanzees that they are capable of crude telegraphic communication at around the level of small children aged two or three. But as we observe the first signs of syntax in children we do so in the knowledge that they are capable of it and will grow up to possess language in the Chomskyian sense. Hints of syntactical ability in chimpanzees cannot be approached with the same assumptions, and support only the most speculative and tentative conclusions.

The Gardners applied stringent scientific modesty to their results with Washoe: "The program we have described avoids the question of whether an animal other than man can acquire language. As comparative psychologists we must reject this question. It is like the question of whether an animal other than man can have thoughts. It depends on the definition of language rather than on what the animals do."

Premack goes further and claims: "We feel justified in concluding that Sarah can understand some symmetrical and hierarchical sentence structures and is therefore competent to some degree in the sentence functions of language." He asserts that Sarah "acquired a language competence apparently comparable in many respects to that of a two to two-and-a-half-year-old child." He adds "man and chimp may conceivably attain comparable limits."

As a layman I shall follow the agnosticism of the Gardners, who say: "Those who have a taste for such questions can decide for themselves whether or not Washoe achieved langauge." And, for those who identify strongly with *homo sapiens,* Premack has the consoling thought that "Since man is required to teach the chimp langauge and not vice versa, we may continue to claim uniqueness."

MARY MIDGLEY

The Concept of Beastliness

Every age has its pet contradictions. Thirty years ago, we used to accept Marx and Freud together, and then wonder, like the chameleon on the tartan, why life was so confusing. Today there is similar trouble over the question whether there is, or is not, something called Human Nature. On the one hand, there has been an explosion of animal behavior studies, and comparisons between animals and men have become immensely popular. People use evidence from animals to decide whether man is naturally aggressive, or naturally territorial; even whether he has an Aggressive or Territorial Instinct. On the other hand, many sociologists and psychologists still seem to hold the Behaviorist view that man is a creature entirely without instincts, and so do existentialist philosophers. If so, all comparison with animals must be irrelevant. (To save space, I have had to simplify both these party lines here, but if anyone thinks I am oversimplifying the behaviorist one, I can only ask him to keep on reading *New Society*.) On that view, man is entirely the product of his culture. He starts off infinitely plastic, and is formed completely by the society in which he grows up. There is no end to the possible variations between cultures; what we take to be man's instincts are just the deep-dug prejudices of our own society. If we form families, fear the dark, or jump at the sight of a spider, these are just results of our conditioning. For Existentialism, at first sight the scene is very different, because the existentialist asserts man's freedom and will not let him call himself the product of anything. But Existentialism too denies that man has a nature; if he had his freedom would not be complete.

From Mary Midgley, "The Concept of Beastliness: Philosophy, Ethics and Animal Behavior," in *Philosophy*, vol. 48 (1973), pp. 111–35.

So Sartre insists that "there is no human nature. . . . Man first of all exists, encounters himself, surges up in the world, and defines himself afterwards. If man as the existentialist sees him is not definable, it is because to begin with he is nothing. He will not be anything until later, and then he will be what he makes himself."[1]

For Existentialism there is only the Human Condition, which is what happens to man and not what he is born like. If we are afraid of the dark, it is because we choose to be cowards; if we care more for our own children than other people's it is because we choose to be partial. We must never talk about human nature or human instincts.

In this paper I want, first, simply to draw attention to this dialectic, which can certainly do with intelligent attention from all sides. Second, I want, myself, to work from the animal behavior angle, which I think is extremely interesting and has not yet been fully used by philosophers. One reason for this is undoubtedly the fear of fatalism; another is the appalling misuse of terms like "instinct" and "human nature" in the past; the third is the dottiness of some ethological propaganda. To dispose of the last first; if we vetoed every science that has had some lunatic exponents we could quickly empty the libraries. What is needed in such cases is to sort the wheat from the chaff. To quote Konrad Lorenz:[2]

> . . . if I have to confess to a sneaking liking for, and even a feeling of gratitude to, my adversaries, I think it only fair to confess that some of my allies make me squirm. Desmond Morris, who is an excellent ethologist and knows better, makes me wince by over-emphasizing, in his book *The Naked Ape*, the beastliness of man. I admit that he does so with the commendable intention of shocking haughty people who refuse to see that man has anything in common with animals at all, but in this attempt he minimizes the unique properties and faculties of man in an effectively misleading manner; the outstanding and biologically relevant property of the human species is neither its partial hairlessness nor its "sexiness," but its faculty for conceptual thought—a fact of which Desmond Morris is, of course, perfectly aware. Another writer who makes me suffer with almost equal intensity, if for different reasons, is Robert Ardrey. . . .

To that mass of knowledge, Lorenz himself adds a clear view of the conceptual scene typical, it must be said, of scientists who have had the foresight to get themselves educated on the continent and not in England or America. (This is also true of Tinbergen and Eibl-Eibesfeldt and of that splendid old person Wolfgang Köhler.[3]) Because of this, and for simplicity, I shall address myself largely to his arguments, and particu-

[1] *Existentialism and Humanism*, 28.
[2] *On Aggression*, 3.
[3] See *The Mentality of Apes*, esp. chs vii and viii.

larly to his book *On Aggression*, without suggesting that he is either isolated or infallible. Like him, however, I have a difficulty of method. The point of my argument is to show how and in what cases comparison between man and other species makes sense, but I must sometimes use such comparisons in the process. Those to whom it is a matter of faith and morals not to consider them, have a problem. I think the circle will prove virtuous, but in advance I suggest the following test. Comparisons make sense only when they are put in the context of the entire character of the species concerned and of the known principles governing resemblances between species. Thus: it is invalid to compare suicide in lemmings or infanticide in hamsters *on their own* with human suicide or infanticide. But when you have looked at the relation of the act to other relevant habits and needs, when you have considered the whole nature of the species, comparison may be possible and helpful.

Now for the other objections.

1. About the fear of fatalism I shall not say much, because it seems to me quite misplaced here. The genetic causes of human behavior need not be seen as overwhelming any more than the social causes; either lot is alarming if you treat it as predestined to win, but no one is committed to doing that by admitting that both lots exist. Knowing that I have a naturally bad temper does not make me lose it; on the contrary it should help me to keep it, by forcing me to distinguish my peevishness from moral indignation. My freedom, therefore, does not seem to be particularly threatened by the admission, nor by any light cast on the meaning of my bad temper by comparison with animals.

2. Words like "instinct" are another matter. Ethologists, particularly Lorenz and Tinbergen, have put in a lot of work on these terms, and I think they are now fit for use again. They are used, not wildly but in a definite and well-organized way, in the detailed, systematic, gruelling studies of animal behavior which have been made by trained zoologists in this century, and have been given the name of Ethology. I shall discuss the use of the terms later.

The general point is that animals clearly lead a much more structured, less chaotic life than people have been accustomed to think, and are therefore, in certain quite definite ways, much less different from men. (There is still plenty of difference, but it is a different difference.) Traditionally, people have congratulated themselves on being an island of order in a sea of chaos. Lorenz and company have shown that this is all my eye and Bishop Wilberforce. There follow various changes in our view of man, because that view has been built up on a supposed contrast between man and animals which was formed by seeing animals, not as they were, but as projections of our own fears and desires. We have thought of a wolf always as he appears to the shepherd at the moment of seizing a lamb from the fold. But this is like judging the shepherd by the impression he makes on the lamb, at the moment when he finally decides to turn it into mutton. Lately, ethologists have taken the trouble to watch wolves systematically, between meal-times, and have found them to be, by human standards, paragons of regularity and virtue. They pair for life, they are faithful and affectionate spouses and parents, they show great loyalty to their pack, great courage and persistence in the face of difficulties, they carefully respect each other's territories, keep their dens clean, and extremely seldom kill anything that they do not need for dinner. If they fight with another wolf, the fight ends with his submission; there is normally a complete inhibition on killing the suppliant and on attacking females and cubs. They have also, like all social animals, a fairly elaborate etiquette, including subtly varied ceremonies of greeting and reassurance, by which friendship is strengthened, co-operation achieved and the wheels of social life generally oiled. All this is not the romantic impressions of casual travellers; it rests on long and careful investigations by trained zoologists, backed up by miles of film, graphs, maps, population surveys, droppings analysis and all the rest of the contemporary toolbag. Moreover, these surveys have often been undertaken by authorities which were initially rather hostile to the wolf, and inclined to hope that it could be blamed for their various troubles. Farley Mowat, doing this work in the Canadian Arctic, had his results rejected time and again because they showed that the sudden drop in the numbers of deer was *not* due to wolves, who had not changed their technique in a number of centuries, but to hunters, who had.[4]

Actual wolves, then, are not much like the folk-figure of the wolf, and the same goes for apes and other creatures. But *it is the folk-figure that has been popular with philosophers.* They have usually taken over the popular notion of lawless cruelty which underlies such terms as "brutal," "bestial," "beastly," "animal desires," etc., and have used it, uncriticized, as a contrast to illuminate the nature of man. Man has been mapped by reference to a landmark which is largely mythical. Because this habit is so ancient, and so deep-rooted, I shall say a little more about it before turning to the philosophic arguments in question. Consideration of its oddity may perhaps prevent us dismissing the whole topic in advance. The fact that some people are silly about animals cannot stop the topic being a serious one. Animals are not just one of the things with which people amuse themselves, like chewing-gum and water-skis, *they are the group to which people belong.* We are not just rather like animals; we *are* animals. Our difference from our relatives may be striking, but

[4]Farley Mowat, *Never Cry Wolf*; Murie, *The Wolves of Mount McKinley.*

the comparison has always been, and must be, crucial to our view of ourselves. It will matter if, as I believe, the gap comes in a slightly different place from where tradition puts it, as well as being rather narrower. The traditional view has certainly distorted argument in ethics, and may have caused mistakes about the possibilities open to humanity.

Turning back then to wolves: the contrast of the ethologist's fully documented picture with the traditional view of the wolf needs no comment. I have read a chatty journalistic book on wolves, whose author described in detail how wolves trapped in medieval France used to be flayed alive, with various appalling refinements. "Perhaps this was rather cruel," he remarked, "but then the wolf is itself a cruel beast." The words sound so natural; it is quite difficult to ask oneself; do wolves in fact flay people alive? Or to take in the fact the only animal that shows the slightest interest in doing this sort of thing is *homo sapiens*. Another complaint that the author made against wolves was their Treachery. They would creep up on people secretly, and then they would attack so suddenly that their victims did not have time to defend themselves. The idea that wolves would starve if they always gave fair warning never strikes him. Wolves, in fact, have traditionally been *blamed* for being carnivores, which is doubly surprising since the people who blamed them normally ate meat themselves, and were not, as the wolf is, compelled by their stomachs to do so.

The restraint apparent in wolves seems to be found in most other carnivores, and well-armed vegetarian creatures too. Where murder is so easy, a species *must* have a rigorous inhibition against it or perish. (*Of course* this inhibition is not a morality, but it works in many ways like one.) Animals less strongly armed do not need this defence. Lorenz[5] gives chilling examples from Roe-deer and Doves, in both of which species stronger members will slowly murder any weaker one if they are kept in captivity with it, because these creatures in a free state save themselves by running away, and not by relying on the inhibition of the victor. And it is painfully clear that Man is nearer to this group than to the wolf.

Man, before his tool-using days, was pretty poorly armed. Without beak or horns, he must have found murder a tedious and exhausting business, and built-in inhibitions against it were therefore not necessary for survival. Then, by the time he invented weapons, it was too late to alter his nature. He had already become a dangerous beast. War and vengeance are primitive human institutions, not late perversions; most cosmogonies postulate strife in Heaven, and bloodshed is taken for granted as much in the Book of Judges as in the *Iliad* or the Sagas.

[5]*King Solomon's Ring*, 192.

There may be non-aggressive societies, as anthropologists assure us, but they are white blackbirds and possibly (as I shall argue later) not so white as they are painted. It seems likely that man shows *more* savagery to his own kind than any other mammal, though among the beasts Lorenz mentions, rats are certainly a competitor. They, it seems, will normally try to kill any rat they meet of another tribe, but in compensation they never kill or seriously fight rats of their own tribe. Rats cannot therefore compete with Cain, or Romulus, still less with Abimelech the son of Gideon, who murdered, on one stone, *all* his brothers, to the number of three-score and ten.[6] An animal who does this is surely rightly labelled "dangerous."

Yet he has always believed otherwise. Man, civilized Western man, has always maintained that in a bloodthirsty world he alone was comparatively harmless. Consider the view of the African jungle given by Victorian hunters. The hunter assumed that every creature he met would attack him, and accordingly shot it at sight. Of course he didn't want to eat it, but he could always stuff it (in order to triumph over his human enemies) and anyway he assumed it was noxious; it would be described in his memoirs as "the great brute." Drawings even exist of Giant Pandas cast in this totally unconvincing role—and shot accordingly. Yet in these days game wardens and photographers habitually treat lions as familiarly as big dogs. It is understood that so long as they are well fed and not provoked they are no more likely to attack you than the average Alsatian. Much the same seems to hold to elephants and other big game. These creatures have their own occupations, and, unless seriously disturbed, are not anxious for a row. Gorillas in particular are peace-loving beasts; Schaller[7] visited a tribe of them for six months without receiving so much as a cross word, or seeing any quarrelling worth naming. In this case, and no doubt in others, Victorian man was deceived by confusing threatening behaviour with attack. Gorillas do threaten, but the point is precisely to avoid combat. By looking sufficiently dreadful, a gorilla patriarch can drive off intruders and defend his family without the trouble and danger of actually fighting. The same thing seems to hold of other simians, and particularly of Howler Monkeys, whose dreadful wailing used to freeze that white hunter's blood. For howlers have reduced the combat business to its lowest and most satisfactory terms. When two groups of them compete for a territory, they both sit down and howl their loudest, and the side which makes the most noise has won. That nervous White Man, with his heart in his mouth and his finger on his trigger, was among the

---

[6]*Judges*, IX, 5.
[7]G. Schaller, *The Year of the Gorilla.*

most dangerous things in the jungle. His weapon was at least as powerful as those of the biggest animals, and while they attacked only what
they could eat, or what was really annoying them, he would shoot at
anything big enough to aim at. Why did he think they were more
savage than he? Why has civilized Western man always thought so?
I am not surprised that early man *disliked* wolves. When an animal
tries to eat you, you cannot be expected to like it, and only a very occasional Buddhist will co-operate. But why did he feel so morally superior? Could he not see that the wolf's hunting him was exactly the
same as his hunting the deer? (There are tribes which do think in this
way: but it is Western thought that I am exploring.) As Lorenz remarks,
people are inclined to disapprove of carnivores even when they eat other
animals and not people, as though other animals all formed one species,
and the carnivores were cannibals. "The average man," he says, "does
not judge the fox that kills a hare by the same standard as the hunter
who shoots one for exactly the same reason, but with the severe censure
that he would apply to a game-keeper who made a practice of shooting
farmers and frying them for supper." This disapproval is very marked
on the occasions when foxes do kill for sport or practice, destroying
more hens than they can eat. You would not guess, to hear people talk
at such times, that people ever hunted foxes. In the same way, it makes
a very disreputable impression when Jane Goodall[8] reports that the
chimpanzees she watched would occasionally catch and eat a baby baboon or colobus monkey, though they all lived amicably together most
of the time and the children even played together. But what else goes on
on the traditional farm?

> Sing, Dilly dilly duckling, come and be killed,
> For you must be stuffed, and my customers filled.

The reason why such parallels are hard to see is, I suggest, that *man has
always been unwilling to admit his own ferocity*, and has tried to deflect
attention from it by making animals out more ferocious than they are.
Sometimes the animals themselves have been blamed and punished.
Such customs as the flaying of wolves were probably intended as pun-
ishments, though it might be hard to separate this intention from magic.
And certainly the Wickedness of animals has often been used to justify
our killing or otherwise interfering with them. It is a cock-eyed sort of
justification, unless Beasts were supposed capable of Deliberation. We
would probably do better to invoke our natural loyalty to our own
species than to rely on our abstract superiority to others. But I am

---

[8]Jane van Lawick Goodall, *My Friends the Wild Chimpanzees*.

more interested for the moment in the philosophic use of the Beast Within than in our treatment of Beasts Without.

The philosopher's Beast Within is a lawless monster to whom nothing is forbidden. It is so described both by moralists like Plato, who are against it, and by ones like Nietzsche, who are for it. Here is a typical passage from Book IX of the *Republic*, where Plato[9] is talking about our nastier desires. These

> ... bestir themselves in dreams, when the gentler part of the soul slumbers, and the control of Reason is withdrawn. Then the Wild Beast in us, full-fed with meat and drink, becomes rampant and shakes off sleep to go in quest of what will gratify its own instincts. As you know, it will cast off all shame and prudence at such moments and stick at nothing. In phantasy it will not shrink from intercourse with a mother or anyone else, man, god or brute, or from forbidden food or any deed of blood. It will go to any lengths of shamelessness and folly.

Consider how odd the image is, in spite of its familiarity. Why not say, "I have these thoughts in my off moments"? Why not at least the Other Man within? What is gained by talking about the Beast?

Here is Nietzsche,[10] speaking of the Lion whom he invokes to break the chain of convention:

> To create for himself freedom for new creation—for this the Lion's strength is sufficient,
> To create for himself freedom, and a holy Nay even to duty; therefore, my brethren, is there need of the Lion.
> Once it loved as holiest Thou Shalt—Now it must see illusion and tyranny even in its holiest, that it may snatch freedom even from its love—
> For this there is need of the Lion. . . .

But in the world there is no such beast. To talk of a Beast is to talk of a thing with its own laws. If lions really did not draw the line at anything—if they went about mating with crocodiles, ignoring territory, eating poisonous snakes and killing their own cubs—they would not *be* lions, nor, as a species, would they last long. This abstract Beast is a fancy on the level of the eighteenth century's abstract Savage, whether Noble or otherwise. (Dr. Johnson: Fanciful people may talk of a mythology being amongst them, but it must be invention. . . . And what account of their religion can you suppose to be learnt from savages?")[11] What anthropology did for this myth, ethology now does for the Beast myth. Kipling's Law of the Jungle is nearer to reality than this fancy

---

[9]*Republic*, IX, 571c.
[10]*Thus Spake Zarathustra*; Discourse of the Three Metamorphoses.
[11]Boswell, *Life of Johnson*, Everyman 2, 34.

of the moralists. What is particularly odd is that beasts are supposed to be so given to sexual licence. It really should not have needed Desmond Morris to point out that, among animal species, *homo sapiens* gives an exceptional amount of time and attention to his sexual life. For most species, a brief mating season and a simple instinctive pattern make of it a seasonal disturbance with a definite routine, comparable to Christmas shopping; it is exactly in human life that it plays, for good or ill, a much more serious and central part. With no other species could a Freudian theory ever have got off the ground. Gorillas, in particular, take so little interest in sex that they really shock Robert Ardrey:[12] he concludes that they are in their decadence. Yet Tolstoy,[13] speaking of the life of systematic sexual indulgence, called it "the ideal of monkeys or Parisians."

If then there is no Lawless Beast outside man, it seems very strange to conclude that there is one inside him. It would be more natural to say, the beast within us gives us partial order; the business of conceptual thought will only be to complete it. But the opposite, *a priori* reasoning was the one that prevailed. If the Beast Within was capable of every iniquity, people reasoned, then Beasts Without probably were so too. This notion made man anxious to exaggerate his difference from all other species, and to ground all activities he valued in capacities unshared by the animals, whether the evidence warranted it or no. In a way this evasion does the species credit, because it reflects our horror at the things we do. Man fears his own guilt, and insists on fixing it on something evidently alien and external. Beasts Within solve the Problem of Evil. It does him credit, because it shows the power of his conscience, but all the same it is a dangerous fib. It is my contention that this use of the Beast Within as a scapegoat for human wickedness has led to some bad confusion, not only about Beasts (which might not matter) but about Man. I suspect that Man began to muddle himself quite badly at the point where he said "The Woman beguiled me, and I did eat," and the Woman said the same about the Serpent. . . .

Aristotle, though in general he was much more convinced of man's continuity with the physical world than Plato, makes some equally odd uses of the contrast between man and beast. In the *Nicomachean Ethics*[14] he asks what the true function of man is, in order to see what his happiness consists in, and concludes that that function is the life of

---

[12]Robert Ardrey, *African Genesis*, 126–127; Schaller, *The Year of the Gorilla*.
[13]L. Tolstoy, *The Kreutzer Sonata*, ch. ii. For further comparison of human sexuality with that of other primate species, see Wickler, "Socio-Sexual Signals," in D. Morris, *Primate Ethology*, 1967. Also, in spite of certain crass and obvious errors, *The Naked Ape*. Eibl-Eibesfeldt in *Love and Hate* sets the whole problem very well in context.
[14]*Nicomachean Ethics I, 7*

reason *because that life only is peculiar to man.* I do not quarrel for the moment with the conclusion but with the argument. If peculiarity to man is the point, why should one not say that the function of man is technology, or the sexual goings-on noted by Desmond Morris, or even being exceptionally ruthless to one's own species? For in all these respects man seems to be unique. It must be shown *separately* that this differentia is itself the best human quality, that it is the point where humanity is excellent as well as exceptional. And it is surely possible *a priori* that the point on which humanity is excellent is one in which it is *not* wholly unique—that at least some aspect of it might be shared with another race of beings? Animals are, I think, used in this argument to point up by contrast the value of reason, to give examples of irrational conduct whose badness will seem obvious to us. But unless we start with a particular view about the importance of Reason in conduct, we shall not necessarily agree. If we prefer, among humans, an impulsively generous act to a cold-blooded piece of calculation, we shall not be moved from our preference by the thought that the generous act is more like an animal's. Nor ought we to be. The claims of Reason must be made good, if at all, within the boundaries of human life itself. They could be strengthened by race-prejudice only if it were true, as sometimes seems to be suggested, that animals were, in fact, invariably wicked. . . .

I have been suggesting that animal life is much more orderly, and ordered in a way closer to human patterns, than tradition suggests. People may grant this, and still ask what it means to attribute this order to Instinct. This must of course be gone into before the term can sensibly be applied to people.

A very useful piece of terminology here is that of Closed and Open Instincts. Closed instincts are behavior patterns fixed genetically in every detail, like the bees' honey-dance, some bird-song, and the nest-building pattern of weaver-birds. Here the same complicated pattern, correct in every detail, will be produced by creatures which have been carefully reared in isolation from any member of their own species, and from any helpful conditioning. Genetic programming here takes the place of intelligence; learning is just maturation. Open instincts on the other hand are general tendencies to certain *kinds* of behavior, such as hunting, tree-climbing, washing, singing or the care of the young. Cats, for example, tend naturally to hunt, they will do so even if deprived of all example. They do it as kittens when they do not need food, and they will go on doing it even if they are kept fully fed; it is not just a means to an end. But their hunting is not a single stereotyped pattern, it covers a wide repertory of movements; a cat will improve greatly in its choice of these during its life, it can invent new ones and pick up tips from other cats. In this sense hunting is learnt. The antithesis between nature and nurture is quite false and unhelpful here; hunting, like most activities of higher animals, is both innate *and* learnt. The creature is born with certain powers and a strong wish to use them, but it will need time, practice, and (often) some example before it can develop them properly. Other powers and wishes it does *not* have and will find it hard to acquire. For instance, swimming is outside the usual range of both cats and monkeys; in spite of their great agility it does not suit them, as it suits men and hippopotami; example will not usually bring them into the water, and they might starve if their food lay beyond it.

Open instincts of this kind are the main equipment of the higher animals. It is to them that we must attribute all the complex behavior which makes the wolf's social life so successful; monogamy, cleanliness, cub care and inability to attack the helpless are loose patterns, but they are built in. Open and closed instincts however are clearly not distinct kinds of things; they are the extremes of a scale with many grades between. For instance, besides the birds with a fixed song pattern, there are others with various powers of imitation. Mocking birds imitate other birds' song and also non-bird noises; their programming is obviously a more complicated matter than a cuckoo's, and must include some power of selection. But imitating itself *is* an instinct with them; they will do it untrained and you cannot teach them to compose instead. Nest-building with the higher animals is like this; they have no fixed stereotype, like the weaver-birds, but a nest they will have, and if there is nothing to build it of they will do the best they can without.[15]

Rats will carry their own tails repeatedly into a corner, still showing the same peculiar movements they would use if they had proper materials. In this way, every gradation is found from the stereotype to the quite general tendency. At the narrow end, perhaps we can say that no instinct can ever be completely closed. Even the weaver-bird must vary things a bit according to the branch and his materials; even the dancing bee adapts to the state of her digestion. At the wide end, what shall we say? Will the notion of Open Instincts make sense when applied to people? Or does it then become so wide as to be vacuous?

When behaviorists say that man has no instincts, they always mean closed instincts. They point to his failure to make standard webs or do standard honey-dances, and ignore his persistent patterns of motivation. Why do people form families? Why do they mind about their homes and quarrel over boundaries? Why do they own property? Why do they gamble, boast, show off, dress up and fear the unknown? Why do they

---

[15]W. H. Thorpe, introduction to Lorenz's *King Solomon's Ring*.

talk so much, and dance, and sing? Why do children play, and for that matter adults too? Why is nobody living in the Republic of Plato? According to Behaviorism, because of cultural conditioning. So (Question 1) who started it? This is like explaining gravitation by saying that whenever something falls, something else pushed it; even if it were true, it wouldn't help. Question 2; why do people ever *resist* their families? Why do they do what everybody is culturally conditioning them *not* to do? I have never seen a proper behaviorist answer to that one, but I gather it would go in terms of subcultures and cultural ambivalences, of society's need for a scapegoat and suchlike. It is a pleasing picture; how do all the children of 18 months pass the news along the grapevine that now is the time to join the subculture, to start climbing furniture, toddling out of the house, playing with fire, breaking windows, taking things to pieces, messing with mud and chasing the ducks? For these are perfectly specific things which *all* healthy children can be depended on to do, not only unconditioned but in the face of all deterrents. Just so, Chomsky asks Skinner how it comes about that small children introduce their own grammatical mistakes into speech, talking in a way that they have never heard and that will be noticed only to be corrected. In dealing with such questions, the behaviorist's hands are tied by his *a priori* assumption. The ethologist, on the other hand, proceeds empirically, which is why I think we ought to like him. When he finds some activity going on among the species he studies, he doesn't look for reasons to regard it as something else, he simply starts photographing and taking notes. He sees it done, and from detailed observation of the context and comparison with other activities he gradually moves towards explaining its relation with other things which are done. (Thus; when herring gulls[16] meet at the borders of their territories they constantly turn aside and pull grass. This is like nest-building behavior, but the bird does not use the grass. Instead it follows other patterns which commonly issue in fighting, and at times does fight. Having thoroughly studied all the things it does, and compared them with its conduct on other occasions, the ethologist tries the hypothesis that this is Displaced Aggression—it is working off its anger on the grass—but does not accept this without careful comparison with other displacement activities and a full analysis of the term and its physiological implications.) He is not postulating any central cure-all explanation. This is where he is better off than many previous people who have made use of the term "human nature." *This* term is suspect because it does suggest cure-all explanations, sweeping theories that man is Basically Sexual, Basically Selfish or Acquisitive, Basically Evil or Basically Good. These theories

[16]N. Tinbergen, *The Herring Gull's World*, 1953, 68.

approach human conduct much as a simple-minded person might approach rising damp. They look for a single place where the water is coming in, a single source of motivation. This hydraulic approach always leads to incredible distortions once the theorist is off his home ground, as can be seen if you look at Marxist theories of art or Freudian explanations of politics. To trace the water back to its only possible source means defying the laws of motion. The ethologist on the other hand doesn't want to say that human nature is basically anything; he wants to see what it consists of. (Even Robert Ardrey doesn't say that man is *basically* territorial.) So, if we must still talk hydraulics, he proceeds more like a surveyor mapping a valley. He notes a spring here, a spring there; he finds that some of them do tend to run together (as, for instance, a cat uses tree-climbing for hunting and caterwauling in courtship). If he finds an apparently isolated activity, with no connexion with the creature's other habits, he simply accumulates information until a connexion appears. Thus the "suicide" of lemmings turns out to be, not an isolated monstrous drive, but part of a very complicated migration pattern. (Lemmings are good swimmers; they often do cross rivers or reach islands, but the reason they set off is that they cannot stand being overcrowded, a condition which drives them to all kinds of desperate escape behaviour.[17]) Thus the grass-pulling gulls were not moved by an isolated monstrous drive for Destruction, but by the interworking of two patterns of motivation—fear and aggression which are connected in certain definite ways in their lives in the context of nesting, and can be roughly mapped to show the general character of the species. *Understanding a habit is seeing what company it keeps.* The meaning is the use. The only assumption made here is the general biologist's one that there ought to be *some* system in an organism, some point in any widespread plant or animal habit. This is justified merely by its success.

The Nature of a Species, then, consists in a certain range of powers and tendencies, a repertoire, inherited and forming a fairly firm characteristic pattern, though conditions after birth will vary the details quite a lot. In this way, baboons are "naturally hierarchical animals," since they travel in bands with a leader and what is pleasingly called a Senate of Elders, and show carefully graded dominance behavior down to the meanest baby baboon. This is not "disproved" by showing that it is not necessarily a brutal "peck order," nor that the hierarchy vary a great deal with different species and conditions.[18] Investigating these subtleties merely strengthens and elucidates the idea of a natural hier-

[17]See W. Marsden, *The Lemming Year*; W. Elton, *Voles, Mice and Lemmings*.
[18]For the variations, see Rowell, "Variations in the Social Organization of Primates," in D. Morris (ed.), *Primate Ethology*.

archical tendency. Nor is it disproved by finding an occasional baboon who is disrespectful or lax about his dignity; baboons "naturally" have fur, and finding a few going bald will not disprove it. . . .

I had better end by saying that I do not of course expect all the facts relevant to the nature of man to be turned up by ethologists. Other disciplines, equally relevant to moral philosophy, have suffered under rather similar tabus. Of course they should not be thought to take over the subject, but all are relevant; we certainly need history, neurology and all the social sciences. If we want to know what is good for man we must know what are his possibilities and roughly what is the price to be paid for each option. But among these studies, perhaps the resistance to ethology has been particularly strong and irrational. As Lorenz remarks, human pride had already taken two nasty knocks from Darwin and Freud; there may be real difficulty in undergoing the third and agreeing that *homo sapiens* is not just mildly interested in animals; he IS an animal. . . .

III

Do Humans Have Obligations To Other Animals?

ARISTOTLE

Animals and Slavery

It is clear that the rule of the soul over the body, and of the mind and the rational element over the passionate, is natural and expedient; whereas the equality of the two or the rule of the inferior is always hurtful. The same holds good of animals in relation to men; for tame animals have a better nature than wild, and all tame animals are better off when they are ruled by man; for then they are preserved. Again, the male is by nature superior, and the female inferior; and the one rules, and the other is ruled; this principle, of necessity, extends to all mankind. Where then there is such a difference as that between soul and body, or between men and animals (as in the case of those whose business is to use their body, and who can do nothing better), the lower sort are by nature slaves, and it is better for them as for all inferiors that they should be under the rule of a master. For he who can be, and therefore is, another's and he who participates in rational principle enough to apprehend, but not to have, such a principle, is a slave by nature. Whereas the lower animals cannot even apprehend a principle; they obey their instincts. And indeed the use made of slaves and of tame animals is not very different; for both with their bodies minister to the needs of life. . . .

Other modes of life are similarly combined in any way which the needs of men may require. Property, in the sense of a bare livelihood, seems to be given by nature herself to all, both when they are first born, and when they are grown up. For some animals bring forth, together with their offspring, so much food as will last until they are able to

From Aristotle, *Politics,* Book I, chapters 5 and 8.

supply themselves; of this the vermiparous or oviparous animals are an instance; and the viviparous animals have up to a certain time a supply of food for their young in themselves, which is called milk. In like manner we may infer that, after the birth of animals, plants exist for their sake, and that the other animals exist for the sake of man, the tame for use and food, the wild, if not all, at least the greater part of them, for food, and for the provision of clothing and various instruments. Now if nature makes nothing incomplete, and nothing in vain, the inference must be that she has made all animals for the sake of man. And so, in one point of view, the art of war is a natural art of acquisition, for the art of acquisition includes hunting, an art which we ought to practise against wild beasts, and against men who, though intended by nature to be governed, will not submit; for war of such a kind is naturally just.

PLUTARCH

Of Eating of Flesh

Tract I

1. You ask of me then for what reason it was that Pythagoras abstained from eating of flesh. I for my part do much admire in what humor, with what soul or reason, the first man with his mouth touched slaughter, and reached to his lips the flesh of a dead animal, and having set before people courses of ghastly corpses and ghosts, could give those parts the names of meat and victuals, that but a little before lowed, cried, moved, and saw; how his sight could endure the blood of the slaughtered, flayed, and mangled bodies; how his smell could bear their scent; and how the very nastiness happened not to offend the taste, while it chewed the sores of others, and participated of the sap and juices of deadly wounds.

> Crept the raw hides, and with a bellowing sound
> Roared the dead limbs; the burning entrails groaned.

This indeed is but a fiction and fancy; but the fare itself is truly monstrous and prodigious—that a man should have a stomach to creatures while they yet bellow, and that he should be giving directions which of things yet alive and speaking is fittest to make food of, and ordering the several manners of the seasoning and dressing them and serving them up to tables. You ought rather, in my opinion, to have enquired who first began this practice, than who of late times left it off.

2. And truly, as for those people who first ventured upon eating of

From Plutarch, *Moral Essays*, 1898.

flesh, it is very probable that the whole reason of their so doing was scarcity and want of other food; for it is not likely that their living together in lawless and extravagant lusts, or their growing wanton and capricious through the excessive variety of provisions then among them, brought them to such unsociable pleasures as these, against Nature. Yea, had they at this instant but their sense and voice restored to them, I am persuaded they would express themselves to this purpose:

"Oh! happy you, and highly favored of the Gods, who now live! Into what an age of the world are you fallen, who share and enjoy among you a plentiful portion of good things! What abundance of things spring up for your use! What fruitful vineyards you enjoy! What wealth you gather from the fields! What delicacies from trees and plants, which you may gather! You may glut and fill yourselves without being polluted. As for us, we fell upon the most dismal and affrighting part of time, in which we were exposed by our first production to manifold and inextricable wants and necessities. As yet the thickened air concealed the heaven from our view, and the stars were as yet confused with a disorderly huddle of fire and moisture and violent fluxions of winds. As yet the sun was not fixed to an unwandering and certain course, so as to distinguish morning and evening, nor did he bring back the seasons in order crowned with wreaths from the fruitful harvest. The land was also spoiled by the inundations of disorderly rivers; and a great part of it was deformed with sloughs, and utterly wild by reason of deep quagmires, unfertile forests, and woods. There was then no production of tame fruits, nor any instruments of art or invention of wit. And hunger gave no time, nor did seed-time then stay for the yearly season. What wonder is it if we made use of the flesh of beasts contrary to Nature, when mud was eaten and the bark of wood, and when it was thought a happy thing to find either a sprouting grass or a root of any plant! But when they had by chance tasted of or eaten an acorn, they danced for very joy about some oak or esculus, calling it by the names of life-giver, mother, and nourisher. And this was the only festival that those times were acquainted with; upon all other occasions, all things were full of anguish and dismal sadness. But whence is it that a certain ravenousness and frenzy drives you in these happy days to pollute yourselves with blood, since you have such an abundance of things necessary for your subsistence? Why do you belie the earth as unable to maintain you? Why do you profane the lawgiver Ceres, and shame the mild and gentle Bacchus, as not furnishing you with sufficiency? Are you not ashamed to mix tame fruits with blood and slaughter? You are indeed wont to call serpents, leopards, and lions savage creatures; but yet yourselves are defiled with blood, and come nothing behind them in cruelty. What they kill is their ordinary nourishment, but what you kill is your better fare."

3. For we eat not lions and wolves by way of revenge; but we let those go, and catch the harmless and tame sort, and such as have neither stings nor teeth to bite with, and slay them; which, so may Jove help us, Nature seems to us to have produced for their beauty and comeliness only.

4. But we are nothing put out of countenance, either by the beauteous gayety of the colors, or by the charmingness of the musical voices, or by the rare sagacity of the intellects, or by the cleanliness and neatness of diet, or by the rare discretion and prudence of these poor unfortunate animals; but for the sake of some little mouthful of flesh, we deprive a soul of the sun and light, and of that proportion of life and time it had been born into the world to enjoy. And then we fancy that the voices it utters and screams forth to us are nothing else but certain inarticulate sounds and noises, and not the several deprecations, entreaties, and pleadings of each of them, as it were saying thus to us: "I deprecate not thy necessity (if such there be), but thy wantonness. Kill me for thy feeding, but do not take me off for thy better feeding." O horrible cruelty! It is truly an affecting sight to see the very table of rich people laid before them, who keep them cooks and caterers to furnish them with dead corpses for their daily fare; but it is yet more affecting to see it taken away, for the mammocks left are more than that which was eaten. These therefore were slain to no purpose. Others there are, who are so sparing of what is set before them that they will not suffer it to be cut or sliced; thus abstaining from them when dead, while they would not spare them when alive.

5. Well then, we understand that that sort of men are used to say, that in eating of flesh they follow the conduct and direction of Nature. But that it is not natural to mankind to feed on flesh, we first of all demonstrate from the very shape and figure of the body. For a human body no ways resembles those that were born for ravenousness; it hath no hawk's bill, no sharp talon, no roughness of teeth, no such strength of stomach or heat of digestion, as can be sufficient to convert or alter such heavy and fleshy fare. But even from hence, that is, from the smoothness of the tongue, and the slowness of the stomach to digest, Nature seems to disclaim all pretence to fleshy victuals. But if you will contend that yourself was born to an inclination to such food as you have now a mind to eat, do you then yourself kill what you would eat. But do it yourself, without the help of a chopping-knife, mallet, or axe —as wolves, bears, and lions do, who kill and eat at once. Rend an ox with thy teeth, worry a hog with thy mouth, tear a lamb or a hare in pieces, and fall on and eat it alive as they do. But if thou hadst rather stay until what thou eatest is to become dead, and if thou art loath to force a soul out of its body, why then dost thou against Nature eat an animate thing? Nay, there is nobody that is willing to eat even a lifeless

and a dead thing as it is; but they boil it, and roast it, and alter it by fire and medicines, as it were, changing and quenching the slaughtered gore with thousands of sweet sauces, that the palate being thereby deceived may admit of such uncouth fare. It was indeed a witty expression of a Lacedaemonian, who, having purchased a small fish in a certain inn, delivered it to his landlord to be dressed; and as he demanded cheese, and vinegar, and oil to make sauce, he replied, if I had had those, I would not have bought the fish.

Tract II

1. Reason persuades us now to return with fresh cogitations and dispositions to what we left cold yesterday of our discourse about flesh-eating. It is indeed a hard and a difficult task to undertake (as Cato once said)to dispute with men's bellies, that have no ears; since most have already drunk that draught of custom, which is like that of Circe.

Of groans and frauds and sorcery replete.

And it is no easy task to pull out the hook of flesh-eating from the jaws of such as have gorged themselves with luxury and are (as it were) nailed down with it. It would indeed be a good action, if as the Egyptians draw out the stomach of a dead body, and cut it open and expose it to the sun, as the only cause of all its evil actions, so we could, by cutting out our gluttony and blood-shedding, purify and cleanse the remainder of our lives. For the stomach itself is not guilty of bloodshed, but is involuntarily polluted by our intemperance. But if this may not be, and we are ashamed by reason of custom to live unblamably, let us at least sin with discretion. Let us eat flesh; but let it be for hunger and not for wantonness. Let us kill an animal; but let us do it with sorrow and pity, and not abusing and tormenting it, as many nowadays are used to do, while some run red-hot spits through the bodies of swine, that by the tincture of the quenched iron the blood may be to that degree mortified, that it may sweeten and soften the flesh in its circulation; others jump and stamp upon the udders of sows that are ready to pig, that so they may trample into one mass (O Piacular Jupiter!) in the very pangs of delivery, blood, milk, and the corruption of the crushed and mangled young ones, and so eat the most inflamed part of the animal; others sew up the eyes of cranes and swans, and so shut them up in darkness to be fattened, and then souse up their flesh with certain monstrous mixtures and pickles.

2. By all which it is most manifest, that it is not for nourishment, or

want, or any necessity, but for mere gluttony, wantonness, and expensiveness, that they make a pleasure of villany. Just as it happens in persons who cannot satiate their intemperance upon women, and having made trial of every thing else and falling into vagaries, at last attempt things not to be mentioned; even so inordinateness in feeding, when it hath once passed the bounds of nature and necessity, studies at last to diversify the lusts of its intemperate appetite by cruelty and villany. For the senses, when they once quit their natural measures, sympathize with each other in their distempers, and are enticed by each other to the same consent and intemperance. ... The beginning of a vicious diet is presently followed by all sorts of luxury and expensiveness,

> Ev'n as a mare is by her thirsty colt.

3. And what meal is not expensive? That for which no animal is put to death. Shall we reckon a soul to be a small expense. I will not say perhaps of a mother, or a father, or of some friend, or child, as Empedocles did; but one participating of feeling, of seeing, of hearing, of imagination, and of intellection; which each animal hath received from Nature for the acquiring of what is agreeable to it, and the avoiding what is disagreeable. Do but consider this with yourself now, which sort of philosophers render us most tame and civil, they who bid people to feed on their children, friends, fathers, and wives, when they are dead; or Pythagoras and Empedocles, that accustom men to be just towards even the other members of the creation. You laugh at a man that will not eat a sheep: but we (they will say again)—when we see you cutting off the parts of your dead father or mother, and sending it to your absent friends, and calling upon and inviting your present friends to eat the rest freely and heartily—shall we not smile?

4. Who then were the first authors of this opinion, that we owe no justice to dumb animals?

> Who first beat out accursed steel,
> And made the lab'ring ox a knife to feel.

In the very same manner oppressors and tyrants begin first to shed blood. For example, the first man that the Athenians ever put to death was one of the basest of all knaves, whom all thought deserving of death; after him they put to death a second and a third. After this, being now accustomed to blood, they patiently saw Niceratus the son of Nicias, and their own general Theramenes, and Polemarchus the philosopher suffer death. Even so, in the beginning, some wild and mischievous beast was killed and eaten, and then some little bird or fish was entrapped. And the love of slaughter, being first experimented and exercised in these, at last passed even to the laboring ox, and the sheep that clothes us, and to the poor cock that keeps the house; until by little and little, unsatiableness being strengthened by use, men came to the slaughter of men, to bloodshed and wars. Now even if one cannot demonstrate and make out, that souls in their regenerations make a promiscuous use of all bodies, and that that which is now rational will at another time be irrational, and that again tame which is now wild—for that Nature changes and transmutes every thing,

> With different fleshy coats new clothing all—

this thing should be sufficient to change and reclaim men, that it is a savage and intemperate habit, that it brings sickness and heaviness upon the body, and that it inclines the mind the more brutishly to bloodshed and destruction, when we have once accustomed ourselves neither to entertain a guest nor keep a wedding nor to treat our friends without blood and slaughter.

5. And if what is argued about the return of souls into bodies is not of force enough to beget faith, yet methinks the very uncertainty of the thing should fill us with apprehension and fear. Suppose, for instance, one should in some night-engagement run on with his drawn sword upon one that had fallen down and covered his body with his arms, and should in the mean time hear one say, that he was not very sure, but that he fancied and believed, that the party lying there was his own son, brother, father, or tent-companion; which were more advisable, think you—to hearken to a false suggestion, and so to let go an enemy under the notion of a friend, or to slight an authority not sufficient to beget faith, and to slay a friend instead of a foe? This you will say would be insupportable. Do but consider the famous Merope in the tragedy, who taking up a hatchet, and lifting it at her son's head, whom she took for her son's murderer, speaks thus as she was ready to give the fatal blow,

> Villain, this pious blow shall cleave thy head;

what a bustle she raises in the whole theatre while she raises herself to give the blow, and what a fear they are all in, lest she should prevent the old man that comes to stop her hand, and should wound the youth. Now if another old man should stand by her and say, "Strike, it is thy enemy," and this, "Hold, it is thy son"; which, think you, would be the greater injustice, to omit the punishing of an enemy for the sake of one's child, or to suffer one's self to be so transported with anger at an enemy as to kill one's child? Since then neither hatred nor wrath nor any revenge nor fear for ourselves carries us to the slaughter of a beast, but the poor sacrifice stands with an inclined neck, only to satisfy thy lust and pleasure, and then one philosopher stands by and tells thee, "Cut him down, it is but an unreasonable animal," and another cries, "Hold, what if there should be the soul of some kinsman or God inclosed in him"?—good Gods! is there the like danger if I refuse to eat flesh, as if I for want of faith murder my child or some other friend?

6. The Stoics' way of reasoning upon this subject of flesh-eating is *Stoics* no way equal nor consonant with themselves. Who is this that hath so many mouths for his belly and the kitchen? Whence comes it to pass, that they so very much womanize and reproach pleasure, as a thing that they will not allow to be either good or preferable, or so much as agreeable, and yet all on a sudden become so zealous advocates for pleasures? It were indeed but a reasonable consequence of their doctrine, that, since they banish perfumes and cakes from their banquets, they should be much more averse to blood and flesh. But now, just as if they would reduce their philosophy to their day-books, they lessen the expenses of their suppers in certain unnecessary and needless matters, but the untamed and murderous part of their expense they nothing boggle at. "Well! What then?" say they. "We have nothing to do with brute beasts." Nor have you any with perfumes, nor with foreign sauces, may some one answer; therefore expel these from your banquets, if you are driving out every thing that is both useless and needless.

7. Let us therefore in the next place consider, whether we owe any justice to the brute beasts. Neither shall we handle this point artificially or like subtle sophisters, but by casting our eye into our own breasts, and conversing with ourselves as men, we will weigh and examine the whole matter. ... [The remainder of the manuscript, if it was ever completed, is missing.]

SAINT THOMAS AQUINAS

On Killing Living Things and the Duty to Love Irrational Creatures

Question 64, Article 1

WHETHER IT IS UNLAWFUL TO KILL ANY LIVING THING

We proceed thus to the First Article:

Objection 1. It would seem unlawful to kill any living thing. For the Apostle says (Rom. xiii. 2): *They that resist the ordinance of God purchase to themselves damnation.* Now Divine providence has ordained that all living things should be preserved, according to Ps. cxlvi. 8, 9, *Who maketh grass to grow on the mountains, . . . Who giveth to beasts their food.* Therefore it seems unlawful to take the life of any living thing.

Obj. 2. Further, Murder is a sin because it deprives a man of life. Now life is common to all animals and plants. Hence for the same reason it is apparently a sin to slay dumb animals and plants.

Obj. 3. Further, In the Divine law a special punishment is not appointed save for a sin. Now a special punishment had to be inflicted, according to the Divine law, on one who killed another man's ox or sheep (Exod. xxii. I). Therefore the slaying of dumb animals is a sin.

On the contrary, Augustine says (*De Civ. Dei* i. 20): *When we hear it said, 'Thou shalt not kill,' we do not take it as referring to trees, for*

From Saint Thomas Aquinas, *Summa Theologica*, literally translated by the English Dominican Fathers (Benziger Brothers, 1918), Part II, Question 64, Article 1, and Question 25, Article 3.

they have no sense, nor to irrational animals, because they have no fellowship with us. Hence it follows that the words, 'Thou shalt not kill' refer to the killing of a man.

I answer that, There is no sin in using a thing for the purpose for which it is. Now the order of things is such that the imperfect are for the perfect, even as in the process of generation nature proceeds from imperfection to perfection. Hence it is that just as in the generation of a man there is first a living thing, then an animal, and lastly a man, so too things, like the plants, which merely have life, are all alike for animals, and all animals are for man. Wherefore it is not unlawful if man use plants for the good of animals, and animals for the good of man, as the Philosopher states (*Polit.* i. 3).

Now the most necessary use would seem to consist in the fact that animals use plants, and men use animals, for food, and this cannot be done unless these be deprived of life: wherefore it is lawful both to take life from plants for the use of animals, and from animals for the use of men. In fact this is in keeping with the commandment of God Himself: for it is written (Gen. i. 29, 30): *Behold I have given you every herb . . . and all trees . . . to be your meat, and to all beasts of the earth:* and again (*ibid.* ix. 3): *Everything that moveth and liveth shall be meat to you.*

Reply Obj. 1. According to the Divine ordinance the life of animals and plants is preserved not for themselves but for man. Hence, as Augustine says (*De Civ. Dei* i. 20), *by a most just ordinance of the Creator, both their life and their death are subject to our use.*

Reply Obj. 2. Dumb animals and plants are devoid of the life of reason whereby to set themselves in motion; they are moved, as it were by another, by a kind of natural impulse, a sign of which is that they are naturally enslaved and accommodated to the uses of others.

Reply Obj. 3. He that kills another's ox, sins, not through killing the ox, but through injuring another man in his property. Wherefore this is not a species of the sin of murder but of the sin of theft or robbery.

Question 65, Article 3

WHETHER IRRATIONAL CREATURES ALSO OUGHT TO BE LOVED OUT OF CHARITY

We proceed thus to the Third Article:

Objection 1. It would seem that irrational creatures also ought to be loved out of charity. For it is chiefly by charity that we are conformed to God. Now God loves irrational creatures out of charity, for He loves all things that are (Wis. xi. 25), and whatever He loves, He loves by

Himself Who is charity. Therefore we also should love irrational creatures out of charity.

Obj. 2. Further, Charity is referred to God principally, and extends
to other things as referable to God. Now just as the rational creature is
referable to God, in as much as it bears the resemblance of image, so
too, are the irrational creatures, in as much as they bear the resemblance
of a trace. Therefore charity extends also to irrational creatures.

Obj. 3. Further, Just as the object of charity is God, so is the object
of faith. Now faith extends to irrational creatures, since we believe that
heaven and earth were created by God, that the fishes and birds were
brought forth out of the waters, and animals that walk, and plants, out
of the earth. Therefore charity extends also to irrational creatures.

On the contrary, The love of charity extends to none but God and
our neighbour. But the word neighbour cannot be extended to irrational
creatures, since they have no fellowship with man in the rational life.
Therefore charity does not extend to irrational creatures.

I answer that, According to what has been stated above (Q. XIII.,
A. 1) charity is a kind of friendship. Now the love of friendship is two-
fold: first, there is the love for the friend to whom our friendship is
given, secondly, the love for those good things which we desire for our
friend. With regard to the first, no irrational creature can be loved out
of charity; and for three reasons. Two of these reasons refer in a general way to friendship, which cannot have an irrational creature for its
object: first because friendship is towards one to whom we wish good
things. While properly speaking, we cannot wish good things to an irrational creature, because it is not competent, properly speaking, to
possess good, this being proper to the rational creature which, through
its free-will, is the master of its disposal of the good it possesses. Hence
the Philosopher says (*Phys.* ii. 6) that we do not speak of good or evil
befalling suchlike things, except metaphorically. Secondly, because all
friendship is based on some fellowship in life; since *nothing is so proper
to friendship as to live together,* as the Philosopher proves (*Ethic* viii. 5).
Now irrational creatures can have no fellowship in human life which is
regulated by reason. Hence friendship with irrational creatures is impossible, except metaphorically speaking. The third reason is proper to
charity, for charity is based on the fellowship of everlasting happiness,
to which the irrational creature cannot attain. Therefore we cannot have
the friendship of charity towards an irrational creature.

Nevertheless we can love irrational creatures out of charity, if we regard them as the good things that we desire for others, in so far, to wit,
as we wish for their preservation, to God's honour and man's use; thus
too does God love them out of charity.

Wherefore the *Reply* to the *First Objection* is evident.

Reply Obj. 2. The likeness by way of trace does not confer the capacity for everlasting life, whereas the likeness of image does: and so the comparison fails.

Reply Obj. 3. Faith can extend to all that is in any way true, whereas the friendship of charity extends only to such things as have a natural capacity for everlasting life; wherefore the comparison fails.

IMMANUEL KANT

Duties to Animals

Baumgarten speaks of duties towards beings which are beneath us and beings which are above us. But so far as animals are concerned, we have no direct duties. Animals are not self-conscious and are there merely as a means to an end. That end is man. We can ask, "Why do animals exist?" But to ask, "Why does man exist?" is a meaningless question. Our duties towards animals are merely indirect duties towards humanity. Animal nature has analogies to human nature, and by doing our duties to animals in respect of manifestations of human nature, we indirectly do our duty towards humanity. Thus, if a dog has served his master long and faithfully, his service, on the analogy of human service, deserves reward, and when the dog has grown too old to serve, his master ought to keep him until he dies. Such action helps to support us in our duties towards human beings, where they are bounden duties. If then any acts of animals are analogous to human acts and spring from the same principles, we have duties towards the animals because thus we cultivate the corresponding duties towards human beings. If a man shoots his dog because the animal is no longer capable of service, he does not fail in his duty to the dog, for the dog cannot judge, but his act is inhuman and damages in himself that humanity which it is his duty to show towards mankind. If he is not to stifle his human feelings, he must practise kindness towards animals, for he who is cruel to animals becomes hard also in his dealing with men. We can judge the heart of a man by his treatment of animals. Hogarth depicts this in his engravings. He shows how cruelty grows and develops. He shows the

From Immanuel Kant, "Duties to Animals and Spirits," in *Lectures on Ethics*, trans. Louis Infield (New York: Harper and Row, 1963), pp. 239–41.

child's cruelty to animals, pinch the tail of a dog or a cat; he then depicts the grown man in his cart running over a child; and lastly, the culmination of cruelty in murder. He thus brings home to us in a terrible fashion the rewards of cruelty, and this should be an impressive lesson to children. The more we come in contact with animals and observe their behaviour, the more we love them, for we see how great is their care for their young. It is then difficult for us to be cruel in thought even to a wolf. Leibnitz used a tiny worm for purposes of observation, and then carefully replaced it with its leaf on the tree so that it should not come to harm through any act of his. He would have been sorry— a natural feeling for a humane man—to destroy such a creature for no reason. Tender feelings towards dumb animals develop humane feelings towards mankind. In England butchers and doctors do not sit on a jury because they are accustomed to the sight of death and hardened. Vivisectionists, who use living animals for their experiments, certainly act cruelly, although their aim is praiseworthy, and they can justify their cruelty, since animals must be regarded as man's instruments; but any such cruelty for sport cannot be justified. A master who turns out his ass or his dog because the animal can no longer earn its keep manifests a small mind. The Greeks' ideas in this respect were highminded, as can be seen from the fable of the ass and the bell of ingratitude. Our duties towards animals, then, are indirect duties towards mankind.

ARTHUR SCHOPENHAUER

A Critique of Kant

§8

ON THE DERIVED FORMS OF THE SUPREME PRINCIPLE
OF THE KANTIAN ETHICS

It is well known that Kant laid down the supreme principle of his ethics in yet a second and quite different form in which it is expressed not merely indirectly as in the first, as an instruction on how it is to to be sought, but directly.[1] Starting at page 63, R. 55, he prepares the way for this, and indeed by very strange, stilted, and even distorted definitions of the concepts *end* and *means*, which, however, may be much more simply and correctly defined thus: *End* is the direct motive of an act of will, *means* the indirect motive (*simplex sigillum veri*). Kant, however, slips through his strange definitions to the proposition: "Man, and in general every rational being, exists *as an end in himself.*" But I must say frankly that "*to exist as an end in oneself*" is an unthinkable expression, a *contradictio in adjecto.* To be an end or aim means to be willed. Every aim or end in view exists only in reference to a will, and is the end of the will, that is (as I have said), the direct motive of it. Only in this relation has the concept *end* any meaning, which

[1]Kant's first formulation of the supreme principle of morality reads: "Act so that maxima of your action may be adopted as a universal law." His second formulation (the one Schopenhauer attacks) reads: "Act so as to treat humanity, both in thine own person and in the person of every other, always as an end, never merely as a means."

it loses as soon as it is torn away. But this essential relation necessarily excludes all *in itself*. "End in itself" is exactly like saying "friend in himself, enemy in himself, uncle in himself, north or east in itself, above or below in itself," and so on. Basically, however, the case is the same with "end in itself" as with the "absolute ought." Secretly, and even unconsciously underlying both, as their condition, is the same idea, namely, the theological. Nor does the *absolute worth* that is said to attach to such an alleged but inconceivable *end in itself* fare any better, for this too I must without mercy stamp as a *contradictio in adjecto*. Every *worth* is a quantity of comparison and even stands necessarily in a double relation. First, it is *relative*, in that it exists *for* someone; and secondly, it is *comparative*, in that it exists in comparison with something else by which it is valued or assessed. Outside these two relations, the concept *worth* loses all meaning; this is so clear that there is no need for further discussion. Now just as those two definitions offend against logic, so is genuine morality outraged by the proposition (page 65, R. 56) that beings devoid of reason (hence animals) are *things* and therefore should be treated merely as *means* that are not at the same time an *end*. In agreement with this, it is expressly stated in the *Metaphysical Principles of the Doctrine of Virtue*, §16, that "man can have no duty to any beings except human"; and then it says in §17 that "cruelty to animals is contrary to man's duty *to himself*, because it deadens in him the feeling of sympathy for their sufferings, and thus a natural tendency that is very useful to morality in relation to *other human beings* is weakened." Thus only for practice are we to have sympathy for animals, and they are, so to speak, the pathological phantom for the purpose of practicing sympathy for human beings. In common with the whole of Asia not tainted with Islam (that is, Judaism), I regard such propositions as revolting and abominable.

§19

CONFIRMATIONS OF THE EXPOUNDED BASIS OF MORALS

Boundless compassion for all living beings is the firmest and surest guarantee of pure moral conduct, and needs no casuistry. Whoever is inspired with it will assuredly injure no one, will wrong no one, will encroach on no one's rights; on the contrary, he will be lenient and patient with everyone, will forgive everyone, will help everyone as much as he can, and all his actions will bear the stamp of justice, philanthropy, and loving-kindness. On the other hand, if we attempt to say, "This man is virtuous but knows no compassion," or, "He is an unjust and malicious man yet he is very compassionate," the contradiction is obvious. Tastes differ, but I know of no finer prayer than the one which ends old Indian dramas (just as in former times English plays ended with a prayer for the King). It runs: "May all living beings remain free from pain." . . .

The moral incentive advanced by me as the genuine, is further confirmed by the fact that *the animals* are also taken under its protection. In other European systems of morality they are badly provided for, which is most inexcusable. They are said to have no rights, and there is the erroneous idea that our behavior to them is without moral significance, or, as it is said in the language of that morality, there are no duties to animals. All this is revoltingly crude, a barbarism of the West, the source of which is to be found in Judaism. In philosophy it rests, despite all evidence to the contrary, on the assumed total difference between man and animal. We all know that such difference was expressed most definitely and strikingly by Descartes as a necessary consequence of his errors. Thus when the philosophy of Descartes, Leibniz, and Wolff built up rational psychology out of abstract concepts and constructed an immortal *anima rationalis,* the natural claims of the animal world obviously stood up against this exclusive privilege, this patent of immortality of the human species, and nature, as always on such occasions, entered her silent protest. With an uneasy intellectual conscience, the philosophers then had to try to support rational psychology by means of the empirical. They were therefore concerned to open up a vast chasm, an immeasurable gulf between man and animal in order to represent them as fundamentally different, in spite of all evidence to the contrary. . . . In the end animals would be quite incapable of distinguishing themselves from the external world and would have no consciousness of themselves, no ego! To answer such absurd statements, we can point simply to the boundless egoism inherent in every animal, even the smallest and lowest, which shows clearly enough how very conscious they are of their ego in face of the world or the non-ego. If any Cartesian were to find himself clawed by a tiger, he would become aware in the clearest possible manner of the sharp distinction such a beast draws between its ego and the non-ego. In keeping with such sophisms of philosophers, we find a popular peculiarity in many languages, especially German, of giving animals special words of their own for eating, drinking, pregnancy, parturition, dying, and their bodies, so that we need not use the same words which describe those acts among human beings: and thus we conceal under a diversity of words the perfect and complete identity of the thing. Since the ancient languages did not recognize any such duplication, but rather frankly and openly denoted the same thing by the same word, that miserable artifice is undoubtedly the work of European priests and parsons. In their profanity these men think they cannot go far enough in disavowing and reviling the eternal essence that lives in all animals, and thus have laid the foundation of that harshness and cruelty to animals which is customary in Europe, but which no native of the Asiatic uplands can look at without righteous horror. In the English language we do not meet with this contemptible trick, doubtless because the Saxons, when they conquered England, were not yet Christians. On the other hand, we do find an analogy to it in the strange fact that in English all animals are of the neuter gender and so are represented by the pronoun "it," just as if they were inanimate things. The effect of this artifice is quite revolting, especially in the case of primates, such as dogs, monkeys, and the like; it is unmistakably a priestly trick for the purpose of reducing animals to the level of things. The ancient Egyptians, whose whole life was dedicated to religious purposes, put the mummies of the ibis, crocodile, and so on, in the same vault with those of human beings. In Europe, however, it is an abomination and a crime for a faithful dog to be buried beside the resting place of his master, though at times, from a faithfulness and attachment not to be found among the human race, he there awaited his own death. Nothing leads more definitely to a recognition of the identity of the essential nature in animal and human phenomena than a study of zoology and anatomy. What, then, are we to say when in these days [1839] a bigoted and canting zootomist has the audacity to emphasize an absolute and radical difference between man and animal, and goes so far as to attack and disparage honest zoologists who keep aloof from all priestly guile, toadyism, and hypocrisy, and pursue their course under the guidance of nature and truth?

One must be really quite blind or totally chloroformed by the *foetor Judaicus* not to recognize that the essential or principal thing in the animal and man is the same, and that what distinguishes the one from the other is not to be found in the primary and original principle, in the archaeus, in the inner nature, in the kernel of the two phenomena, such kernel being in both alike the *will* of the individual; but only in the secondary, in the intellect, in the degree of the cognitive faculty. In man this degree is incomparably higher through the addition of the faculty of *abstract* knowledge, called *reason*. Yet this superiority is traceable only to a greater cerebral development, and hence to the somatic difference of a single part, the brain, and in particular, its quantity. On the other hand, the similarity between animal and man is incomparably greater, both psychically and somatically. And so we must remind the Western, Judaized despiser of animals and idolater of the faculty of reason that, just as he was suckled by *his* mother, so too was the dog by *his*. Even Kant fell into this mistake of his contemporaries and countrymen; this I have already censured. The morality of Christianity has no consideration for animals, a defect that is better admitted than perpetuated. . . .

Since compassion for animals is so intimately associated with goodness of character, it may be confidently asserted that whoever is cruel to animals cannot be a good man. This compassion also appears to have sprung from the same source as the virtue that is shown to human beings has. Thus, for example, persons of delicate feelings, on realizing that in a bad mood, in anger, or under the influence of wine, they unnecessarily or excessively, or beyond propriety, ill-treated their dog, horse, or monkey—these people will feel the same remorse, the same dissatisfaction with themselves as is felt when they recall a wrong done to human beings, where it is called the voice of reproving conscience.

JEREMY BENTHAM

A Utilitarian View

IV. What other agents then are there, which, at the same time that they are under the influence of man's direction, are susceptible of happiness? They are of two sorts: (1) Other human beings who are styled persons. (2) Other animals, which, on account of their interests having been neglected by the insensibility of the ancient jurists, stand degraded into the class of *things*.

Under the Hindu and Mahometan religions, the interests of the rest of the animal creation seem to have met with some attention. Why have they not, universally, with as much as those of human creatures, allowance made for the difference in point of sensibility? Because the laws that are have been the work of mutual fear; a sentiment which the less rational animals have not had the same means as man has of turning to account. Why *ought* they not? No reason can be given. If the being eaten were all, there is very good reason why we should be suffered to eat such of them as we like to eat: we are the better for it, and they are never the worse. They have none of those long-protracted anticipations of future misery which we have. The death they suffer in our hands commonly is, and always may be, a speedier, and by that means a less painful one, than that which would await them in the inevitable course of nature. If the being killed were all, there is very good reason why we should be suffered to kill such as molest us: we should be the worse for their living, and they are never the worse for being dead. But is there any reason why we should be suffered to torment them? Not any that I can see. Are there any why we should *not* be suffered to tor-

From Jeremy Bentham, *The Principles of Morals and Legislation* (1789), Chapter XVII, Section 1.

ment them? Yes, several. The day has been, I grieve to say in many places it is not yet past, in which the greater part of the species, under the denomination of slaves, have been treated by the law exactly upon the same footing as, in England for example, the inferior races of animals are still. The day *may come*, when the rest of the animal creation may acquire those rights which never could have been withholden from them but by the hand of tyranny. The French have already discovered that the blackness of the skin is no reason why a human being should be abandoned without redress to the caprice of a tormentor. It may come one day to be recognized, that the number of the legs, the villosity of the skin, or the termination of the *os sacrum*, are reasons equally insufficient for abandoning a sensitive being to the same fate. What else is it that should trace the insuperable line? Is it the faculty of reason, or, perhaps, the faculty of discourse? But a full-grown horse or dog is beyond comparison a more rational, as well as a more conversable animal, than an infant of a day, or a week, or even a month, old. But suppose the case were otherwise, what would it avail? the question is not, Can they *reason*? nor, Can they *talk*? but, Can they *suffer*?

JOHN STUART MILL

A Defense of Bentham

Dr. Whewell puts the last hand to his supposed refutation of Bentham's principle, by what he thinks a crushing *reductio ad absurdum*. The reader might make a hundred guesses before discovering what this is. We have not yet got over our astonishment, not at Bentham, but at Dr. Whewell. See, he says, to what consequences your greatest-happiness principle leads! Bentham says that it is as much a moral duty to regard the pleasures and pains of other animals as those of human beings. . . .

This noble anticipation, in 1780, of the better morality of which a first dawn has been seen in the laws enacted nearly fifty years afterwards against cruelty to animals, is in Dr. Whewell's eyes the finishing proof that the morality of happiness is absurd!

> The pleasures of animals are elements of a very different order from the pleasures of man. We are bound to endeavour to augment the pleasures of men, not only because they are pleasures, but because they are human pleasures. We are bound to men by the universal tie of humanity, of human brotherhood. We have no such tie to animals. [*Lectures*, p. 223.]

This then is Dr. Whewell's noble and disinterested ideal of virtue. Duties, according to him, are only duties to ourselves and our like.

> We are to be *humane* to them, because we are *human*, not because we and they alike feel *animal* pleasures. . . . The morality which depends

From John Stuart Mill, "Whewell on Moral Philosophy," in Mill's *Collected Works*, vol. X, pp. 185–87.

upon the increase of pleasure alone, would make it our duty to increase the pleasure of pigs or of geese rather than that of men, if we were sure that the pleasures we could give them were greater than the pleasures of men. . . . It is not only not an obvious, but to most persons not a tolerable doctrine, that we may sacrifice the happiness of men provided we can in that way produce an overplus of pleasure to cats, dogs, and hogs. (Pp. 223–5.)

It is "to most persons" in the Slave States of America not a tolerable doctrine that we may sacrifice any portion of the happiness of white men for the sake of a greater amount of happiness to black men. It would have been intolerable five centuries ago "to most persons" among the feudal nobolity, to hear it asserted that the greatest pleasure or pain of a hundred serfs ought not to give way to the smallest of a nobleman. According to the standard of Dr. Whewell the slavemasters and the nobles were right. They too felt themselves "bound" by a "tie of brotherhood" to the white men and to the nobility, and felt no such tie to the negroes and serfs. And if a feeling on moral subjects is right because it is natural, their feeling was justifiable. Nothing is more natural to human beings, nor, up to a certain point in cultivation, more universal, than to estimate the pleasures and pains of others as deserving of regard exactly in proportion to their likeness to ourselves. These superstitions of selfishness had the characteristics by which Dr. Whewell recognizes his moral rules; and his opinion on the rights of animals shows that in this case at least he is consistent. We are perfectly willing to stake the whole question on this one issue. Granted that any practice causes more pain to animals than it gives pleasure to man; is that practice moral or immoral? And if, exactly in proportion as human beings raise their heads out of the slough of selfishness, they do not with one voice answer "immoral," let the morality of the principle of utility be for ever condemned.

ALBERT SCHWEITZER

The Ethic of
Reverence for Life

Descartes tells us that philosophizing is based on the judgment: "I think, therefore I am." From this meagre and arbitrarily selected beginning it is inevitable that it should wander into the path of the abstract. It does not find the entrance to the ethical realm, and remains held fast in a dead view of the world and of life. True philosophy must commence with the most immediate and comprehensive facts of consciousness. And this may be formulated as follows: "I am life which wills to live, and I exist in the midst of life which wills to live." This is no mere excogitated subtlety. Day after day and hour after hour I proceed on my way invested in it. In every moment of reflection it forces itself on me anew. A living world- and life-view, informing all the facts of life, gushes forth from it continually, as from an eternal spring. A mystically ethical oneness with existence grows forth from it unceasingly.

Just as in my own will-to-live there is a yearning for more life, and for that mysterious exaltation of the will-to-live which is called pleasure, and terror in face of annihilation and that injury to the will-to-live which is called pain; so the same obtains in all the will-to-live around me, equally whether it can express itself to my comprehension or whether it remains unvoiced.

Ethics thus consists in this, that I experience the necessity of practising the same reverence for life toward all will-to-live, as toward my own. Therein I have already the needed fundamental principle of moral-

From Albert Schweitzer, *Civilization and Ethics* (Part II of *The Philosophy of Civilization*), trans. John Naish. Reprinted by permission of A. & C. Black Ltd. and Macmillan Publishing Co., Inc.

ity. It is *good* to maintain and cherish life; it is *evil* to destroy and to check life.

As a matter of fact, everything which in the usual ethical valuation of inter-human relations is looked upon as good can be traced back to the material and spiritual maintenance or enhancement of human life and to the effort to raise it to its highest level of value. And contrariwise everything in human relations which is considered as evil, is in the final analysis found to be material or spiritual destruction or checking of human life and slackening of the effort to raise it to its highest value. Individual concepts of good and evil which are widely divergent and apparently unconnected fit into one another like pieces which belong together, the moment they are comprehended and their essential nature is grasped in this general notion.

The fundamental principle of morality which we seek as a necessity for thought is not, however, a matter only of arranging and deepening current views of good and evil, but also of expanding and extending these. A man is really ethical only when he obeys the constraint laid on him to help all life which he is able to succour, and when he goes out of his way to avoid injuring anything living. He does not ask how far this or that life deserves sympathy as valuable in itself, nor how far it is capable of feeling. To him life as such is sacred. He shatters no ice crystal that sparkles in the sun, tears no leaf from its tree, breaks off no flower, and is careful not to crush any insect as he walks. If he works by lamplight on a summer evening, he prefers to keep the window shut and to breathe stifling air, rather than to see insect after insect fall on his table with singed and sinking wings.

If he goes out into the street after a rainstorm and sees a worm which has strayed there, he reflects that it will certainly dry up in the sunshine, if it does not quickly regain the damp soil into which it can creep, and so he helps it back from the deadly paving stones into the lush grass. Should he pass by an insect which has fallen into a pool, he spares the time to reach it a leaf or stalk on which it may clamber and save itself.

He is not afraid of being laughed at as sentimental. It is indeed the fate of every truth to be an object of ridicule when it is first acclaimed. It was once considered foolish to suppose that coloured men were really human beings and ought to be treated as such. What was once foolishness has now become a recognized truth. Today it is considered as exaggeration to proclaim constant respect for every form of life as being the serious demand of a rational ethic. But the time is coming when people will be amazed that the human race was so long before it recognized thoughtless injury to life as incompatible with real ethics. Ethics is in its unqualified form extended responsibility with regard to everything that has life.

The general idea of ethics as a partaking of the mental atmosphere of reverence for life is not perhaps attractive. But it is the only complete notion possible. Mere sympathy is too narrow a concept to serve as the intellectual expression of the ethical element. It denotes, indeed, only a sharing of the suffering of the will-to-live. But to be ethical is to share the whole experience of all the circumstances and aspirations of the will-to-live, to live with it in its pleasures, in its yearnings, in its struggles toward perfection.

Love is a more inclusive term, since it signifies fellowship in suffering, in joy, and in effort. But it describes the ethical element only as it were by a simile, however natural and profound that simile may be. It places the solidarity created by ethics in analogy to that which nature has caused to come into being in a more or less superficial physical manner, and with a view to the fulfilment of their destiny, between two sexually attracted existences, or between these and their offspring.

Thought must strive to find a formula for the essential nature of the ethical. In so doing it is led to characterize ethics as self-devotion for the sake of life, motivated by reverence for life. Although the phrase "reverence for life" may perhaps sound a trifle unreal, yet that which it denotes is something which never lets go its hold of the man in whose thought it has once found a place. Sympathy, love, and, in general, all enthusiastic feeling of real value are summed up in it. It works with restless vitality on the mental nature in which it has found a footing and flings this into the restless activity of a responsibility which never ceases and stops nowhere. Reverence for life drives a man on as the whirling thrashing screw forces a ship through the water.

The ethic of reverence for life, arising as it does out of an inward necessity, is not dependent on the question as to how far or how little it is capable of development into a satisfactory view of life. It does not need to prove that the action of ethical men, as directed to maintaining, enhancing and exalting life, has any significance for the total course of the world-process. Nor is it disturbed by the consideration that the preservation and enhancement of life which it practises are of almost no account at all beside the mighty destruction of life which takes place every moment as the result of natural forces. Determined as it is to act, it is yet able to ignore all the problems raised as to the result of its action. The fact that in the man who has become ethical a will informed by reverence for life and self-sacrifice for the sake of life exists in the world, is itself significant for the world.

The universal will-to-live experiences itself in my personal will-to-live otherwise than it does in other phenomena. For here it enters on an individualization, which, so far as I am able to gather in trying to view it from the outside, struggles only to live itself out, and not at all to become one with will-to-live external to itself. The world is indeed the grisly drama of will-to-live at variance with itself. One existence survives at the expense of another of which it yet knows nothing. But in me the will-to-live has become cognizant of the existence of other will-to-live. There is in it a yearning for unity with itself, a longing to become universal.

Why is it that the will-to-live has this experience only in myself? Is it a result of my having become capable of reflection about the totality of existence? Whither will the evolution lead which has thus begun in me?

There is no answer to these questions. It remains a painful enigma how I am to live by the rule of reverence for life in a world ruled by creative will which is at the same time destructive will, and by destructive will which is also creative.

I can do no other than hold on to the fact that the will-to-live appears in me as will-to-live which aims at becoming one with other will-to-live. This fact is the light which shines for me in the darkness. My ignorance regarding the real nature of the objective world no longer troubles me. I am set free from the world. I have been cast by my reverence for life into a state of unrest foreign to the world. By this, too, I am placed in a state of beatitude which the world cannot give. If in the happiness induced by our independence of the world I and another afford each other mutual help in understanding and in forgiveness, when otherwise will would harass other will, then the will-to-live is no longer at variance with itself. If I rescue an insect from a pool of water, then life has given itself for life, and again the self-contradiction of the will-to-live has been removed. Whenever my life has given itself out in any way for other life, my eternal will-to-live experiences union with the eternal, since all life is one. I possess a cordial which secures me from dying of thirst in the desert of life.

Therefore I recognize it as the destiny of my existence to be obedient to the higher revelation of the will-to-live which I find in myself. I choose as my activity the removal of the self-contradiction of the will-to-live, as far as the influence of my own existence extends. Knowing as I do the one thing needful, I am content to offer no opinion about the enigma of the objective world and my own being.

Thought becomes religious when it thinks itself out to the end. The ethic of reverence for life is the ethic of Jesus brought to philosophical expression, extended into cosmical form, and conceived as intellectually necessary.

The surmising and longing of all deeply religious personalities is comprehended and contained in the ethic of reverence for life. This, however, does not build up a world-view as a completed system, but resigns itself to leave the cathedral perforce incomplete. It is only able to finish the choir. Yet in this true piety celebrates a living and continuous divine service. . . .

What does reverence for life teach us about the relations of man and the nonhuman animals?

Whenever I injure life of any kind I must be quite clear as to whether this is necessary or not. I ought never to pass the limits of the unavoidable, even in apparently insignificant cases. The countryman who has mowed down a thousand blossoms in his meadow as fodder for his cows should take care that on the way home he does not, in wanton pastime, switch off the head of a single flower growing on the edge of the road, for in so doing he injures life without being forced to do so by necessity.

Those who test operations or drugs on animals, or who inoculate them with diseases so that they may be able to help human beings by means of the results thus obtained, ought never to rest satisfied with the general idea that their dreadful doings are performed in pursuit of a worthy aim. It is their duty to ponder in every separate case whether it is really and truly necessary thus to sacrifice an animal for humanity. They ought to be filled with anxious care to alleviate as much as possible the pain which they cause. How many outrages are committed in this way in scientific institutions where narcotics are often omitted to save time and trouble! How many also when animals are made to suffer agonizing tortures, only in order to demonstrate to students scientific truths which are perfectly well known. The very fact that the animal, as a victim of research, has in his pain rendered such services to suffering men, has itself created a new and unique relation of solidarity between him and ourselves. The result is that a fresh obligation is laid on each of us to do as much good as we possibly can to all creatures in all sorts of circumstances. When I help an insect out of his troubles all that I do is to attempt to remove some of the guilt contracted through these crimes against animals.

Wherever any animal is forced into the service of man, the sufferings which it has to bear on that account are the concern of every one of us. No one ought to permit, in so far as he can prevent it, pain or suffering for which he will not take the responsibility. No one ought to rest at ease in the thought that in so doing he would mix himself up in affairs which are not his business. Let no one shirk the burden of his responsibility. When there is so much maltreatment of animals, when the cries of thirsting creatures go up unnoticed from the railway trucks, when

there is so much roughness in our slaughter-houses, when in our kitch-
ens so many animals suffer horrible deaths from unskilful hands, when
animals endure unheard-of agonies from heartless men, or are delivered
to the dreadful play of children, then we are all guilty and must bear
the blame.

We are afraid of shocking or offending by showing too plainly how
deeply we are moved by the sufferings which man causes to the nonhuman creatures. We tend to reflect that others are more "rational" than
we are, and would consider that which so disturbs us as customary and
as a matter of course. And then, suddenly, they let fall some expression
which shows us that they, too, are not really satisfied with the situation.
Strangers to us hitherto, they are now quite near our own position. The
masks, in which we had each concealed ourselves from the other, fall off.
We now know that neither of us can cut ourselves free from the horrible necessity which plays ceaselessly around us. What a wonderful
thing it is thus to get to know each other!

The ethic of reverence for life forbids any of us to deduce from the
silence of our contemporaries that they, or in their case we, have ceased
to feel what as thinking men we all cannot but feel. It prompts us to
keep a mutual watch in this atmosphere of suffering and endurance,
and to speak and act without panic according to the responsibility which
we feel. It inspires us to join in a search for opportunities to afford help
of some kind or other to the animals, to make up for the great amount
of misery which they endure at our hands, and thus to escape for a
moment from the inconceivable horrors of existence.

HENRY S. SALT

The Humanities of Diet

Some years ago, in an article entitled "Wanted, a New Meat," the *Spectator* complained that dietetic provision is made nowadays "not for man as humanised by schools of cookery, but for a race of fruit-eating apes." We introduce bananas, pines, Italian figs, pomegranates, and a variety of new fruits, but what is really wanted is "some new and large animal, something which shall combine the game flavour with the substantial solidity of a leg of mutton"* Surmising that there must exist "some neglected quadruped, which will furnish what we seek," the *Spectator* proceeded to take anxious stock of the world's resources, subjecting in turn the rodents, the pachyderms, and the ruminants to a careful survey, in which the claims even of the wart-hog were conscientiously debated. In the end the ruminants won the day, and the choice fell upon the Eland, which was called to the high function of supplying a new flesh-food for "humanised" man.

This is not the sense in which I am about to speak of the "humanities" of diet. I have not been fired by the *Spectator's* enthusiasm for the rescue of some "neglected quadruped," nor have I any wish to see eviscerated Elands hanging a-row in our butchers' shops. On the contrary, I suggest that in proportion as man is truly "humanised," not by schools of cookery but by schools of thought, he will abandon the barbarous habit of his flesh-eating ancestors, and will make gradual progress towards a purer, simpler, more humane, and therefore more civilised diet-system.

From Henry S. Salt, *The Humanities of Diet* (Manchester: The Vegetarian Society, 1914).

*Cf. Richard Jefferies's complaint of "the ceaseless round of mutton and beef to which the dead level of civilisation reduces us." Yet Vegetarians are supposed to lack "variety"!

There are many signs that the public is awaking to the fact that there is such a thing as food-reform. The reception of a new idea of this sort is always a strange process, and has to pass through several successive phases. First, there is tacit contempt; secondly, open ridicule; then a more or less respectful opposition; and lastly, a partial acceptance. During the third period, the one at which the Vegetarian question has now arrived, discussion is often complicated by the way in which the opponents of the new idea fail to grasp the *real* object of the reformers, and pleasantly substitute some exaggerated, distorted, or wholly imaginary concept of their own; after which they proceed to argue from a wrong basis, crediting their antagonists with mistaken aims and purposes, and then triumphantly impugning their consistency or logic. It is therefore of importance that, in debating the problem of food-reform, we should know exactly what the reformers themselves are aiming at.

Let me first make plain what I mean by calling Vegetarianism a *new* idea. Historically, of course, it is not new at all, either as a precept or a practice. A great portion of the world's inhabitants have always been practically Vegetarians, and some whole races and sects have been so upon principle. The Buddhist canon in the east, and the Pythagorean in the west, enjoined abstinence from flesh-food on humane, as on other grounds; and in the writings of such "pagan" philosophers as Plutarch and Porphyry we find a humanitarian ethic of the most exalted kind, which, after undergoing a long repression during medieval churchdom, reappeared, albeit but weakly and fitfully at first, in the literature of the Renaissance, to be traced more definitely in the eighteenth century school of "sensibility." But it was not until after the age of Rousseau, from which must be dated the great humanitarian movement of the past century, that Vegetarianism began to assert itself as a system, a reasoned plea for the disuse of flesh-food. In this sense it is a new ethical principle, and its import as such is only now beginning to be generally understood.

I say *ethical* principle, because it is beyond doubt that the chief motive of Vegetarianism is the humane one. Questions of hygiene and of economy both play their part, and an important part, in a full discussion of food reform; but the feeling which underlies and animates the whole movement is the instinctive horror of butchery, especially the butchery of the more highly organized animals, so human, so near akin to man. Let me quote a short passage from the preface to Mr. Howard Williams's "Ethics of Diet," an acknowledged text-book of Vegetarianism.

> "It has been well said," remarks Mr. Williams, "that there are steps on the way to the summit of dietetic reform, and if only one step be taken, yet that single step will not be without importance and without influence in the world. The step which leaves for ever behind it the

barbarism of slaughtering our fellow beings, the mammals and birds, is, it is superfluous to add, the most important and influential of all."

Let it therefore be clearly understood that this step—the "first step," as Tolstoy has called it, in a scheme of humane living—has been the main object of all Vegetarian propaganda since the establishment of the Vegetarian Society in 1847. To secure the discontinuance of the shocking and inhuman practices that are inseparable from the slaughter-house— this, and no abstract theory of abstinence from all "animal" substances, no fastidious abhorrence of contact with the "evil thing," has been the purpose of modern food-reformers. They are, moreover, well aware that a change of this sort, which involves a reconsideration of our whole attitude towards the "lower animals," can only be gradually realised; nor do they invite the world, as their opponents seem to imagine, to an immediate hard-and-fast decision, a revolution in national habits which is to be discussed, voted, and carried into effect the day after to-morrow, to the grievous jeopardy and dislocation of certain time-honoured interests. They simply point to the need of progression towards humaner diet, believing, with Thoreau, that "it is part of the destiny of the human race, in its gradual improvement, to leave off eating animals, as surely as the savage tribes have left off eating each other, when they came in contact with the more civilised."

There are, however, many critics of Vegetarianism who have not grasped this ethical principle, and whose contentions are, therefore, quite irrelevant. It has been said, for example, that "the most enthusiastic Vegetarians scarcely venture to deny that the destruction of many animals is requisite for human existence. What Vegetarian would allow his premises to be swarming with mice, rats, and similar pests? Does he permit caterpillars, snails, and slugs to devour the produce of his vegetable garden? Perhaps he satisfies his conscience with the reflection that the destruction of vermin is a necessary act."

Perhaps the Vegetarian draws a distinction between the avowedly necessary destruction of garden and household pests, and the quite unnecessary (from the Vegetarian standpoint) butchery of oxen and sheep, who are bred for no other purpose than that of the slaughter-house, where they are killed in a most barbarous manner! *Perhaps* the Vegetarian "satisfies his conscience" with this distinction! I should rather think he did.

No wonder that food-reformers seem a strange and unreasonable folk to those who have thus failed to apprehend the very *raison d'être* of food-reform, and who persist in arguing as if the choice between the old diet and the new were a mere matter of personal caprice or professional adjustment, into which the moral question scarcely enters at all.

To this same misunderstanding is due the futile outcry that is raised every now and then against the term "Vegetarian," when some zealous opponent undertakes to "expose the delusions of those who boast that they live on vegetables, and yet take eggs, butter, and milk as regular articles of diet." Of course the simple fact is that Vegetarians are neither boastful of their diet, nor enamoured of their name; it was invented, wisely or unwisely, a full half-century ago, and, whether we like it or not, has evidently "come to stay" until we find something better. It is worth observing that the objection is seldom or never made in actual everyday life, where the word "Vegetarian" carries with it a quite definite meaning, viz., one who abstains from flesh-food but not necessarily from animal products; the verbal pother is always made by somebody who is sitting down to write an article against food-reform, and has nothing better to say. It all comes from the notion that Vegetarians are bent on some barren, logical "consistency," rather than on practical progress towards a more humane method of living—the only sort of "consistency" which in this, or any other branch of reform, is either possible in itself, or worth a moment's attention from a sensible man.

To show, however, that this question of the temporary use of animal products has not been shirked by food-reformers, I quote the following from my "Plea for Vegetarianism," published nearly thirty years ago.

> The immediate object which food-reformers aim at is not so much the disuse of animal substances in general, as the abolition of flesh-meat in particular; and if they can drive their opponents to make the important admission that actual flesh-food is unnecessary, they can afford to smile at the trivial retort that animal substance is still used in eggs and milk. . . . They are well aware that even dairy produce is quite unnecessary, and will doubtless be dispensed with altogether under a more natural system of diet. In the meantime, however, one step is sufficient. Let us first recognize the fact that the slaughter-house, with all its attendant horrors, might easily be abolished; that point gained, the question of the total disuse of all animal products is one that will be decided hereafter. What I wish to insist on is that it is not 'animal' food which we primarily abjure, but nasty food, expensive food, and unwholesome food.

If medical men, instead of quibbling about the word "Vegetarian," would recommend to their clients the use of animal products, as a substitute for "butchers' meat," there would be a great gain to the humanities of diet. Incidentally, it must be remarked, the doctors quite admit the efficiency of such substitutes; for in their eagerness to convict Vegetarians of inconsistency in using animal products, they guilelessly give away their own case by arguing that, of course, on *this* diet the Vegetarians do well enough! As for those ultra-consistent persons who sometimes write as if it were not worth while to discontinue the practice of cow-killing, unless we also immediately discontinue the practice of using milk—that is to say, who think the greater reform is worthless without the lesser and subsequent one—I can only express my respectful astonishment at such reasoning. It is as though a traveller were too "consistent" to start on a journey because he might be required to "change carriages" on the way.

But it is said, why not introduce "humane" methods of slaughtering, and so remedy the chief evil in the present system of diet? Well, in the first place, "humane slaughtering," if it be once admitted that there is no necessity to slaughter at all, is a contradiction in terms. But letting that pass, and recognising, as Vegetarians gladly do, that there would be a great reduction of suffering, if all flesh-eaters would combine for the abolition of *private* slaughter-houses and the substitution of well-ordered municipal abattoirs, we are still faced by the difficulty that these changes will take a long time to carry out, opposed as they are by powerful private interests, and that, even under the best possible conditions, the butchering of the larger animals must always be a horrible and inhuman business. Vegetarianism, as a movement, has nothing whatever to fear from the introduction of improved slaughtering; indeed, Vegetarians may take the credit of having worked quite as zealously as flesh-eaters in that direction, feeling, as they do, that in our complex society no individuals can exempt themselves from a share in the general responsibility—the brand of the slaughterer is on the brow of every one of us. But there is no half-way resting-place in humane progress; and we may be quite sure that when the public conscience is once aroused on this dreadful subject of the slaughter-house, it will maintain its interest to a much more thorough solution of the difficulty than a mere improvement of methods.

One thing is quite certain. It is impossible for flesh-eaters to find any justification of their diet in the plea that animals *might* be slaughtered humanely; it is an obvious duty to carry out the improvements first, and to make the excuses afterwards. Those who admit that the Vegetarian, in his indictment of the slaughter-house, hits a grievous blot in our civilisation, often try to escape from the inevitable conclusion on the ground that such allegations tell not against the use of animal food, but against the ignorance, carelessness, and brutality too often displayed in the slaughter-houses. This, however, is a libel on the working men who have to earn a livelihood by the disgusting occupation of butchering. The ignorance, carelessness, and brutality are not only in the rough-handed slaughtermen, but in the polite ladies and gentlemen whose dietetic habits render the slaughtermen necessary. The real responsibility rests not on the wage slave, but on the employer. "I'm only doing your dirty work," was the reply of a Whitechapel butcher to a gentleman who expressed the same sentiments as those I have quoted. "It's such as *you* makes such as *us*."

At this point it would presumably be the right thing to give some detailed description of the horrors enacted in our shambles, of which I might quote numerous instances from perfectly trust-worthy witnesses. If I do not do so, I can assure my readers that it is not from any desire to spare their feelings, for I think it might fairly be demanded of those who eat beef and mutton that they should not shrink from an acquaintance with facts of their own making; also we have often been told that it is the Vegetarians, not the flesh-eaters, who are the "sentimentalists" in this matter. I refrain for the simple reason that I fear, if I narrated the facts, this chapter would go unread. So, before passing on, I will merely add this, that in some ways the evils attendant on slaughtering grow worse, and not better, as civilisation advances, because of the more complex conditions of town life, and the increasingly long journeys to which animals are subjected in their transit from the grazier to the slaughterman. The cattle-ships of the present day reproduce, in an aggravated form, some of the worst horrors of the slave-ship of fifty years back. I take it for granted, then, as not denied by our opponents, that the present system of killing animals for food is a very cruel and barbarous one, and a direct outrage on what I have termed the "humanities of diet."

It is also an outrage on every sense of refinement and good taste, for in this question the aesthetics are not to be dissociated from the humanities. Has the artist ever considered the history of the "chop" which is brought so elegantly to his studio? Not he. He would not be able to eat it if he thought about it. He has first employed a slaughterman ("It's such as you makes such as us") to convert a beautiful living creature into a hideous carcase, to be displayed with other carcases in that ugliest product of civilisation, a butcher's shop, and then he has employed a cook to conceal, as far as may be, the work of the slaughterman. This is what the *Spectator* calls being "humanised" by schools of cookery; I should call it being de-humanised. In passing a butcher's I have seen a concert-programme pinned prominently on the corpse of a pig, and I have mused on that suggestive though unintended allegory of the Basis of Art. I deny that it is the right basis, and I maintain that there will necessarily be something porcine in the art that is so upheld and exhibited. Nine-tenths of our literary and artistic gatherings, our social functions, and most sumptuous entertainments, are tainted from the same source. You take a beautiful girl down to supper, and you offer her—a ham sandwich! It is proverbial folly to cast pearls before swine. What are we to say of the politeness which casts swine before pearls?

It is no part of my purpose to argue in detail the *possibility* of a

Vegetarian diet; nor is there any need to do so. The proofs of it are everywhere—in the history of races, in the rules of monastic orders, in the habits of large numbers of working populations, in biographies of well-known men, in the facts and instances of every-day life. The medical view of Vegetarianism, which at first (as in the similar case of tee-totalism) was expressed by a severe negative and ominous head-shake, has very largely changed during the past ten or twenty years, and, in so far as it is still hostile, dwells rather on the superiority of the "mixed" diet than on the insufficiency of the other, while the solemn warnings which used to be addressed to the venturesome individual who had the hardihood to leave off eating his fellow-beings, have now lapsed into more general statements as to the probable failure of Vegetarianism in the long run, and on a more extended trial. Well, we know what that means. It is what has been said of every vital movement that the world has seen. It means that ordinary people, and dull people, and learned people, and specialists, need time to envisage new truths; but they *do* envisage them, some day. Already the medical preference for a flesh diet may be summed up under two heads—that flesh is more digestible, more easily assimilated, than vegetables, and that it is unwise to limit the sources of food which (to quote Sir Henry Thompson) "Nature has abundantly provided."

The first argument, as to the superior digestibility of flesh, is flatly denied by food-reformers on the plain grounds of experience, the notion that Vegetarians are in the habit of eating a greater bulk of food, in order to obtain an equal amount of nutriment, being one of those amazing superstitions which could not survive a day's comparative study of the parties in question. My own conviction is that the average flesh-eater eats at least twice as much in bulk as the average Vegetarian; and I know that the experience of Vegetarians bears witness to a great reduction, instead of a great increase, in the amount of their diet. As for the second medical argument, the unwisdom of rejecting any of Nature's bounties, it ignores the very existence of the ethical question, which is the Vegetarian's chief contention; nor does this appeal to "Nature" strike one as being very "scientific," inasmuch as (ethics apart) it might just as well justify cannibalism as flesh-eating. We can imagine how the medicine-men of some old anthropophagous tribe might deprecate the new-fangled civilised notion of abstinence from human flesh, on the ground that it is foolish to refuse the benefits which "Nature" has abundantly provided.

But what of the failures of those who have attempted the Vegetarian diet? Is not the movement hopelessly blocked by Mr. So-and So's six weeks' experiment? He became so very weak, you know, until his friends were quite alarmed about him, and he was really *obliged* to take something more nourishing. All of which symptoms, I would remark, could be matched by thousands of similar instances from the records of the temperance movement, and prove clearly enough, not that abstinence from flesh food or alcohol is impossible, but that (as any thoughtful person might have foreseen) a great change in the habits of a people cannot be effected suddenly, or without its inevitable percentage of failures. Every propagandist movement, religious, social, or dietetic, is sure to attract to itself a motley crowd of adherents, many of whom, after a trial of the new principles—some after a genuine trial, others after a very superficial one—revert to their former position. Let it be freely granted that a habit so ingrained as that of flesh-eating is likely, and, indeed certain, in some particular cases to be very hard to eradicate. What then? Is not that exactly what might have been expected in a change of this kind? And, on the other side, it is equally certain that a large number of the reported failures—nine-tenths of them, I should say—are caused by the half-hearted or ill-advised manner in which the attempt is made. It is just as possible to commit suicide on a Vegetarian diet as on any other, if you are bent on that conclusion; and really one might almost imagine, from the extraordinary folly sometimes shown in the selection of a diet, that certain experimentalists were "riding for a fall" in their dealings with Vegetarianism—taking up the thing in order to be able to say, "I tried it, and see the result!" I knew a man, a master at a great public school, who "tried Vegetarianism," and he tried it by making cabbage and potato the substitute for flesh, and after a month's trial he felt "very flabby," and then he gave it up.

An important factor in the success of a change of diet is the spirit in which such change is undertaken. As far as the mere chemistry of food is concerned, the majority of people may doubtless, with ordinary wisdom in the conduct of the change, substitute a Vegetarian for a "mixed" diet without inconvenience. But in some cases, owing perhaps to the temperament of the individual, or the nature of his surroundings, the change is much more difficult; and here it will make all the difference whether he have really at heart a sincere wish to take the first step towards a humaner diet, or whether he be simply experimenting out of curiosity or some other trivial motive. It is one more proof that the *moral* basis of Vegetarianism is the one that sustains the rest.

But are there not other reasons alleged against the practice of Vegetarianism? Ah, those dear old Fallacies, so immemorial yet ever new, how can I speak disrespectfully of what has so often refreshed and entertained me! Every food-reformer is familiar with them—the "law of nature" arguments, which would approximate human ethics to the standard of the tiger-cat or rattle-snake; the "necessity-of-taking-life" argument, which conscientiously ignores the practice of *un*necessary killing; the blubber argument, or, to put it more exactly, the "what-would-become-of-the-Esquimaux"? to which the only adequate answer is, a system of State-aided emigration; the "for-my-sake" argument, which may be called the family fallacy; the "what-should-we-do-without-leather?" that lurid picture of a shoeless world instantaneously converted to Vegetarianism; and the disinterested "what-would-become-of-the-animals?" which foresees the grievous wanderings of homeless herds who can find no kind protector to eat them. Best of all, I think, is what may be termed the logic of the larder, beloved of learned men, which urges that the animals would prefer to live and be eaten than not to live at all—an imaginary ante-natal choice in an imaginary ante-natal condition!

I have now shown what I mean by those "humanities of diet," without which, as it seems to me, it is idle to dispute over the question of the "rights" of animals. A lively argument was lately raging between zoophilists and Jesuits, as to whether animals are "persons;" I would put it to both parties, is not the battle an unreal one, so long as the "persons" in question are by common agreement handed over to the tender mercies of the butcher, who will make exceeding short work of their "personality"?

I advance no exaggerated or fanciful claim for Vegetarianism. It is not, as some have asserted, a "panacea" for human ills; it is something much more rational—an essential part of the modern humanitarian movement, which can make no true progress without it. Vegetarianism is the diet of the future, as flesh-food is the diet of the past. In that striking and common contrast, a fruit shop side by side with a butcher's, we have a most significant object lesson. There, on the one hand, are the barbarities of a savage custom—the headless carcases, stiffened into a ghastly semblance of life, the joints and steaks and gobbets with their sickening odour, the harsh grating of the bone-saw, and the dull thud of the chopper—a perpetual crying protest against the horrors of flesh-eating. And, as if this were not witness sufficient, here, close alongside, is a wealth of golden fruit, a sight to make a poet happy, the only food that is entirely congenial to the physical structure and the natural instincts of mankind, that can entirely satisfy the highest human aspirations. Can we doubt, as we gaze at this contrast, that whatever intermediate steps may need to be gradually taken, whatever difficulties to be overcome, the path of progression from the barbarities to the humanities of diet lies clear and unmistakable before us?

PETER SINGER
All Animals Are Equal

In recent years a number of oppressed groups have campaigned vigorously for equality. The classic instance is the Black Liberation movement, which demands an end to the prejudice and discrimination that
has made blacks second-class citizens. The immediate appeal of the
black liberation movement and its initial, if limited, success made it a
model for other oppressed groups to follow. We became familiar with
liberation movements for Spanish-Americans, gay people, and a variety
of other minorities. When a majority group—women—began their cam-
paign, some thought we had come to the end of the road. Discrimination on the basis of sex, it has been said, is the last universally accepted
form of discrimination, practiced without secrecy or pretense even in
those liberal circles that have long prided themselves on their freedom
from prejudice against racial minorities.

One should always be wary of talking of "the last remaining form of
discrimination." If we have learnt anything from the liberation movements, we should have learnt how difficult it is to be aware of latent
prejudice in our attitudes to particular groups until this prejudice is
forcefully pointed out.

A liberation movement demands an expansion of our moral horizons
and an extension or reinterpretation of the basic moral principle of
equality. Practices that were previously regarded as natural and inevitable come to be seen as the result of an unjustifiable prejudice. Who can
say with confidence that all his or her attitudes and practices are beyond

From *Philosophic Exchange*, vol. 1, no. 5 (Summer 1974). Parts of this article appeared in a review of *Animals, Men and Morals*, Godlovitch and Harris (eds.), in
The New York Review of Books, April 5, 1973.

criticism? If we wish to avoid being numbered amongst the oppressors, we must be prepared to re-think even our most fundamental attitudes. We need to consider them from the point of view of those most disadvantaged by our attitudes, and the practices that follow from these attitudes. If we can make this unaccustomed mental switch we may discover a pattern in our attitudes and practices that consistently operates so as to benefit one group—usually the one to which we ourselves belong—at the expense of another. In this way we may come to see that there is a case for a new liberation movement. My aim is to advocate that we make this mental switch in respect of our attitudes and practices towards a very large group of beings: members of species other than our own—or, as we popularly though misleadingly call them, animals. In other words, I am urging that we extend to other species the basic principle of equality that most of us recognize should be extended to all members of our own species.

All this may sound a little far-fetched, more like a parody of other liberation movements than a serious objective. In fact, in the past the idea of "The Rights of Animals" really has been used to parody the case for women's rights. When Mary Wollstonecroft, a forerunner of later feminists, published her *Vindication of the Rights of Women* in 1792, her ideas were widely regarded as absurd, and they were satirized in an anonymous publication entitled *A Vindication of the Rights of Brutes*. The author of this satire (actually Thomas Taylor, a distinguished Cambridge philosopher) tried to refute Wollstonecroft's reasonings by showing that they could be carried one stage further. If sound when applied to women, why should the arguments not be applied to dogs, cats, and horses? They seemed to hold equally well for these "brutes"; yet to hold that brutes had rights was manifestly absurd; therefore the reasoning by which this conclusion had been reached must be unsound, and if unsound when applied to brutes, it must also be unsound when applied to women, since the very same arguments had been used in each case.

One way in which we might reply to this argument is by saying that the case for equality between men and women cannot validly be extended to nonhuman animals. Women have a right to vote, for instance, because they are just as capable of making rational decisions as men are; dogs, on the other hand, are incapable of understanding the significance of voting, so they cannot have the right to vote. There are many other obvious ways in which men and women resemble each other closely, while humans and other animals differ greatly. So, it might be said, men and women are similiar beings, and should have equal rights, while humans and nonhumans are different and should not have equal rights.

The thought behind this reply to Taylor's analogy is correct up to a point, but it does not go far enough. There *are* important differences between humans and other animals, and these differences must give rise to *some* differences in the rights that each have. Recognizing this obvious fact, however, is no barrier to the case for extending the basic principle of equality to nonhuman animals. The differences that exist between men and women are equally undeniable, and the supporters of Women's Liberation are aware that these differences may give rise to different rights. Many feminists hold that women have the right to an abortion on request. It does not follow that since these same people are campaigning for equality between men and women they must support the right of men to have abortions too. Since a man cannot have an abortion, it is meaningless to talk of his right to have one. Since a pig can't vote, it is meaningless to talk of its right to vote. There is no reason why either Women's Liberation or Animal Liberation should get involved in such nonsense. The extension of the basic principle of equality from one group to another does not imply that we must treat both groups in exactly the same way, or grant exactly the same rights to both groups. Whether we should do so will depend on the nature of the members of the two groups. The basic principle of equality, I shall argue, is equality of consideration; and equal consideration for different beings may lead to different treatment and different rights.

So there is a different way of replying to Taylor's attempt to parody Wollstonecroft's arguments, a way which does not deny the differences between humans and nonhumans, but goes more deeply into the question of equality, and concludes by finding nothing absurd in the idea that the basic principle of equality applies to so-called "brutes." I believe that we reach this conclusion if we examine the basis on which our opposition to discrimination on grounds of race or sex ultimately rests. We will then see that we would be on shaky ground if we were to demand equality for blacks, women, and other groups of oppressed humans while denying equal consideration to nonhumans.

When we say that all human beings, whatever their race, creed or sex, are equal, what is it that we are asserting? Those who wish to defend a hierarchical, inegalitarian society have often pointed out that by whatever test we choose, it simply is not true that all humans are equal. Like it or not, we must face the fact that humans come in different shapes and sizes; they come with differing moral capacities, differing intellectual abilities, differing amounts of benevolent feeling and sensitivity to the needs of others, differing abilities to communicate effectively, and differing capacities to experience pleasure and pain. In short, if the demand for equality were based on the actual equality of all human beings, we would have to stop demanding equality. It would be an unjustifiable demand.

Still, one might cling to the view that the demand for equality among human beings is based on the actual equality of the different races and sexes. Although humans differ as individuals in various ways, there are no differences between the races and sexes *as such*. From the mere fact that a person is black, or a woman, we cannot infer anything else about that person. This, it may be said, is what is wrong with racism and sexism. The white racist claims that whites are superior to blacks, but this is false—although there are differences between individuals, some blacks are superior to some whites in all of the capacities and abilities that could conceivably be relevant. The opponent of sexism would say the same: a person's sex is no guide to his or her abilities, and this is why it is unjustifiable to discriminate on the basis of sex.

This is a possible line of objection to racial and sexual discrimination. It is not, however, the way that someone really concerned about equality would choose, because taking this line could, in some circumstances, force one to accept a most inegalitarian society. The fact that humans differ as individuals, rather than as races or sexes, is a valid reply to someone who defends a hierarchical society like, say, South Africa, in which all whites are superior in status to all blacks. The existence of individual variations that cut across the lines of race or sex, however, provides us with no defence at all against a more sophisticated opponent of equality, one who proposes that, say, the interests of those with I.Q. ratings above 100 be preferred to the interests of those with I.Q.s below 100. Would a hierarchical society of this sort really be so much better than one based on race or sex? I think not. But if we tie the moral principle of equality to the factual equality of the different races or sexes, taken as a whole, our opposition to racism and sexism does not provide us with any basis for objecting to this kind of inegalitarianism.

There is a second important reason why we ought not to base our opposition to racism and sexism on any kind of factual equality, even the limited kind which asserts that variations in capacities and abilities are spread evenly between the different races and sexes: we can have no absolute guarantee that these abilities and capacities really are distributed evenly, without regard to race or sex, among human beings. So far as actual abilities are concerned, there do seem to be certain measurable differences between both races and sexes. These differences do not, of course, appear in each case, but only when averages are taken. More important still, we do not yet know how much of these differences is really due to the different genetic endowments of the various races and sexes, and how much is due to environmental differences that are the result of past and continuing discrimination. Perhaps all of the important differences will eventually prove to be environmental rather than genetic. Anyone opposed to racism and sexism will certainly hope that this will be so, for it will make the task of ending discrimination a lot easier; nevertheless it would be dangerous to rest the case against racism and sexism on the belief that all significant differences are environmental in origin. The opponent of, say, racism who takes this line will be unable to avoid conceding that if differences in ability did after all prove to have some genetic connection with race, racism would in some way be defensible.

It would be folly for the opponent of racism to stake his whole case on a dogmatic commitment to one particular outcome of a difficult scientific issue which is still a long way from being settled. While attempts to prove that differences in certain selected abilities between races and sexes are primarily genetic in origin have certainly not been conclusive, the same must be said of attempts to prove that these differences are largely the result of environment. At this stage of the investigation we cannot be certain which view is correct, however much we may hope it is the latter.

Fortunately, there is no need to pin the case for equality to one particular outcome of this scientific investigation. The appropriate response to those who claim to have found evidence of genetically-based differences in ability between the races or sexes is not to stick to the belief that the genetic explanation must be wrong, whatever evidence to the contrary may turn up: instead we should make it quite clear that the claim to equality does not depend on intelligence, moral capacity, physical strength, or similar matters of fact. Equality is a moral ideal, not a simple assertion of fact. There is no logically compelling reason for assuming that a factual difference in ability between two people justifies any difference in the amount of consideration we give to satisfying their needs and interests. The principle of the equality of human beings is not a description of an alleged actual equality among humans: it is a prescription of how we should treat humans.

Jeremy Bentham incorporated the essential basis of moral equality into his utilitarian system of ethics in the formula: "Each to count for one and none for more than one." In other words, the interests of every being affected by an action are to be taken into account and given the same weight as the like interests of any other being. A later utilitarian, Henry Sidgwick, put the point in this way: "The good of any one individual is of no more importance, from the point of view (if I may say so) of the Universe, than the good of any other."[1] More recently, the leading figures in contemporary moral philosophy have shown a great deal of agreement in specifying as a fundamental presupposition of

[1] *The Methods of Ethics* (7th Ed.), p. 382.

their moral theories some similar requirement which operates so as to give everyone's interests equal consideration—although they cannot agree on how this requirement is best formulated.[2]

It is an implication of this principle of equality that our concern for others ought not to depend on what they are like, or what abilities they possess—although precisely what this concern requires us to do may vary according to the characteristics of those affected by what we do. It is on this basis that the case against racism and the case against sexism must both ultimately rest; and it is in accordance with this principle that speciesism is also to be condemned. If possessing a higher degree of intelligence does not entitle one human to use another for his own ends, how can it entitle humans to exploit nonhumans?

Many philosophers have proposed the principle of equal consideration of interests, in some form or other, as a basic moral principle; but, as we shall see in more detail shortly, not many of them have recognised that this principle applies to members of other species as well as to our own. Bentham was one of the few who did realize this. In a forward-looking passage, written at a time when black slaves in the British dominions were still being treated much as we now treat nonhuman animals, Bentham wrote:

> The day *may* come when the rest of the animal creation may acquire those rights which never could have been witholden from them but by the hand of tyranny. The French have already discovered that the blackness of the skin is no reason why a human being should be abandoned without redress to the caprice of a tormentor. It may one day come to be recognized that the number of the legs, the villosity of the skin, or the termination of the *os sacrum*, are reasons equally insufficient for abandoning a sensitive being to the same fate. What else is it that should trace the insuperable line? Is it the faculty of reason, or perhaps the faculty of discourse? But a full-grown horse or dog is beyond comparison a more rational, as well as a more conversable animal, than an infant of a day, or a week, or even a month, old. But suppose they were otherwise, what would it avail? The question is not, Can they reason? nor Can they *talk*? but, *Can they suffer*?[3]

In this passage Bentham points to the capacity for suffering as the vital characteristic that gives a being the right to equal consideration. The capacity for suffering—or more strictly, for suffering and/or enjoy-

[2]For example, R. M. Hare, *Freedom and Reason* (Oxford, 1963) and J. Rawls, *A Theory of Justice* (Harvard, 1972); for a brief account of the essential agreement on this issue between these and other positions, see R. M. Hare, "Rules of War and Moral Reasoning," *Philosophy and Public Affairs*, vol. I, no. 2 (1972).

[3]*Introduction to the Principles of Morals and Legislation*, ch. XVII.

ment or happiness—is not just another characteristic like the capacity for language, or for higher mathematics. Bentham is not saying that those who try to mark "the insuperable line" that determines whether the interests of a being should be considered happen to have selected the wrong characteristic. The capacity for suffering and enjoying things is a pre-requisite for having interests at all, a condition that must be satisfied before we can speak of interests in any meaningful way. It would be nonsense to say that it was not in the interests of a stone to be kicked along the road by a schoolboy. A stone does not have interests because it cannot suffer. Nothing that we can do to it could possibly make any difference to its welfare. A mouse, on the other hand, does have an interest in not being tormented, because it will suffer if it is.

If a being suffers, there can be no moral justification for refusing to take that suffering into consideration. No matter what the nature of the being, the principle of equality requires that its suffering be counted equally with the like suffering—in so far as rough comparisons can be made—of any other being. If a being is not capable of suffering, or of experiencing enjoyment or happiness, there is nothing to be taken into account. This is why the limit of sentience (using the term as a convenient, if not strictly accurate, shorthand for the capacity to suffer or experience enjoyment or happiness) is the only defensible boundary of concern for the interests of others. To mark this boundary by some characteristic like intelligence or rationality would be to mark it in an arbitrary way. Why not choose some other characteristic, like skin color?

The racist violates the principle of equality by giving greater weight to the interests of members of his own race, when there is a clash between their interests and the interests of those of another race. Similarly the speciesist allows the interests of his own species to override the greater interests of members of other species.[4] The pattern is the same in each case. Most human beings are speciesists. I shall now very briefly describe some of the practices that show this.

For the great majority of human beings, especially in urban, industrialized societies, the most direct form of contact with members of other species is at meal-times: we eat them. In doing so we treat them purely as means to our ends. We regard their life and well-being as subordinate to our taste for a particular kind of dish. I say "taste" deliberately—this is purely a matter of pleasing our palate. There can be no defence of eating flesh in terms of satisfying nutritional needs, since it has been established beyond doubt that we could satisfy our need for protein and other essential nutrients far more efficiently with a diet that

---

[4] I owe the term "speciesism" to Richard Ryder.

replaced animal flesh by soy beans, or products derived from soy beans, and other high-protein vegetable products.[5]

It is not merely the act of killing that indicates what we are ready to do to other species in order to gratify our tastes. The suffering we inflict on the animals while they are alive is perhaps an even clearer indication of our speciesism than the fact that we are prepared to kill them.[6] In order to have meat on the table at a price that people can afford, our society tolerates methods of meat production that confine sentient animals in cramped, unsuitable conditions for the entire durations of their lives. Animals are treated like machines that convert fodder into flesh, and any innovation that results in a higher "conversion ratio" is liable to be adopted. As one authority on the subject has said, "cruelty is acknowledged only when profitability ceases."[7] . . .

Since, as I have said, none of these practices cater for anything more than our pleasures of taste, our practice of rearing and killing other animals in order to eat them is a clear instance of the sacrifice of the most important interests of other beings in order to satisfy trivial interests of our own. To avoid speciesism we must stop this practice, and each of us has a moral obligation to cease supporting the practice. Our custom is all the support that the meat-industry needs. The decision to cease giving it that support may be difficult, but it is no more difficult than it would have been for a white Southerner to go against the traditions of his society and free his slaves: if we do not change our dietary habits, how can we censure those slaveholders who would not change their own way of living?

The same form of discrimination may be observed in the widespread

---

[5]In order to produce 1 lb. of protein in the form of beef or veal, we must feed 21 lbs. of protein to the animal. Other forms of livestock are slightly less inefficient, but the average ratio in the U.S. is still 1:8. It has been estimated that the amount of protein lost to humans in this way is equivalent to 90% of the annual world protein deficit. For a brief account, see Frances Moore Lappé, *Diet for a Small Planet* (Friends of The Earth/Ballantine, New York 1971) pp. 4–11.

[6]Although one might think that killing a being is obviously the ultimate wrong one can do to it, I think that the infliction of suffering is a clearer indication of speciesism because it might be argued that at least part of what is wrong with killing a human is that most humans are conscious of their existence over time, and have desires and purposes that extend into the future—see, for instance, M. Tooley, "Abortion and Infanticide," *Philosophy and Public Affairs*, vol. 2, no. 1 (1972). Of course, if one took this view one would have to hold—as Tooley does —that killing a human infant or mental defective is not in itself wrong, and is less serious than killing certain higher mammals that probably do have a sense of their own existence over time.

[7]Ruth Harrison, *Animal Machines* (Stuart, London, 1964). For an account of farming conditions, see my *Animal Liberation* (New York Review Company, 1975) from which "Down on the Factory Farm," is reprinted in this volume.

practice of experimenting on other species in order to see if certain substances are safe for human beings, or to test some psychological theory about the effect of severe punishment on learning, or to try out various new compounds just in case something turns up. . . .

In the past, argument about vivisection has often missed this point, because it has been put in absolutist terms: Would the abolitionist be prepared to let thousands die if they could be saved by experimenting on a single animal? The way to reply to this purely hypothetical question is to pose another: Would the experimenter be prepared to perform his experiment on an orphaned human infant, if that were the only way to save many lives? (I say "orphan" to avoid the complication of parental feelings, although in doing so I am being overfair to the experimenter, since the nonhuman subjects of experiments are not orphans.) If the experimenter is not prepared to use an orphaned human infant, then his readiness to use nonhumans is simple discrimination, since adult apes, cats, mice and other mammals are more aware of what is happening to them, more self-directing and, so far as we can tell, at least as sensitive to pain, as any human infant. There seems to be no relevant characteristic that human infants possess that adult mammals do not have to the same or a higher degree. (Someone might try to argue that what makes it wrong to experiment on a human infant is that the infant will, in time and if left alone, develop into more than the nonhuman, but one would then, to be consistent, have to oppose abortion, since the fetus has the same potential as the infant—indeed, even contraception and abstinence might be wrong on this ground, since the egg and sperm, considered jointly, also have the same potential. In any case, this argument still gives us no reason for selecting a nonhuman, rather than a human with severe and irreversible brain damage, as the subject for our experiments.)

The experimenter, then, shows a bias in favor of his own species whenever he carries out an experiment on a nonhuman for a purpose that he would not think justified him in using a human being at an equal or lower level of sentience, awareness, ability to be self-directing, etc. No one familiar with the kind of results yielded by most experiments on animals can have the slightest doubt that if this bias were eliminated the number of experiments performed would be a minute fraction of the number performed today.

Experimenting on animals, and eating their flesh, are perhaps the two major forms of speciesism in our society. By comparison, the third and last form of speciesism is so minor as to be insignificant, but it is perhaps of some special interest to those for whom this article was written. I am referring to speciesism in contemporary philosophy.

Philosophy ought to question the basic assumptions of the age.

Thinking through, critically and carefully, what most people take for granted is, I believe, the chief task of philosophy, and it is this task that makes philosophy a worthwhile activity. Regrettably, philosophy does not always live up to its historic role. Philosophers are human beings and they are subject to all the preconceptions of the society to which they belong. Sometimes they succeed in breaking free of the prevailing ideology: more often they become its most sophisticated defenders. So, in this case, philosophy as practiced in the universities today does not challenge anyone's preconceptions about our relations with other species. By their writings, those philosophers who tackle problems that touch upon the issue reveal that they make the same unquestioned assumptions as most other humans, and what they say tends to confirm the reader in his or her comfortable speciesist habits.

I could illustrate this claim by referring to the writings of philosophers in various fields—for instance, the attempts that have been made by those interested in rights to draw the boundary of the sphere of rights so that it runs parallel to the biological boundaries of the species *homo sapiens*, including infants and even mental defectives, but excluding those other beings of equal or greater capacity who are so useful to us at mealtimes and in our laboratories. I think it would be a more appropriate conclusion to this article, however, if I concentrated on the problem with which we have been centrally concerned, the problem of equality.

It is significant that the problem of equality, in moral and political philosophy, is invariably formulated in terms of human equality. The effect of this is that the question of the equality of other animals does not confront the philosopher, or student, as an issue itself—and this is already an indication of the failure of philosophy to challenge accepted beliefs. Still, philosophers have found it difficult to discuss the issue of human equality without raising, in a paragraph or two, the question of the status of other animals. The reason for this, which should be apparent from what I have said already, is that if humans are to be regarded as equal to one another, we need some sense of "equal" that does not require any actual, descriptive equality of capacities, talents or other qualities. If equality is to be related to any actual characteristics of humans, these characteristics must be some lowest common denominator, pitched so low that no human lacks them—but then the philosopher comes up against the catch that any such set of characteristics which covers *all* humans will not be possessed *only by humans*. In other words, it turns out that in the only sense in which we can truly say, as an assertion of fact, that all humans are equal, at least some members of other species are also equal—equal, that is, to each other and to humans. If, on the other hand, we regard the statement "All humans

are equal" in some non-factual way, perhaps as a prescription, then, as
I have already argued, it is even more difficult to exclude non-humans
from the sphere of equality.

This result is not what the egalitarian philosopher originally intended
to assert. Instead of accepting the radical outcome to which their own
reasonings naturally point, however, most philosophers try to reconcile
their beliefs in human equality and animal inequality by arguments that
can only be described as devious.

As a first example, I take William Frankena's well-known article
"The Concept of Social Justice." Frankena opposes the idea of basing
justice on merit, because he sees that this could lead to highly inegalitarian results. Instead he proposes the principle that

> . . . all men are to be treated as equals, not because they are equal, in
> any respect, but simply because they are human. They are human be-
> cause they have emotions and desires, and are able to think, and hence
> are capable of enjoying a good life in a sense in which other animals
> are not.[8]

But what is this capacity to enjoy the good life which all humans
have, but no other animals? Other animals have emotions and desires,
and appear to be capable of enjoying a good life. We may doubt that
they can think—although the behavior of some apes, dolphins and even
dogs suggests that some of them can—but what is the relevance of
thinking? Frankena goes on to admit that by "the good life" he means
"not so much the morally good life as the happy or satisfactory life,"
so thought would appear to be unnecessary for enjoying the good life;
in fact to emphasise the need for thought would make difficulties for
the egalitarian since only some people are capable of leading intellectually satisfying lives, or morally good lives. This makes it difficult to see
what Frankena's principle of equality has to do with simply being *human*. Surely every sentient being is capable of leading a life that is
happier or less miserable than some alternative life, and hence has a
claim to be taken into account. In this respect the distinction between
humans and nonhumans is not a sharp division, but rather a continuum
along which we move gradually, and with overlaps between the species,
from simple capacities for enjoyment and satisfaction, or pain and suffering, to more complex ones.

Faced with a situation in which they see a need for some basis for the
moral gulf that is commonly thought to separate humans and animals,
but can find no concrete difference that will do the job without under-
mining the equality of humans, philosophers tend to waffle. They resort

---

[8]In R. Brandt (ed.) *Social Justice* (Prentice-Hall, Englewood Cliffs, 1962), p. 19.

to high-sounding phrases like "the intrinsic dignity of the human individual";[9] They talk of the "intrinsic worth of all men" as if men (humans?) had some worth that other beings did not,[10] or they say that humans, and only humans, are "ends in themselves," while "everything other than a person can only have value for a person."[11]

This idea of a distinctive human dignity and worth has a long history; it can be traced back directly to the Renaissance humanists, for instance to Pico della Mirandola's *Oration on the Dignity of Man*. Pico and other humanists based their estimate of human dignity on the idea that man possessed the central, pivotal position in the "Great Chain of Being" that led from the lowliest forms of matter to God himself; this view of the universe, in turn, goes back to both classical and Judeo-Christian doctrines. Contemporary philosophers have cast off these metaphysical and religious shackles and freely invoke the dignity of mankind without needing to justify the idea at all. Why should we not attribute "intrinsic dignity" or "intrinsic worth" to ourselves? Fellow-humans are unlikely to reject the accolades we so generously bestow on them, and those to whom we deny the honor are unable to object. Indeed, when one thinks only of humans, it can be very liberal, very progressive, to talk of the dignity of all human beings. In so doing, we implicitly condemn slavery, racism, and other violations of human rights. We admit that we ourselves are in some fundamental sense on a par with the poorest, most ignorant members of our own species. It is only when we think of humans as no more than a small sub-group of all the beings that inhabit our planet that we may realize that in elevating our own species we are at the same time lowering the relative status of all other species.

The truth is that the appeal to the intrinsic dignity of human beings appears to solve the egalitarian's problems only as long as it goes unchallenged. Once we ask *why* it should be that all humans—including infants, mental defectives, psychopaths, Hitler, Stalin and the rest—have some kind of dignity or worth that no elephant, pig, or chimpanzee can ever achieve, we see that this question is as difficult to answer as our original request for some relevant fact that justifies the inequality of humans and other animals. In fact, these two questions are really one: talk of intrinsic dignity or moral worth only takes the problem back one step, because any satisfactory defence of the claim that all and only humans have intrinsic dignity would need to refer to some relevant capacities or characteristics that all and only humans possess. Philoso-

[9]Frankena, *op. cit.*, p. 23.

[10]H. A. Bedau, "Egalitarianism and the Idea of Equality" in *Nomos IX: Equality*, ed. J. R. Pennock and J. W. Chapman, New York, 1967.

[11]G. Vlastos, "Justice and Equality" in Brandt, *Social Justice*, p. 48.

phers frequently introduce ideas of dignity, respect and worth at the point at which other reasons appear to be lacking, but this is hardly good enough. Fine phrases are the last resource of those who have run out of arguments.

In case there are those who still think it may be possible to find some relevant characteristic that distinguishes all humans from all members of other species, I shall refer again, before I conclude, to the existence of some humans who quite clearly are below the level of awareness, self-consciousness, intelligence, and sentience, of many non-humans. I am thinking of humans with severe and irreparable brain damage, and also of infant humans. To avoid the complication of the relevance of a being's potential, however, I shall henceforth concentrate on permanently retarded humans.

Philosophers who set out to find a characteristic that will distinguish humans from other animals rarely take the course of abandoning these groups of humans by lumping them in with the other animals. It is easy to see why they do not. To take this line without re-thinking our attitudes to other animals would entail that we have the right to perform painful experiments on retarded humans for trivial reasons; similarly it would follow that we had the right to rear and kill these humans for food. To most philosophers these consequences are as unacceptable as the view that we should stop treating nonhumans in this way.

Of course, when discussing the problem of equality it is possible to ignore the problem of mental defectives, or brush it aside as if somehow insignificant.[12] This is the easiest way out. What else remains? My final example of speciesism in contemporary philosophy has been selected to show what happens when a writer is prepared to face the question of human equality and animal inequality without ignoring the existence of mental defectives, and without resorting to obscurantist mumbo-jumbo. Stanley Benn's clear and honest article "Egalitarianism and Equal Consideration of Interests"[13] fits this description.

Benn, after noting the usual "evident human inequalities" argues, correctly I think, for equality of consideration as the only possible basis for egalitarianism. Yet Benn, like other writers, is thinking only of "equal consideration of human interests." Benn is quite open in his defence of this restriction of equal consideration:

> . . . not to possess human shape *is* a disqualifying condition. However faithful or intelligent a dog may be, it would be a monstrous sentimen-

[12]For example, Bernard Williams, "The Idea of Equality," in *Philosophy, Politics and Society* (second series), ed. P. Laslett and W. Runciman (Blackwell, Oxford, 1962), p. 118; J. Rawls, *A Theory of Justice*, pp. 509–10.
[13]*Nomos IX: Equality*; the passages quoted are on p. 62ff.

tality to attribute to him interests that could be weighed in an equal
balance with those of human beings ... if, for instance, one had to decide between feeding a hungry baby or a hungry dog, anyone who chose
the dog would generally be reckoned morally defective, unable to recognize a fundamental inequality of claims.

This is what distinguishes our attitude to animals from our attitude
to imbeciles. It would be odd to say that we ought to respect equally
the dignity or personality of the imbecile and of the rational man ...
but there is nothing odd about saying that we should respect their interests equally, that is, that we should give to the interests of each the
same serious consideration as claims to considerations necessary for
some standard of well-being that we can recognize and endorse.

Benn's statement of the basis of the consideration we should have for
imbeciles seems to me correct, but why should there be any fundamental inequality of claims between a dog and a human imbecile? Benn sees
that if equal consideration depended on rationality, no reason could be
given against using imbeciles for research purposes, as we now use
dogs and guinea pigs. This will not do: "But of course we do distinguish
imbeciles from animals in this regard," he says. That the common distinction is justifiable is something Benn does not question; his problem
is how it is to be justified. The answer he gives is this:

> ... we respect the interests of men and give them priority over dogs not
> *insofar* as they are rational, but because rationality is the human norm.
> We say it is *unfair* to exploit the deficiencies of the imbecile who falls
> short of the norm, just as it would be unfair, and not just ordinarily
> dishonest, to steal from a blind man. If we do not think in this way
> about dogs, it is because we do not see the irrationality of the dog as a
> deficiency or a handicap, but as normal for the species. The characteris-
> tics, therefore, that distinguish the normal man from the normal dog
> make it intelligible for us to talk of other men having interests and
> capacities, and therefore claims, of precisely the same kind as we make
> on our own behalf. But although these characteristics may provide the
> point of the distinction between men and other species, they are not in
> fact the qualifying conditions for membership, or the distinguishing cri-
> teria of the class of morally considerable persons; and this is precisely
> because a man does not become a member of a different species, with
> its own standards of normality, by reason of not possessing these char-
> acteristics.

The final sentence of this passage gives the argument away. An imbecile, Benn concedes, may have no characteristics superior to those of
a dog; nevertheless this does not make the imbecile a member of "a different species" as the dog is. *Therefore* it would be "unfair" to use
the imbecile for medical research as we use the dog. But why? That the
imbecile is not rational is just the way things have worked out, and the

same is true of the dog—neither is any more responsible for their mental level. If it is unfair to take advantage of an isolated defect, why is it
fair to take advantage of a more general limitation? I find it hard to see
anything in this argument except a defence of preferring the interests
of members of our own species because they are members of our own
species. To those who think there might be more to it, I suggest the
following mental exercise. Assume that it has been proven that there is
a difference in the average, or normal, intelligence quotient for two different races, say whites and blacks. Then substitute the term "white"
for every occurrence of "men" and "black" for every occurrence of
"dog" in the passage quoted; and substitute "high I.Q." for "rationality" and when Benn talks of "imbeciles" replace this term by "dumb
whites"—that is, whites who fall well below the normal white I.Q. score.
Finally, change "species" to "race." Now re-read the passage. It has become a defence of a rigid, no-exceptions division between whites and
blacks, based on I.Q. scores, *not withstanding an admitted overlap*
between whites and blacks in this respect. The revised passage is, of
course, outrageous, and this is not only because we have made fictitious
assumptions in our substitutions. The point is that in the original passage Benn was defending a rigid division in the amount of consideration
due to members of different species, despite admitted cases of overlap.
If the original did not, at first reading strike us as being as outrageous
as the revised version does, this is largely because although we are not
racists ourselves, most of us are speciesists. Like the other articles,
Benn's stands as a warning of the ease with which the best minds can
fall victim to a prevailing ideology.

ROBERT J. WHITE

A Defense of Vivisection

The humanity which would prevent human suffering is a deeper and truer humanity than the humanity which would save pain or death in the animal.

—Charles W. Eliot

The quotation above from that distinguished intellectual and former Harvard University president, written decades ago, continues to crystallize clearly the basic position of medical science toward the employment of animals in research and teaching. I would state it more simply: the alleviation of human suffering justifies the sacrifice of lower animals. Because this statement is as valid today as it was then, and yet has so little impact on the public conscience, I am almost reluctant to shed the mantle of clinical and professional detachment and take up the cudgels against that ill-defined, elusive Hydra—the antivivisection movement. To a degree, my inertia is also derived from my conviction that medical science has always seemed to assume a low-profile posture in justifying the utilization of lower animals for research and education (as it has so often done with other public health issues); it has invariably waited until one of those vigorous cyclic antivivisection campaigns, using the most advanced techniques in news management, has reached its apogee before attempting to combat the pernicious effects on public and congressional opinion. And then, unfortunately, it has employed almost exclusively its own scientific journals as the instruments for presenting its position to an already prejudiced audience. While the scientific com-

From Robert J. White, "Antivivisection: The Reluctant Hydra," *The American Scholar*, vol. 40, no. 3 (Summer 1971). Copyright © 1971 by the United Chapters of Phi Beta Kappa. Reprinted by permission of the publishers.

munity has lobbied successfully in congressional committees against restrictive legislation directed at medical research, it has neglected to present to the American public its case for the continuation of animal experimentation with sufficient force and clarity to eliminate the ever-present danger of government control of biological research through the limitation of animal availability and experimental design. The intelligent citizenry of this country must be educated not only regarding the already multiple advantages of medical research but, what is more important, the absolute necessity of continued proliferation of biological research.

Man, in a sense, has unwittingly painted himself into an ecological corner, and without the opportunity of biological testing in lower animals he may be unable to extract himself from his polluted environment. Acknowledging man's equally wanton disregard of animal life, as he has slowly but inevitably poisoned this planet (to say nothing of our careless attrition of individual species to the point of extinction), I do not intend that this essay should be, by any stretch of the imagination, construed as an indictment of the broad humanitarian movement; quite the contrary, for many of its objectives, particularly in the ecological field, are not only most laudable but fully subscribed to by many within the scientific community. Rather, my proprietary interest here is to emphasize need for animal experimentation in neurological research. As a consequence, my confrontation is exclusively with those societies, collectively known as the antivivisection movement, whose single unifying principle is the almost religiously held tenet that it is morally wrong to use lower animals in medical research and teaching. Professor Saul Bevolson, in tracing the historical development of the antivivisection movement in this country, demonstrates that the movement, while spawned and nurtured by the humanitarian establishment, is, in reality, separate in organizational structure. Dr. Maurice Visscher has felt the necessity of characterizing the antivivisection movement as a spectrum with certain gradations of moral and ethical absoluteness with regard to man's right to sacrifice lower animal life for scientific knowledge and medical advancement. Thus, this philosophical spectrum is anchored at one end by the abolitionist who sees no justification under any circumstances for the employment of the nonhuman animal for scientific study, and at the other extreme by the regulatory antivivisectionists who would place external controls (obviously governmental) on medical research by limiting the type and number of animals utilized, and demanding review of the experimental methods with particular reference to purpose and duplication. Make no mistake, in spite of their highly publicized concern for the housing and veterinary care of research animals, the true thrust of these organizations is directed toward the eventual elimination from medical investigation and research of all nonhuman subjects.

As a concerned scientist and as a practicing neurosurgeon, I am simply unable to plumb the depths of a philosophy that places such a premium on animal life even at the expense of human existence and improvement. It would appear that this preoccupation with the alleged pain and suffering of the animals used in medical research may well represent, at the very least, social prejudice against medicine or, more seriously, true psychiatric aberrations. Regardless of the social or psychiatric shortcomings of the antivivisectionists, it has always amazed me that the biological profession is forced into a position of periodically preparing defense briefs on animal experimentation (unfortunately appearing only in scientific journals) as a result of the Herculean efforts of these societies, while the meat-packing industry, which slaughters millions of animals annually, seldom if ever finds it necessary to defend its activities.

As I write this article, I relive my vivid experiences of yesterday when I removed at operation a large tumor from the cerebellum and brain stem of a small child. This was a surgical undertaking that would have been impossible a few decades ago, highly dangerous a few years ago, but is today, thanks to extensive experimentation on the brains of lower animals, routinely accomplished with a high degree of safety.

The human brain is the most complex, the most superbly designed structure known. Before it, all human scientific and engineering accomplishment pales. Our understanding of its intimate functions, such as intelligence and memory, is extremely limited. Even the more easily characterized capabilities of sensory reception and motor activity are only now being elucidated. Without the use of the experimental animal, particularly a species whose central nervous system is similar to that of man, we simply cannot decipher the mysteries of cerebral performance. Without this knowledge of brain function, we will never be able to develop new and improved methods for the treatment of neurological diseases, so many of which now must be placed in an incurable category. Even today the surgery of the brain is in its infancy, and on many occasions the critical tolerance between success and failure in human cerebral operations is narrow. Yet this gap can be significantly increased through properly oriented research. These serious considerations moved Dr. Harvey Cushing, the eminent brain surgeon, to remark, "Those who oppose the employment of animals for such purposes . . . leave us the only alternative of subjecting our fellow man, as a lesser creature, to our first crude manipulations."

In a more personal sense, I have a score of my own to settle with these misguided societies that for decades have been attempting to confuse the public about the true purpose of animal experimentation by depicting the medical and veterinary scientist as the most cruel of men, seeking every opportunity to visit pain and suffering on defenseless laboratory creatures. The more aggressive of these organizations, which are committed to the total abolition of animal research, have recently installed me as their célèbre terrible, monster-scientist, perpetrator of abominable crimes. And thus I join the distinguished company of such legendary scientists as Claude Bernard, Louis Pasteur, Lord Lister, Victor Horsley and Alfred Blalock! Dr. Catherine Roberts herself has already prejudged my work and me by earnestly stating, "The details of his experiments are so horrifying that they seem to reach the limits of scientific depravity." Fortunately, my researches do not stand alone in her sweeping condemnation of medical science, for in the same article she described organ transplantation and profound hypothermia as "life degrading scientific achievements." I am sure that she, as well as other staunch antivivisectionists, would be willing to include in this list: open-heart surgery, control of infection, surgical metabolism and shock studies since literally thousands of animals were sacrificed in the development of these lifesaving techniques. In a sense, condemnation of these achievements amounts to condemnation of the most meaningful advances in medicine and surgery in the last thirty years.

What of our own experiments, which have evoked such vituperative treatment at the hands of the antivivisection press? Here are the "shocking" details.

In 1964, we were successful for the first time in medical history in totally isolating the subhuman primate brain outside of its body and sustaining it in a viable state by connecting it with the vascular system of another monkey or with a mechanical perfusion circuit that incorporated engineering units designed to perform the functions of the heart, lungs and kidneys while simultaneously circulating blood to and from the brain. We were overjoyed since scientists had attempted to construct such a model surgically for the last one hundred years without success. As late as the 1930s Dr. Alexis Carrel, the Nobel laureate, with the collaboration of Colonel Charles Lindbergh, had been able to support the viability of almost all body organs in an isolated state with simple perfusion equipment that forcefully propelled nonsanguineous nutrient fluid through the blood vessels of the separated tissue. Only the nervous system, because of its complexity and delicacy, escaped their magnificent scientific capabilities. Parenthetically, it should be mentioned that Dr. Carrel had his problems with the antivivisectionists of his time.

With further refinements in operative technique, perfusion/structural design and blood processing, we were able to demonstrate normalization of intrinsic electrical activity and metabolic performance of the isolated monkey brain for extended periods of time. We now had the methodology to unlock many of the subtle mysteries surrounding cerebral function that heretofore had resisted all attempts at solution because of the difficulties of neurogenically and vascularly isolating the entire brain *in situ*. What is perhaps of greater importance in terms of understanding and treating neurological disease, we could now easily impose on our brain models abnormal clinical states such as infarction, circulatory arrest, infection and malignancy with absolute control of environmental circumstances and with a real hope of elucidating their effects on brain tissue alone. Once the characteristics of these states were defined, these same models would be of inestimable value in developing new and meaningful therapeutic regimens aimed at eliminating these clinical disease states.

As we set about exploring and documenting the capabilities of the isolated brain in an atmosphere not unlike the conditions described for the fifth level in Michael Crichton's book, *The Andromeda Strain*, we gradually became aware of a growing public interest in the preparation, an interest that intensified after our success in transplanting the brain in the experimental animal in 1966. A succession of competent medical journalists visited our laboratories and subsequently prepared a number of highly informative and reasoned articles dealing with our investigative efforts. I personally have always approved of this kind of interchange. In spite of our best efforts to assist in the preparation of the textual material, however, an unreviewed and unauthorized article written by Orianna Fallachi appeared in *Look* (November 28, 1967), in which this well-known interviewer attempted to humanize the monkey by depicting it as a small child. This single article (or lengthy excerpts from it) has now enjoyed world-wide publication and translation. Besides her treatment of the monkey as a small patient, Miss Fallachi's detailed description of the preoperative preparation (including the induction of anesthesia) and her vivid portrayal of the isolated brain model apparently struck a sympathetic and responsive chord among the membership of the antivivisection societies in this country as well as throughout the world. Like Mary Shelley, Miss Fallachi had created a Doctor Frankenstein and an up-to-date monster, at least as far as the antivivisectionists are concerned. True, this tale has its amusing—if not outlandish—elements, but its overall effect is tragic, since Miss Fallachi's creations are not only as factitious as Mary Shelley's, but in reality the direct antithesis of the Frankenstein legend.

Admittedly, the nervous system is the most difficult body organ system to investigate, not only because of its intrinsic complexity but also because, somewhere within its billions of cells and fibers, pain and suffering are represented. For this reason, the neurophysiologist is, on occasion, unable to avoid producing some discomfort in his animal when he is specifically studying pain in any or all of its complicated ramifications within the neural system. Actually, the isolated brain model is completely denervated by virtue of the fact that all pain pathways have been surgically severed; consequently, this brain model enjoys a completely painless existence by all known physiological criteria.

Since the isolated brain is incapable of perceiving these modalities, one can only wonder at the creditability and objectivity of the antivivisection prose, which has been so uncomplimentary in its descriptions of this subhuman research model.

The nervous system—the repository, so to speak, of pain and suffering, but, more important, of the qualities and capabilities that uniquely distinguish an organism—is most critical to this discussion since direct surgical or electronic manipulation or chemical modification of this system in the experimental animal offers to the antivivisectionist the most logical area for condemnation of biological research. At issue here would not be the indiscriminate infliction of pain and suffering (these experiments are basically free of pain), but rather purposeful alteration of the innate behavior of the organism in order to advance our knowledge of emotion, memory and intelligence, with the final phase again being the interpretive extrapolation of this information to the human and to human mental functioning. As yet we have heard little from the antivivisectionists regarding the inappropriateness of these experiments with reference to animal welfare. It may be, however, that their historical fixation on the "twin sins" of pain and suffering in neurological investigation has blinded them to the realities of modern experimental research. Just as I must vigorously dissent from the antivivisection philosophy (and the belief of certain physiologists) that the production of some pain, no matter how minimal, is never justified, so too I cannot conceive of the development of a valid argument opposing behavioral research, if only for the simple reason that mental illness cannot successfully be treated until mental performance is understood.

To circumvent the employment of nonhuman animals in medical research, the antivivisection movement has recently turned for assistance to science itself. It has been suggested that many of the physiological and biochemical studies conducted on animals could be programmed for computer analysis and thereby reduce and eventually eliminate the need for the living experimental preparations. Actually, computers, since their inception, have been used in biological research and, with their growing complexity, have markedly extended the frontiers of investigation. If anything, computer availability has contributed to the increasing demand for animals for research.

An equally unrealistic approach to the elimination of animal experimentation has been based on the cell culture work of Professor Sureyat Aygun, Director of the Bacteriological Institute of the University of Ankara, and a leading antivivisection proponent. The theory here is that, with proper culture techniques, cells or embryos could eventually be developed into entire organ systems. The technological advances and expense necessary to accomplish such a program to replace present-day animal research facilities are unachievable. There is no more need to seek alternatives to the use of lower animals for medical research than to search for nonflesh substitutions for meat in our diets. While it may well be true that ecological "facts of life" could eventually require the elimination of certain endangered species from both the laboratory and commercial market, there is nothing to suggest that some suitable species cannot be substituted. Even Dr. Albert Schweitzer recognized in his own unique philosophical scheme of things that scientific experiments with animals were necessary for the alleviation of human ills.

The American public demonstrates its overwhelming support of medical research by annually contributing millions of dollars through direct federal financing and private subscription; yet this same public is tragically unaware that progress in medical science is continually threatened by the antivivisection movement. At the urging of a small but determined group of antivivisectionists, the United States Congress is constantly considering legislation that, if enacted into law, will seriously restrict the freedom of individual scientists participating in medical research, in the same way that laws have so seriously hampered similar research in Britain. Since, through research grants to qualified individuals and institutions, the federal government provides the major financial support for medical investigation in this country, all laws affecting the conduct of such research are of paramount importance to the health of the entire citizenry. Unless American medicine and its allied biological professions cast off their mantles of detachment and undertake the responsibility of educating through established lines of communication our citizens to the necessities of medical research, the antivivisection movement may eventually win the day.

In the final analysis, there is no way that I can personally resolve or even arbitrate the impasse that exists between the theology of the antivivisection movement and the immutable stance of practicality maintained by biological research, since like R. D. Guthrie, I believe that the inclusion of lower animals in our ethical system is philosophically meaningless and operationally impossible and that, consequently, antivivisection theory and practice have no moral or ethical basis.

IV

Do Animals Have Rights?

HENRY S. SALT

Animals' Rights

Have the lower animals "rights"? Undoubtedly—if men have. That is the point I wish to make evident in this opening chapter. But have men rights? Let it be stated at the outset that I have no intention of discussing the abstract theory of rights, which at the present time is looked upon with suspicion and disfavour by many social reformers, since it has not unfrequently been made to cover the most extravagant and contradictory assertions. But though its phraseology is vague, there is nevertheless a solid truth underlying it—a truth which has always been clearly apprehended by the moral faculty, however difficult it may be to establish it on an unassailable logical basis. If men have not "rights"—well, they have an unmistakable intimation of something very similar; a sense of justice which marks the boundary-line where acquiescence ceases and resistance begins; a demand for freedom to live their own lives, subject to the necessity of respecting the equal freedom of other people.

Such is the doctrine of rights as formulated by Herbert Spencer. "Every man," he says, "is free to do that which he wills, provided he infringes not the equal liberty of any other man." And again, "Whoever admits that each man must have a certain restricted freedom, asserts that it is *right* he should have this restricted freedom. ... And hence the several particular freedoms deducible may fitly be called, as they commonly are called, his *rights*" ("Justice," pp. 46, 62).

The fitness of this nomenclature is disputed, but the existence of some real principle of the kind can hardly be called in question; so that

From Henry S. Salt, *Animals' Rights* (London: The Humanitarian League, 1912), excerpts from Chapter 1, "The Principle of Animals' Rights."

the controversy concerning "rights" is little else than an academic battle over words, which leads to no practical conclusion. I shall assume, therefore, that men are possessed of "rights," in the sense of Herbert Spencer's definition; and if any of my readers object to this qualified use of the term, I can only say that I shall be perfectly willing to change the word as soon as a more appropriate one is forthcoming. The immediate question that claims our attention is this—if men have rights, have animals their rights also? . . .

So anomalous is the attitude of man towards the lower animals, that it is no marvel if many humane thinkers have wellnigh despaired over this question. "The whole subject of the brute creation," wrote Dr. Arnold, "is to me one of such painful mystery, that I dare not approach it"; and this (to put the most charitable interpretation on their silence) appears to be the position of the majority of moralists and teachers at the present time. Yet there is urgent need of some solution of the problem; and in no other way can this be found than by the admission of the lower races within the pale of human sympathy. All the promptings of our best and surest instincts point us in this direction. "It is abundantly evident," says Lecky, "both from history and from present experience, that the instinctive shock, or natural feelings of disgust, caused by the sight of the sufferings of men, is not generically different from that which is caused by the sight of the suffering of animals." If this be so, can it be seriously contended that the same humanitarian tendency which has already emancipated the slave, will not ultimately benefit the lower races also? Here, again, the historian of "European Morals" has a significant remark:

> At one time the benevolent affections embrace merely the family, soon the circle expanding includes first a class, then a nation, then a coalition of nations, then all humanity; and finally its influence is felt in the dealings of man with the animal world. In each of these cases a standard is formed, different from that of the preceding stage, but in each case the same tendency is recognized as virtue.

But, it may be argued, vague sympathy with the lower animals is one thing, and a definite recognition of their "rights" is another; what reason is there to suppose that we shall advance from the former phase to the latter? Just this; that every great liberating movement has proceeded exactly on such lines. Oppression and cruelty are invariably founded on a lack of imaginative sympathy; the tyrant or tormentor can have no true sense of kinship with the victim of his injustice. When once the sense of affinity is awakened, the knell of tyranny is sounded, and the ultimate concession of "rights" is simply a matter of time. The present condition of the more highly organized domestic animals is in many ways very analogous to that of the negro slaves of a hundred years ago: look back, and you will find in their case precisely the same exclusion from the common pale of humanity; the same hypocritical fallacies, to justify that exclusion; and, as a consequence, the same deliberate stubborn denial of their social "rights." Look back—for it is well to do so—and then look forward, and the moral can hardly be mistaken.

We find so great a thinker as Aristotle seriously pondering, in his "Ethics," whether a slave may be considered as a fellow-being. In emphasizing the point that friendship is founded on propinquity, he expresses himself as follows:

> Neither can men have friendships with horses, cattle, or slaves, considered merely as such; for a slave is merely a living instrument, and an instrument a lifeless slave. Yet, considered as a man, a slave may be an object of friendship, for certain rights seem to belong to all those capable of participating in law and engagement.

Slaves, says Bentham,

> have been treated by the law exactly upon the same footing as in England, for example, the inferior races of animals are still. The day may come when the rest of the animal creation may acquire those rights which could never have been withholden from them but by the hand of tyranny.

Let us unreservedly admit the immense difficulties that stand in the way of this animal enfranchisement. Our relation towards the animals is complicated and embittered by innumerable habits handed down through centuries of brutality and mistrust; we cannot, in all cases, suddenly relax these habits, or do full justice even where we see that justice will have to be done. A perfect ethic of humaneness is therefore impracticable, if not unthinkable; and we can attempt to do no more than to indicate in a general way the main principle of animals' rights, noting at the same time the most flagrant particular violations of those rights, and the lines on which the only valid reform can hereafter be effected. But, on the other hand, it may be remembered for the comfort and encouragement of humanitarian workers, that these obstacles are, after all, only such as are inevitable in each branch of social improvement; for at every stage of every great reformation it has been repeatedly argued, by indifferent or hostile observers, that further progress is impossible; indeed, when the opponents of a great cause begin to demonstrate its "impossibility," experience teaches us that that cause is already on the high road to fulfilment.

As for the demand so frequently made on reformers, that they should first explain the details of their scheme—how this and that point will be arranged, and by what process all kinds of difficulties, real or imagined, will be circumvented—the only rational reply is that it is absurd to expect to see the end of a question when we are now but at its beginning. The persons who offer this futile sort of criticism are usually those who under no circumstances would be open to conviction; they purposely ask for an explanation which, by the very nature of the case, is impossible because it necessarily belongs to a later period of time. It would be equally sensible to request a traveller to enumerate beforehand all the particular things he will see by the way, on pain of being denounced as an unpractical visionary, although he may have a quite sufficient general knowledge of his course and destination.

Our main principle is now clear. If "rights" exist at all—and both feeling and usage indubitably prove that they do exist—they cannot be consistently awarded to men and denied to animals, since the same sense of justice and compassion apply in both cases. "Pain is pain," says Humphry Primatt, "whether it be inflicted on man or on beast; and the creature that suffers it, whether man or beast, being sensible of the misery of it while it lasts, suffers evil; and the sufferance of evil, unmeritedly, unprovokedly, where no offence has been given, and no good can possibly be answered by it, but merely to exhibit power to gratify malice, is Cruelty and Injustice in him that occasions it."

I commend this outspoken utterance to the attention of those ingenious moralists who quibble about the "discipline" of suffering, and deprecate immediate attempts to redress what, it is alleged, may be a necessary instrument for the attainment of human welfare. It is perhaps a mere coincidence, but it may be observed that those who are most forward to disallow the rights of others, and to argue that suffering and subjection are the natural lot of all living things, are usually themselves exempt from the operation of this beneficent law, and that the beauty of self-sacrifice is most loudly belauded by those who profit most largely at the expense of their fellow-beings.

But "nature is one with rapine," say some, and this utopian theory of "rights," if too widely extended, must come in conflict with that iron rule of internecine competition by which the universe is regulated. But is the universe so regulated? We note that this very objection, which was confidently relied on a few years back by many opponents of the emancipation of the working-classes, is not heard of in that connection now. Our learned economists and men of science, who set themselves to play the defenders of the social *status quo*, have seen their own weapons of "natural selection," "survival of the fittest," and what not, snatched from their hands and turned against them, and are therefore beginning to explain to us, in a scientific manner, what we untutored humanitarians had previously felt to be true, viz., that competition is not by any means the sole governing law among the human race. We are not greatly dismayed, then, to find the same old bugbear trotted out as an argument against animals' rights—indeed, we see already unmistakable signs of a similar reversal of the scientific judgment.

The charge of "sentimentalism" is frequently brought against those who plead for animals' rights. Now "sentimentalism," if any meaning at all can be attached to the word, must signify an inequality, an ill balance of sentiment, an inconsistency which leads men into attacking one abuse, while they ignore or condone another where a reform is equally desirable. That this weakness is often observable among "philanthropists" on the one hand, and "friends of animals" on the other, and most of all among those acute "men of the world," whose regard is only for themselves, I am not concerned to deny; what I wish to point out is, that the only real safeguard against sentimentality is to take up a consistent position towards the rights of men and of the lower animals alike, and to cultivate a broad sense of universal justice (not "mercy") for all living things. Herein, and herein alone, is to be sought the true sanity of temperament.

It is an entire mistake to suppose that the rights of animals are in any way antagonistic to the rights of men. Let us not be betrayed for a moment into the specious fallacy that we must study human rights first, and leave the animal question to solve itself hereafter; for it is only by a wide and disinterested study of *both* subjects that a solution of either is possible. "For he who loves all animated nature," says Porphyry, "will not hate any one tribe of innocent beings, and by how much greater his love for the whole, by so much the more will he cultivate justice towards a part of them, and that part to which he is most allied." To omit all worthier reasons, it is too late in the day to suggest the indefinite postponement of a consideration of animals' rights, for from a moral point of view, and even from a legislative point of view, we are daily confronted with the problem, and the so-called "practical" people who affect to ignore it are simply shutting their eyes to facts which they find it disagreeable to confront.

Once more then, animals have rights, and these rights consist in the "restricted freedom" to live a natural life—a life, that is, which permits of the individual development—subject to the limitations imposed by the permanent needs and interests of the community. There is nothing quixotic or visionary in this assertion; it is perfectly compatible with a readiness to look the sternest laws of existence fully and honestly in the face. If we must kill, whether it be man or animal, let us kill and have done with it; if we must inflict pain, let us do what is inevitable, without hypocrisy, or evasion, or cant. But (here is the cardinal point) let us first be assured that it *is* necessary; let us not wantonly trade on the needless miseries of other beings, and then attempt to lull our consciences by a series of shuffling excuses which cannot endure a moment's candid investigation. As Leigh Hunt well says:

> That there is pain and evil, is no rule
> That I should make it greater, like a fool.

JOSEPH RICKABY

Of the So-called Rights of Animals

1. Brute beasts, not having understanding and therefore not being persons, cannot have any rights. The conclusion is clear. They are not autocentric. They are of the number of *things*, which are another's: they are chattels, or cattle. We have no duties to them—not of justice, as is shown: not of religion, unless we are to worship them, like the Egyptians of old; not of fidelity, for they are incapable of accepting a promise. The only question can be of charity. Have we duties of charity to the lower animals? Charity is an extension of the love of ourselves to beings like ourselves, in view of our common nature and our common destiny to happiness in God. (c. iv., nn. 1, 2, p. 239.) It is not for the present treatise to prove, but to assume, that our nature is not common to brute beasts, but immeasurably above theirs, higher indeed above them than we are below the angels. Man alone speaks, man alone worships, man alone hopes to contemplate for ever, if not—in the natural order—the Face of his Father in Heaven, at least the reflected brightness of that Divine Face. (*Ethics*, c. ii., s. iv., nn. 3, 4.) We have then no duties of charity, nor duties of any kind, to the lower animals, as neither to sticks and stones.

2. Still we have duties *about* stones, not to fling them through our neighbour's windows; and we have duties *about* brute beasts. We must not harm them, when they are our neighbour's property. We must not break out into paroxysms of rage and impatience in dealing with them. It is a miserable way of showing off human pre-eminence, to torture

From Father Joseph Rickaby, S. J., *Moral Philosophy* (1901), "Ethics and Natural Law."

poor brutes in malevolent glee at their pain and helplessness. Such wanton cruelty is especially deplorable, because it disposes the perpetrators to be cruel also to men. As St. Thomas says (1a 2ae, q. 102, art. 6, ad 8):

"Because the passion of pity arises from the afflictions of others, and it happens even to brute animals to feel pain, the affection of pity may arise in man even about the afflictions of animals. Obviously, whoever is practised in the affection of pity towards animals, is thereby more disposed to the affection of pity towards men: whence it is said in Proverbs xii. 10: 'The just regardeth the lives of his beasts, but the bowels of the wicked are cruel.' And therefore the Lord, seeing the Jewish people to be cruel, that He might reclaim them to pity, wished to train them to pity even toward brute beasts, forbidding certain things to be done to animals which seem to touch upon cruelty. And therefore He forbade them to seethe the kid in the mother's milk (Deut. xiv 21), or to muzzle the treading ox (Deut. xxv. 4), or to kill the old bird with the young." (Deut. xxii. 6, 7.) *disturb*

3. It is wanton cruelty to vex and annoy a brute beast *for sport*. This is unworthy of man, and disposes him to inhumanity towards his own species. Yet the converse is not to be relied on: there have been cruel men who have made pets of the brute creation. But there is no shadow of evil resting on the practice of causing pain to brutes *in sport*, where the pain is not the sport itself, but an incidental concomitant of it. Much more in all that conduces to the sustenance of man may we give pain to brutes, as also in the pursuit of science. Nor are we bound to any anxious care to make this pain as little as may be. Brutes are as *things* in our regard: so far as they are useful to us, they exist for us, not for themselves; and we do right in using them unsparingly for our need and convenience, though not for our wantonness. If then any special case of pain to a brute creature be a fact of considerable value for observation in biological science or the medical art, no reasoned considerations of morality can stand in the way of man making the experiment, yet so that even in the quest of science he be mindful of mercy.

4. Altogether it will be found that a sedulous observance of the rights and claims of other men, a mastery over one's own passions, and a reverence for the Creator, give the best assurance of a wise and humane treatment of the lower animals. But to preach kindness to brutes as a primary obligation, and capital point of amendment in the conversion of a sinner, is to treat the symptom and leave unchecked the inward malady.

D. G. RITCHIE

Why Animals Do Not Have Rights

If rights are determined solely by reference to human society, it follows that the lower animals, not being members of human society, cannot have rights. This conclusion is resented by many modern humanitarians who, feeling that in some sense or other we may be said to have duties towards the lower animals, or at least duties in respect of our conduct towards them, conclude that the animals in their turn must have rights against us. If a utilitarian theory be based on a consideration of the pleasures of all *sentient* existence, then, whether or not the phraseology of natural rights be used, all animals must be taken into account in our judgments of right and wrong. Very difficult questions of casuistry will, indeed, arise because of the difference in grades of sentience; and the undoubted difference in degree of acuteness of feeling among human beings ought most assuredly to be taken account of also. If the recognition of Animal Rights is compatible with the kindly use of a horse as a beast of burden, would not a kindly negro-slavery be also perfectly compatible with the recognition of Natural Rights generally? And if we discriminate between what may be rightly done to the mollusc from what may be rightly done to the mammal, on grounds of different grades of sentience, should we not also—if sentience be our sole guiding principle—discriminate between what may be rightly done to lower and higher races among mankind—the lower and less civilised being undoubtedly less capable of acute feeling? An ethical theory which is based on the social nature of man is not directly troubled by these difficulties, though in the details of practical conduct these grades

From D. G. Ritchie, *Natural Rights* (London: Allen & Unwin, 1894).

of sentience do enter in as one of the factors determining our moral judgments.

The most recent English book of which I know on the subject of *Animals' Rights* is that of Mr. H. S. Salt. "Have the lower animals 'rights'?" he asks, and answers his question, "Undoubtedly—if men have." But the question whether and in what sense men have rights, Mr. Salt refuses to discuss. He takes for granted that in some sense they have rights, and treats the controversy about rights as "little else than an academic battle over words, which leads to no practical conclusion." The term "academic" is apparently used as a term of dispraise. For this, unfortunately, the past traditions of learned societies may be to blame; or is a disparagement of logic and of all careful use of language merely one of the notes of the higher barbarism of the new school of Rousseauists? I have tried to show that there is a sense in which the term "natural rights" may be harmlessly used, but it is a sense which needs caution; and therefore, if the term be used at all, it should not be used except in "academic" discussions. Otherwise its use can only be regarded as a rhetorical device for gaining a point without the trouble of proving it— a device which may be left to the stump-orator or party-journalist, but which should be discredited in all serious writing. Mr. Salt's justification for his assertion, that animals have rights if men have, must be discovered incidentally. First of all, I note that he appeals to the actual state of the law in England. "It is scarcely possible, in the face of this legislation [for the prevention of cruelty to animals], to maintain that 'rights' are a privilege with which none but human beings can be invested; for if *some* animals are already included within the pale of protection, why should not more and more be so included in the future?" Because a work of art or some ancient monument is protected by law from injury, do we speak of the "rights" of pictures or stones? Further, are animals capable of being parties to a lawsuit? It might be answered, they are on the same footing permanently on which human "infants" are temporarily (*i.e.* until they attain full age). But if there are rights, there are correlative duties. And whereas infants may be tried on a criminal charge, I do not know, apart from a *cause célèbre* in Aristophanes, of any such trial of animals in any advanced legal system. Thus it will hardly do to appeal to existing law in proof that animals have rights in any *legal* sense. Again, I note that Mr. Salt quotes with approbation the maxim of the "Buddhist and Pythagorean canons"—"Not to kill or injure any innocent animal," and the words of Bentham: "We have begun by attending to the condition of slaves; we shall finish by softening that of all the animals which assist our labours or supply our wants." Why these limitations of the *jus animalium*? If the animal as such has rights, who are we to pronounce judgment, according to our own human convenience, on his "innocence"? What is the "guilt" from the tiger's point of view of her raid on a human village? Why do we commend a cat that kills mice and punish her if she attacks a tame bird? If the animals were consulted, they would choose to be tried by a jury of their peers, before the question of guilt or innocence were decided. The most despotic kings have always been quite willing to leave in peace those of their subjects who contributed to their convenience, or whom they regarded as harmless. The Czar of Russia does not oppress any one whom he regards as "innocent." The claim of natural rights among men has meant something very much more than a claim that the innocent should be kindly treated, the arbitrary government against which they protested being free to decide the question of innocence.

It may be admitted, however, that towards the lower animals we must always stand in the relation of despots; but it may be urged that our despotism ought to be guided by a recognition of their rights. Well, then, in our exercise of our power and in our guardianship of the rights of animals, must we not protect the weak among them against the strong? Must we not put to death blackbirds and thrushes because they feed on worms, or (if capital punishment offends our humanitarianism) starve them slowly by permanent captivity and vegetarian diet? What becomes of the "return to nature" if we must prevent the cat's nocturnal wanderings, lest she should wickedly slay a mouse? Are we not to vindicate the rights of the persecuted prey of the stronger? or is our declaration of the rights of every creeping thing to remain a mere hypocritical formula to gratify pug-loving sentimentalists, who prate about a nature they will not take the trouble to understand—a nature whose genuine students they are ready to persecute? Mr. Salt injures a needed protest against certain barbarities of "sport," and against the habitual callousness of the ignorant in their treatment of animals, by his attacks on men of science and his opposition to the use of animal food. If all the world were Jews, it has been well said, there would be no pigs in existence; and if all the world were vegetarians, would there be any sheep or cattle, well cared for and guarded against starvation? Perhaps a stray specimen in a zoological garden: turnips being all needed for human food. Cruelty to animals is rightly supposed to be an offence against *humanitarian* feeling. Our duty to the animals is a duty to human society. It is an offence against civilised life to cause any unnecessary suffering, or to do any unnecessary damage—"unnecessary" meaning, as it means even in Mr. Salt's theory, unnecessary for *human* well-being. This consideration will explain also why we regard cruelty to domestic animals, especially to pets, with more horror than cruelty to wild animals—especially to dangerous or injurious wild animals. We have admitted certain animals to a sort of honorary membership of our society; and we come to think of them as standing in a quasi-human relation to ourselves, especially when we give them names of their own, as if they were persons. Of Schopenhauer, that poodle-loving hater of man, it might almost be said that he and his dog (the reigning sovereign for the time) formed a society by themselves. In a metaphorical sense we may be said to have duties towards these honorary human beings.

Pain is in itself an evil, not in the special moral sense of the term "evil," but in the sense that it is an impediment to the maintenance and development of life: it is an impediment which every normal sentient being "naturally," *i.e.* by mere instinct, strives to escape, and this instinct is kept alert by natural selection. The growth of sympathy and of imagination makes it possible for human beings to feel mental pain at the sufferings of other human beings, even of those not specially connected with them, and of other animals, in a manner and to an extent impossible in a more primitive stage of existence. (The real savage and our sentimental neo-savage are very different persons in this respect.) And thus the avoidance of pain for other beings capable of feeling it, as well as for oneself, comes to be thought of as a duty, except when the infliction of such pain is necessary and unavoidable in the interests of human society and human progress. Thus we may be said to have duties of *kindness towards* the animals; but it is incorrect to represent these as strictly *duties towards* the animals themselves, as if they had rights against us. If the animals had in any proper sense rights, we should no more be entitled to put them to death without a fair trial, unless in strict self-defence, than to torture them for our amusement. It is our duty to put animals to death as painlessly as possible, when we wish their death for any human end; and similarly in experiments on living animals for scientific purposes, it is right to prefer the less highly organised animal to the more highly organised, wherever the lower type is clearly sufficient for the purposes of the experiment. It is a duty also not to cause any suffering which is unnecessary for the properly scientific purpose of the experiment. The evil of pain is the element of permanent truth in the Hedonist protest against Asceticism; but to make the mere fact of sentience the determining principle of right and wrong in ethics is the abstraction that renders Hedonism, even in its universalistic form, an inadequate ethical theory. I have already suggested the difficulties which would be involved in any consistent attempt to recognise in animals equal rights with human beings: on the other hand, to fix a scale of unequal rights solely from the point of view of human convenience is practically to give up basing ethics on the mere fact of sentience, and implicitly to recognise the interests of human society as our ultimate criterion of right and wrong.

HENRY S. SALT

Logic of the Larder

It is often said, as an excuse for the slaughter of animals, that it is better for them to live and to be butchered than not to live at all. Now, obviously, if such reasoning justifies the practice of flesh-eating, it must equally justify *all* breeding of animals for profit or pastime, when their life is a fairly happy one. The argument is frequently used by sportsmen, on the ground that the fox would long ago have become extinct in this country had not they, his true friends, "preserved" him for purposes of sport. Vivisectors, who breed guinea-pigs for experimentation, also have used it, and they have as much right to it as flesh-eaters; for how, they may say, can a few hours of suffering be set in the balance against the enormous benefit of life? In fact, if we once admit that it is an *advantage* to an animal to be brought into the world, there is hardly any treatment that cannot be justified by the supposed terms of such a contract.

Also, the argument must apply to mankind. It has, in fact, been the plea of the slave-breeder; and it is logically just as good an excuse for slave-holding as for flesh-eating. It would justify parents in almost any treatment of their children, who owe them, for the great boon of life, a debt of gratitude which no subsequent services can repay. We could hardly deny the same merit to cannibals, if they were to breed their human victims for the table, as the early Peruvians are said to have done.

It is on record, in no less authentic a work than "Hansard" (March 7, 1883), that when Sir Herbert Maxwell argued in Parliament that a

From Henry S. Salt, *The Humanities of Diet* (Manchester: The Vegetarian Society, 1914).

"blue rock" would prefer to be sport for pigeon-shooters than not to exist at all, Mr. W. E. Forster satirically remarked that what we have to consider is not a blue rock *before* existence, but a blue rock *in* existence. There, in brief, is the key to the whole matter. The fallacy lies in the confusion of thought which attempts to compare existence with non-existence. A person who is already in existence may feel that he would rather have lived than not, but he must first have the *terra firma* of existence to argue from; the moment he begins to argue as if from the abyss of the non-existent, he talks nonsense, by predicating good or evil, happiness or unhappiness, of that of which we can predicate nothing.

When, therefore, we talk of "bringing a being," as we vaguely express it, "into the world," we cannot claim from that being any *gratitude* for our action, or drive a bargain with him, and a very shabby one, on that account; nor can our duties to him be evaded by any such quibble, in which the wish is so obviously father to the thought. Nor, in this connection, is it necessary to enter on the question of ante-natal existence, because, if such existence there be, we have no reason for assuming that it is less happy than the present existence; and thus equally the argument falls to the ground. It is absurd to compare a supposed preexistence, or non-existence, with actual individual life as known to us here. All reasoning based on such comparison must necessarily be false, and will lead to grotesque conclusions.

Take the case, as it stands, between the Philosopher and the Pig. Is it not adding insult to injury that this much-massacred animal should not only be *eaten* by the Philosopher, but should also be made the subject of a far from disinterested beatification—"Blessed is the Pig, for the Philosopher is fond of bacon."[1] We can imagine how the Philosopher, when he passes a butcher's shop, which, according to his showing, is a very shrine and centre of humaneness, since without it there "would be no pigs at all," must pause in serene self-satisfaction to felicitate the pallid carcase laid out there, with the mockery of an ornamental orange in its mouth. "I have been a benefactor to this Pig," he must say, "inasmuch as I ate a portion of his predecessor; and now I will be a benefactor to some yet unborn pig, by eating a portion of this one."

This, then, is the benign attitude of the Philosopher towards the Pig;

---

[1] "Of all the arguments for Vegetarianism none is so weak as the argument from humanity. The pig has a stronger interest than anyone in the demand for bacon. If all the world were Jewish, there would be no pigs at all."—Leslie Stephen in "Social Rights and Duties."

"If all the world were Jews, it has been well said, there would be no pigs in existence; and if all the world were Vegetarians, would there be any sheep or cattle, well cared for, and guarded against starvation?"—Professor D. G. Ritchie in "Natural Rights."

and what shall be the reply of the Pig to the Philosopher? "Revered moralist," he might plead, "it were unseemly for me, who am to-day a pig, and to-morrow but ham and sausages, to dispute with a master of ethics, yet to my porcine intellect it appeareth that having first determined to kill and devour me, thou hast afterwards bestirred thee to find a moral reason. For mark, I pray thee, that in my entry into the world my own predilection was in no wise considered, nor did I purchase life on condition of my own butchery. If, then, thou art firm set on pork, so be it, for pork I am: but though thou hast not spared my life, at least spare me thy sophistry. It is not for *his* sake, but for *thine*, that in his life the Pig is filthily housed and fed, and at the end barbarously butchered."

From whatever point one looks at this sophism, it is seen to be equally hollow. For even apart from the philosophical flaw which vitiates it, there is the practical consideration that a far greater number of human lives can be supported on a grain and fruit-growing district than on one which rears cattle; so that if a larger area of England were devoted to the rearing of "livestock," we should actually be lessening human life that there might be more beef and mutton; that is, we should be increasing the lower existence at the expense of the higher. It is worth noting, too, that the life of animals doomed to the slaughter is of a far lower quality than it would be if the same animals were either entirely wild, or domesticated to some rational purpose by friendly association with man; the very fact that an animal is going to be eaten seems to remove it from the category of intelligent beings, and causes it to be regarded as mere animated "meat." "To keep a man, slave, or servant," says Edward Carpenter, "for your own advantage merely, to keep an animal, that you may *eat* it, is a lie; you cannot look that animal in the face." The existence of bullocks, for example, can scarcely be called life; they are "live-stock," but they do not *live*. And what of the "fat beasts" that are yearly exhibited at the Agricultural Hall, and elsewhere, at the season of peace and goodwill? Are these wretched victims of human gluttony to be grateful for the boon of life? Are crammed fowls and Strasburg geese to be grateful? And the calf and the lamb—are *they* to be felicitated on the rather short term allowed them in the ghoulish contract, or must we except the eaters of veal and lamb from the list of animal benefactors?

Let us heartily accept all that may be said of "the joyfulness of life." But what is the moral to be drawn from that fact? Surely not that we are justified in outraging and destroying life, to pamper our selfish appetites, because forsooth we shall then produce more of it! But rather that we should respect the beauty and sanctity of life in others as in ourselves, and strive as far as possible to secure its fullest natural development. This logic of the larder is the very negation of a true reverence for life; for it implies that the real lover of animals is he whose larder is fullest of them:

> He prayeth best, who *eateth* best
> All things both great and small.

It is the philosophy of the wolf, the shark, the cannibal. If there be any truth in such an argument, let those who believe it have the courage of their convictions, and face the inevitable conclusion. The Ogre has hitherto been a much misunderstood character, but now at last Philosophy and Science are doing justice to his beneficence. His organization has been defective, perhaps, but his spirit has been wholly commendable. He is *par excellence* the zoophilist, the philanthropist, the saint.[2]

But enough of this quibbling! Vegetarianism would save the actual animals, who have been brought into this actual world, from the very real suffering that is inseparable from the cattle-ship and the slaughterhouse; and if its only inhumanity is that which it perpetrates on nonexistent races by not arranging for their birth, it may bear the charge with equanimity. If there were any unkindness, or any lack of kindness, in *not* breeding animals, the enormity of our sins of omission would be more than the human conscience could endure, for the number of the unborn is limitless, and to wade through slaughter to a throne, "and shut the gates of mercy on mankind," would be a trifle in comparison with this cold-blooded shutting of the gates of life on the poor, neglected nonexistent!

It is interesting to note that this fallacy—the assumption that it is a *kindness* to bring a being into the world–is as old as the time of Lucretius, who deals with it, in another connection, in a passage of his great philosophical poem, *De Rerum Natura* (v. 176–180), which may be rendered thus:

> What loss were ours, if we had known not birth?
> Let living men to longer life aspire,
> While fond affection binds their hearts to earth:

---

[2]"If the motive that might produce the greatest number of the happiest cattle would be the eating of beef, then beef-eating, so far, must be commended. And while, heretofore, the motive has not been for the sake of cattle, it is conceivable that, if Vegetarian convictions should spread much further, love for cattle would (if it be not psychologically incompatible) blend with the love of beef in the minds of the opponents of Vegetarianism. With deeper insight, new and higher motives may replace or supplement old ones, and perpetuate but ennoble ancient practices."—Dr. Stanton Coit.

But whoso ne'er hath tasted life's desire,
Unborn, impersonal, can feel no dearth.

We see, then, that a vulgar sophism of to-day was clearly exposed nearly two thousand years ago. It is quite possible that fools may be repeating it two thousand years hence.

JOEL FEINBERG

Can Animals Have Rights?

To have a right is to have a claim[1] *to* something and *against* someone the recognition of which is called for by legal (or other institutional) rules, or in the case of moral rights, by the principles of an enlightened conscience. In the familiar cases of rights, the claimant is a competent adult human being, and the claimee is an office-holder in an institution or else a private individual, in either case, another competent adult human being. Normal adult human beings, then, are obviously the sorts of beings of whom rights can meaningfully be predicated. Everyone would agree to that, even extreme misanthropes who deny that anyone in fact has rights. On the other hand, it is absurd to say that rocks can have rights, not because rocks are morally inferior things unworthy of rights (that statement makes no sense either), but because rocks belong to a category of entities of whom rights cannot be meaningfully predicated. That is not to say that there are no circumstances in which we ought to treat rocks carefully, but only that the rocks themselves cannot claim good treatment from us. In between the clear cases of rocks and normal human beings, however, is a spectrum of less obvious cases, including some bewildering borderline ones. Is it meaningful or conceptually possible to ascribe rights to our dead ancestors? to individual animals? to whole species of animals? to plants? to idiots and madmen? to fetuses? to generations yet unborn? Until we know how to settle these puzzling

From Joel Feinberg, "The Rights of Animals and Future Generations," an expanded version of the paper of the same title that appears in *Philosophy and Environmental Crisis*, ed. William Blackstone (Athens, Georgia: University of Georgia Press, 1974).
[1] I shall leave the concept of a claim unanalysed here, but for a detailed discussion, see my "The Nature and Value of Rights," *Journal of Value Inquiry*, Winter 1971.

cases, we cannot claim fully to grasp the concept of a right, or to know the shape of its logical boundaries.

One way to approach these riddles is to turn one's attention first to the most familiar and unproblematic instances of rights, note their most salient characteristics, and then compare the borderline cases with them, measuring as closely as possible the points of similarity and difference. In the end, the way we classify the borderline cases may depend on whether we are more impressed with the similarities or the differences between them and the cases in which we have the most confidence.

It will be useful to consider the problem of individual animals first, because their case is the one that has already been debated with the most thoroughness by philosophers so that the dialectic of claim and rejoinder has now unfolded to the point where disputants can get to the end game quickly and isolate the crucial point at issue. When we understand precisely what *is* at issue in the debate over animal rights, I think we will have the key to the solution of all the other riddles about rights.

Almost all modern writers agree that we ought to be kind to animals, but that is quite another thing from holding that animals can claim kind treatment from us as their due. Statutes making cruelty to animals a crime are now very common, and these, of course, impose legal duties on people not to mistreat animals; but that still leaves open the question whether the animals as beneficiaries of those duties, possess rights correlative to them. We may very well have duties *regarding* animals that are not at the same time duties *to* animals, just as we may have duties regarding rocks, or buildings, or lawns, that are not duties *to* the rocks, buildings, or lawns. Some legal writers have taken the still more extreme position that animals themselves are not even the intended direct beneficiaries of statutes prohibiting cruelty to animals. During the Nineteenth Century, for example, it was commonly said that such statutes were designed to protect human beings by preventing the growth of cruel habits that could later threaten human beings with harm too. Professor Louis B. Schwartz finds the rationale of the cruelty-to-animals prohibition in its protection of animal lovers from affronts to their sensibilities. "It is not the mistreated dog who is the ultimate object of concern, . . ." he writes. "Our concern is for the feelings of other human beings, a large proportion of whom, although accustomed to the slaughter of animals for food, readily identify themselves with a tortured dog or horse and respond with great sensitivity to its sufferings."[2] This seems to me to be factitious. How much more natural it is to say with John Chipman Gray that the true purpose of cruelty-to-animals statutes is

[2]Louis B. Schwartz, "Morals, Offenses and the Model Penal Code," *Columbia Law Review*, Vol. 63 (1963), p. 673.

"to preserve the dumb brutes from suffering."[3] The very people whose sensibilities are invoked in the alternative explanation, a group that no doubt now includes most of us, are precisely those who would insist that the protection belongs primarily to the animals themselves, not merely to their own tender feelings. Indeed, it would be difficult even to account for the existence of such feelings in the absence of a belief that the animals deserve the protection in their own right and for their own sakes.

Even if we allow, as I think we must, that animals are the directly intended beneficiaries of legislation forbidding cruelty to animals, it does not follow directly that animals have legal rights; and Gray himself, for one,[4] refused to draw this further inference. Animals cannot have rights, he thought, for the same reason they cannot have duties, namely, that they are not genuine "moral agents." Now, it is relatively easy to see why animals cannot have duties, and this matter is largely beyond controversy. Animals cannot be "reasoned with" or instructed in their responsibilities; they are inflexible and unadaptable to future contingencies; they are incapable of controlling instinctive impulses. Hence, they cannot enter into contractual agreements, or make promises; they cannot be trusted; and they cannot (except within very narrow limits and for purposes of conditioning) be blamed for what would be called "moral failures" in a human being. They are therefore incapable of being moral subjects, of acting rightly or wrongly in the moral senses, of having, discharging, or breaching duties and obligations.

But what is there about the intellectual incompetence of animals (which admittedly disqualifies them for duties) that makes them logically unsuitable for rights? The most common reply to this question is that animals are incapable of *claiming* rights on their own. They cannot make motion, on their own, to courts to have their claims recognized or enforced; they cannot initiate, on their own, any kind of legal proceedings; nor are they capable of even understanding when their rights are being violated, or distinguishing harm from wrongful injury, and responding with indignation and an outraged sense of justice instead of mere anger or fear.

No one can deny any of these allegations; but to the claim that they are the ground of animal disqualification for rights, philosophers on the other side of this controversy have made convincing rejoinders. It is simply not true, says W. D. Lamont,[5] that the ability to understand what

[3]John Chipman Gray, *The Nature and Sources of the Law*, 2nd ed. (Boston: Beacon Press, 1963), p. 43.

[4]And W. D. Ross for another. See *The Right and the Good* (Oxford: Clarendon Press, 1930), Appendix I, pp. 48–56.

[5]W. D. Lamont, *Principles of Moral Judgment* (Oxford: Clarendon Press, 1946), pp. 83–85.

a right is and the ability to set legal machinery in motion by one's own initiative are necessary for the possession of legal rights. If that were the case, then neither human idiots nor wee babies would have any legal rights at all. Yet it is manifest that both of these classes of intellectual incompetents have legal rights recognized and easily enforced by the courts. Children and idiots start legal proceedings, not on their own direct initiative, but rather through the actions of proxies or attorneys who are empowered to speak in their names. If there is no conceptual absurdity in this situation, why should there be in the case where a proxy makes a claim on behalf of an animal? People commonly enough make wills leaving money to trustees for the care of animals. Is it not natural to speak of the animal's right to his inheritance in cases of this kind? If a trustee embezzles money from the animal's account,[6] and a proxy speaking in the dumb brute's behalf presses the animal's claim, can he not be described as asserting the animal's *rights*? More exactly, the animal itself claims its rights through the vicarious actions of a human proxy speaking in its name and in its behalf. There appears to be no reason why we should require the animal to understand what is going on (so the argument concludes) as a condition for regarding it as a possessor of rights.

Some writers protest at this point that the legal relation between a principal and an agent cannot hold between animals and human beings. Between humans, the relation of agency can take two very different forms, depending upon the degree of discretion granted to the agent, and there is a continuum of combinations between the extremes. On the one hand, there is the agent who is the mere "mouthpiece" of his principal. He is a "tool" in much the same sense as is a typewriter or telephone; he simply transmits the instructions of his principal. Human beings could hardly be the agents or representatives of animals in this sense, since the dumb brutes could no more use human "tools" than mechanical ones. On the other hand, an agent may be some sort of expert hired to exercise his professional judgment on behalf of, and in the name of, the principal. He may be given, within some limited area of expertise, complete independence to act as he deems best, binding his principal to all the beneficial or detrimental consequences. This is the role played by trustees, lawyers, and ghost-writers. This type of representation requires that the agent have great skill, but makes little or no demand upon the principal, who may leave everything to the judgment of his agent. Hence, there appears, at first, to be no reason why an animal cannot be a totally passive principal in this second kind of agency relationship.

[6]Cf. H. J. McCloskey, "Rights," *Philosophical Quarterly*, Vol. 15 (1965), pp. 121, 124.

There are, however, still some important disanalogies. In the typical instance of agency-representation, even of the second, highly discretionary, kind, the agent is *hired* by a principal who enters into an *agreement* or *contract* with him; the principal tells his agent that within certain carefully specified boundaries "You may speak for me," subject always to the principal's *approval*, his right to give new directions, or to *cancel* the whole arrangement. No dog or cat could possibly do any of those things. Moreover, if it is the assigned task of the agent to defend the principal's rights, the principal may often decide to *release* his claimee, or to *waive* his own rights, and *instruct* his agent accordingly. Again, no mute cow or horse can do that. But although the possibility of hiring, agreeing, contracting, approving, directing, canceling, releasing, waiving, and instructing is present in the typical (all human) case of agency representation, there appears to be no reason of a logical or conceptual kind why that *must* be so, and indeed there are some special examples involving human principals where it is not in fact so. I have in mind, for example, legal rules that require that a defendant be represented at his trial by an attorney, and impose a state-appointed attorney upon reluctant defendants, or upon those tried *in absentia*, whether they like it or not. Moreover, small children and mentally deficient and deranged adults are commonly represented by trustees and attorneys even though they are incapable of granting their own consent to the representation, or of entering into contracts, of giving directions, or waiving their rights. It may be that it is unwise to permit agents to represent principals without the latters' knowledge or consent. If so, then no one should ever be permitted to speak for an animal, at least in a legally binding way. But that is quite another thing than saying that such representation is logically incoherent or conceptually incongruous—the contention that is at issue.

H. J. McCloskey,[7] I believe, accepts the argument up to this point; but he presents a new and different reason for denying that animals can have legal rights. The ability to make claims, whether directly or through a representative, he implies, is essential to the possession of rights. Animals obviously cannot press their claims on their own; so if they have rights, these rights must be assertable by agents. Animals, however, cannot be represented, McCloskey contends, and not for any of the reasons already discussed, but rather because representation, in the requisite sense, is always of interests; and *animals* (he says) *are incapable of having interests*.

Now, there is a very important insight expressed in the requirement

---

[7] *Ibid.*

that a being have interests if he is to be a logically proper subject of rights. This can be appreciated if we consider just why it is that mere things cannot have rights. Consider a very precious "mere thing"—a beautiful natural wilderness, or a complex and ornamental artifact, like the Taj Mahal. Such things ought to be cared for, because they would sink into decay if neglected, depriving some human beings or perhaps even *all* human beings, of something of great value. Certain persons may even have as their own special job the care and protection of these valuable objects. But we are not tempted in these cases to speak of "thing-rights" correlative to custodial duties, because, try as we might, we cannot think of mere things as possessing *interests* of their own. Some people may have a duty to preserve, maintain, or improve the Taj Mahal; but they can hardly have a duty to help or hurt it, benefit or aid it, succor or relieve it. Custodians may protect it for the sake of a nation's pride and art lovers' fancy; but they don't keep it in good repair for "its own sake," or for "its own true welfare," or "well-being." A mere thing, however valuable to others, has no good of its own. The explanation of that fact, I suspect, is that mere things have no conative life; neither conscious wishes, desires, and hopes; nor urges and impulses; nor unconscious drives, aims, goals; nor latent tendencies, directions of growth, and natural fulfillments. Interests must be compounded somehow out of conations; hence mere things have no interests. *A fortiori*, they have no interests to be protected by legal or moral rules. And without interests a creature can have no "good" of its own, the achievement of which can be its due.

So far McCloskey (as I have reconstructed his argument) is on solid ground; but one can quarrel with his denial that any animals but humans have interests. I should think that the trustee of funds willed to a dog or cat is more than a mere custodian of the animal he protects. Rather his job is to look out for the interests of the animal and make sure no one denies it its due. The animal itself is the beneficiary of his dutiful services. Many of the higher animals at least have appetites, conative urges, and rudimentary purposes, the integrated satisfaction of which constitutes their welfare or good. We can, of course, with consistency treat animals as mere pests and deny that they have any rights; and for most animals, especially those of the lower orders, we have little choice but to do so. But it seems clear to me, nevertheless, that in general, animals *are* among the sorts of beings of whom rights can meaningfully be predicated and denied.

Now, if a person agrees with the conclusion of the argument thus far, that animals are the sorts of beings that *can* have rights, and further, if he accepts the moral judgment that we ought to be kind to animals, only one further premise is needed to yield the conclusion that some animals do in fact have rights. We must now ask ourselves for whose sake ought we to treat (some) animals with consideration and humaneness? If we conceive our duty to be one of obedience to authority, or to one's own conscience merely, or one of consideration for tender human sensibilities only, then we might still deny that animals have rights, even though we admit that they are the kinds of beings that *can* have rights. But if we hold not only that we ought to treat animals humanely but also that we should do so for the animal's *own sake*, that such treatment is something we *owe* animals as their *due*, something that can be *claimed* for them, something the withholding of which would be an *injustice* and a *wrong*, and not merely a cause of damage, then it follows that we do ascribe rights to animals. I suspect that the moral judgments most of us make about animals do pass these phenomenological tests, so that most of us do believe that animals have rights, but are reluctant to say so because of the conceptual confusions about the notion of a right that I have attempted to dispel above.

TOM REGAN

Do Animals Have
a Right to Life?

My argument in this section turns on considerations about the natural "right to life" that we humans are sometimes said uniquely to possess, and to possess to an equal degree. My strategy here will be similar to my strategy in the previous section. What I will try to show is that arguments that might be used in defense of the claim that all human beings have this natural right, to an equal extent, would also show that animals are possessors of it, whereas arguments that might be used to show that animals do not have this right would also show that not all human beings do either. Just as in the preceding section, however, so here too, a disclaimer to completeness is in order. I have not been able to consider all the arguments that might be advanced in this context; all that I have been able to do is consider what I think are the most important ones.

Let us begin, then, with the idea that all humans possess an equal natural right to life. And let us notice, once again, that it is an *equal natural* right that we are speaking of, one that we cannot acquire or have granted to us, and one that we all are supposed to have just because we are human beings. On what basis, then, might it be alleged that all and only human beings possess this right to an equal extent? Well, a number of familiar possibilities come immediately to mind. It might be argued that all and only human beings have an equal right to life because either (a) all and only human beings have the capacity to reason, or (b) all and only human beings have the capacity to make free choices, or

From "The Moral Basis of Vegetarianism," *The Canadian Journal of Philosophy*, October, 1975. Reprinted by permission of the publisher.

(c) all and only human beings have a concept of "self," or (d) all and only human beings have all or some combination of the previously mentioned capacities. And it is easy to imagine how someone might argue that, since animals do not have any of these capacities, *they* do not possess a right to life, least of all one that is equal to the one possessed by humans.

I have already touched upon some of the difficulties such views must inevitably encounter. Briefly, it is not clear, first, that no nonhuman animals satisfy any one (or all) of these conditions, and, second, it is reasonably clear that not all human beings satisfy them. The severely mentally feeble, for example, fail to satisfy them. Accordingly, *if* we want to insist that they have a right to life, then we cannot also maintain that they have it because they satisfy one or another of these conditions. Thus, *if* we want to insist that they have an equal right to life, despite their failure to satisfy these conditions, we cannot consistently maintain that animals, because they fail to satisfy these conditions, therefore lack this right.

Another possible ground is that of sentience, by which I understand the capacity to experience pleasure and pain. But this view, too, must encounter a familiar difficulty—namely, that it could not justify restricting the right *only* to human beings.

What clearly is needed, then, if we are to present any plausible argument for the view that all and only human beings have an equal natural right to life, is a basis for this right that is invariant and equal in the case of all human beings and only in their case. It is against this backdrop, I think, that the following view naturally arises.[1] This is the view that the life of every human being has "intrinsic worth—that, in Kant's terms, each of us exists as "an end in himself"—*and* that this intrinsic worth which belongs *only* to human beings, is shared *equally* by all. "Thus," it might be alleged, "it is because of the equal intrinsic worth of all human beings that we all have an equal right to life."

This view, I think, has a degree of plausibility which those previously discussed lack. For by saying that the worth that is supposed to attach to a being just because he or she is human is intrinsic, and that it is because of this that we all have an equal natural right to life, this view rules out the possibility that one human being might give this right to or withhold it from another. It would appear, therefore, that this view could make sense of the alleged *naturalness* of the right in question. Moreover, by resting the equal right to life on the idea of the *equal in-*

---

[1]For an example of this kind of argument, see Gregory Vlastos's "Justice and Equality" in *Social Justice*, edited by Richard B. Brandt (Englewood Cliffs, N.J.: Prentice-Hall, Inc., 1962).

trinsic worth of all human beings, this view may succeed, where the others have failed, in accounting for the alleged *equality* of this right.

Despite these apparent advantages, however, the view under consideration must face certain difficulties. One difficulty lies in specifying just what it is supposed to mean to say that the life of every human being is "intrinsically worthwhile."[2] Now, it cannot mean that "each and every human being has a natural right to life." For the idea that the life of each and every human being has intrinsic worth was introduced in the first place to provide a basis for saying that each and every human being has an equal right to life. Accordingly, if, say, "Jones's life is intrinsically worthwhile" ends up *meaning* "Jones has an equal right to life," then the claim that the life of each and every individual is equally worthwhile, judged intrinsically, cannot be construed as a *basis* for saying that each and every human being has an equal right to life. For the two claims would mean the same thing, and one claim can never be construed as being the basis for another, if they both mean the same.

But a second and, for our purposes, more important difficulty is this: On what grounds is it being alleged that each and every human being, and only human beings, are intrinsically worthwhile? Just what is there, in other words, about being human, and only about being human, that underlies this ascription of unique worth? Well, one possible answer here is that there isn't "anything" that underlies this worth. The worth in question, in short, just belongs to anyone who is human, and only to those who are. It is a worth that we simply recognize or intuit, whenever we carefully examine that complex of ideas we have before our minds when we think of the idea, "human being." I find this view unsatisfactory, both because it would seem to commit us to an ontology of value that is very difficult to defend, and because I, for one, even after the most scrupulous examination I can manage, fail to intuit the unique worth in question. I do not know how to prove that the view in question is mistaken in a few swift strokes, however. All I can do is point out the historic precedents of certain groups of human beings who have claimed to "intuit" a special worth belonging to their group and not to others within the human family, and say that it is good to remember that alluding to a special, intuitive way of "knowing" such things could only serve the purpose of giving an air of intellectual respectability to unreasoned prejudices. And, further, I can only register here my own suspicion that the same is true in this case, though to a much wider extent. For I think that falling into talk about the "intuition of the unique intrinsic worth of being human" would be the last recourse of men who, having found

[2]This is a point that first became clear to me in discussion with Donald Van-DeVeer.

no good reason to believe that human beings have a unique intrinsic worth, would go on believing that they do anyhow.

Short of having recourse to intuition, then, we can expect those who believe that human beings uniquely possess intrinsic worth to tell us what there is about being human, in virtue of which this worth is possessed. The difficulty here, however, as can be anticipated, is that some familiar problems are going to raise their tiresome heads. For shall we say that it is the fact that humans can speak, or reason, or make free choices, or form a concept of their own identity that underlies this worth? These suggestions will not work here, anymore than they have before. For there are some beings who are human who cannot do these things, and there very well may be some beings who are not human who can. None of these capacities, therefore, could do the job of providing the basis for a kind of worth that all humans and only humans are supposed to possess.

But suppose we try to unpack this notion of intrinsic worth in a slightly different way.[3] Suppose we say that the reasons we have for saying that all and only human beings exist as ends in themselves are, first, that every human being has various positive interests, such as desires, goals, hopes, preferences and the like, the satisfaction or realization of which brings intrinsic value to their lives, in the form of intrinsically valuable experiences; and, second, that the intrinsic value brought to the life of any one man, by the satisfaction of his desires or the realization of his goals, is just as good, judged in itself, as the intrinsic value brought to the life of any other man by the satisfaction or realization of those comparable desires and goals he happens to have. In this sense, then, all men are equal, and it is because of this equality among all men, it might be alleged, that each man has as much right as any other to seek to satisfy his desires and realize his goals, so long, at least, that, in doing so, he does not violate the rights of any other human being. "Now, since," this line of argument continues, "no one can seek to satisfy his desires or realize his goals if he is dead, and in view of the fact that every man has as much right as any other to seek to satisfy his desires and realize his goals, then to take the life of any human being will always be prima facie to violate a right which he shares equally with all other human beings—namely, his right to life."

What shall we make of this argument? I am uncertain whether it can withstand careful scrutiny. Whether it can or not, however, is not a matter I feel compelled to try to decide here. What I do want to point out is, of the arguments considered here, this one has a degree of plausi-

---

[3]Vlastos, *op. cit.*

bility the others lack, not only because, as I have already remarked, it addresses itself both to the alleged naturalness and the alleged equality of the right in question, but also because it rests on what I take to be a necessary condition of being human—namely, that a being must have interests. For these reasons, then, I do not think I can be accused of "straw-man" tactics by choosing this as the most plausible among a cluster of possible arguments that might be urged in support of the contention that all human beings have an equal natural right to life. At the same time, however, as can be anticipated, I believe that, whatever plausibility this argument might have in this connection, it would also have in connection with the claim that animals, too, have an equal natural right to life.

For even if it is true that this argument provides us with adequate grounds for ascribing a natural right to life equally to all human beings, there is nothing in it that could tend to show that this is a right that belongs *only* to those beings who are human. On the contrary, the argument in question would equally well support the claim that any being who has positive interests which, when satisfied, bring about experiences that are just as intrinsically valuable as the satisfaction of the comparable interests of any other individual, would have an equal right to life. In particular, then, it would support the view that animals have an equal right to life, if they meet the conditions in question. And a case can be made for the view that they do. For, once again, it seems clear that animals have positive interests, the satisfaction or realization of which would appear to be just as intrinsically worthwhile, judged in themselves, as the satisfaction or realization of any comparable interest a human being might have. True, the interests animals have may be of a comparatively low grade, when we compare them to, say, the contemplative interests of Aristotle's virtuous man. But the same is true of many human beings: their interests may be largely restricted to food and drink, with occasional bursts of sympathy for a few. Yet we would not say that such a man has less of a right to life than another, assuming that all men have an equal right to life. Neither, then, can we say that animals, because of their "base" interests, have any less of a right to life.

One way to avoid this conclusion . . . is to deny that animals have interests.[4] But on what basis might this denial rest? A by now familiar basis is that animals cannot speak; they cannot use words to formulate or express anything; thus, they cannot have an interest in anything. But this objection obviously assumes that only those beings who are able to

---

[4]See, for example, H. J. McCloskey's "Rights," *Philosophical Quarterly* (1965). McCloskey denies that animals have interests, but does not, so far as I can see, give any reason for believing that this is so.

use words to formulate or express something can have interests, and this, even ignoring the possibility that at least some animals might be able to do this, seems implausible. For we do not suppose that infants, for example, have to learn to use a language before they can have any interests. Moreover, the behavior of animals certainly seems to attest to the fact that they not only can, but that they actually do have interests. Their behavior presents us with many cases of preferential choice and goal-directed action, in the face of which, and in the absence of any rationally compelling argument to the contrary, it seems both arbitrary and prejudicial to deny the presence of interests in them.

The most plausible argument for the view that humans have an equal natural right to life, therefore, seems to provide an equally plausible justification for the view that animals have this right also. But just as in saying that men and animals have an equal right to be spared unde-served pain, so here, too, we would not imply that the right in question can never be overridden. For there may arise circumstances in which an individual's right to life could be outweighed by other, more pressing moral demands, and where, therefore, we would be justified in taking the life of the individual in question. But even a moment's reflection will reveal that we would not condone a practice which involved the routine slaughter of human beings simply on the grounds that it brought about this or that amount of pleasure, or this or that amount of intrinsi-cally good experiences for others, no matter how great the amount of good hypothesized. For to take the lives of individuals, for this reason, is manifestly not to recognize that their life is just as worthwhile as any-body else's, or that they have just as much right to life as others do. Nor need any of this involve considerations about the amount of pain that is caused the persons whose lives are taken. Let us suppose that these per-sons are killed painlessly; that still would not alter the fact that they have been treated wrongly and that the practice in question is immoral.

If, then, the argument in the present section is sound; and assuming that no other basis is forthcoming which would support the view that humans do, but animals do not, have an equal right to life; then the same is true of any practice involving the slaughter of animals, and we have, therefore, grounds for responding to the two objections raised, but not answered, at the end of the first section. These objections were, first, that since the only thing wrong with the way animals are treated in the course of being raised and slaughtered is that they are caused a lot of undeserved pain, the thing to do is to desensitize them so that they don't feel anything. What we can see now, however, is that the undeserved pain animals feel is not the only morally relevant consideration; it is also the fact that they are killed that must be taken into account.

Similarly, to attempt to avoid the force of my argument for conditional vegetarianism by buying meat from farms that do not practice intensive rearing methods or by hunting and killing animals oneself— expedients that formed the basis of the second objection at the end of Section I—these expedients will not meet the total challenge vegetarians can place before their meat-eating friends. For the animals slaughtered on even the most otherwise idyllic farms, as well as those shot in the wild, are just as much killed, and just as much dead, as the animals slaughtered under the most ruthless of conditions.

Unless or until, then, we are given a rationally compelling argument that shows that all and only human beings have an equal right to life; and so long as any plausible argument that might be advanced to support the view that all human beings have this right can be shown to support, to the same extent, the view that animals have this right also; and so long as we believe we are rationally justified in ascribing this right to humans and to make reference to it in the course of justifying our judgment that it is wrong to kill a given number of human beings simply for the sake of bringing about this or that amount of good for this or that number of people; given all these conditions, then, I believe we are equally committed to the view that we cannot be justified in killing any one or any number of animals for the intrinsic good their deaths may bring to us. I do not say that there are no possible circumstances in which we would be justified in killing them. What I do say is that we cannot justify doing so in their case, anymore than we can in the case of the slaughter of human beings, by arguing that such a practice brings about intrinsically valuable experiences for others.

Once again, therefore, the onus of justification lies, not on the shoulders of those who are vegetarians, but on the shoulders of those who are not. If the argument of the present section is sound, it is the nonvegetarian who must show us how he can be justified in eating meat, when he knows that, in order to do so, an animal has had to be killed. It is the nonvegetarian who must show us how his manner of life does not contribute to practices which systematically ignore the right to life which animals possess, if humans are supposed to possess it on the basis of the most plausible argument considered here. And it is the nonvegetarian who must do all this while being fully cognizant of the fact that he cannot defend his way of life merely by summing up the intrinsic goods— the delicious taste of meat, for example—that come into being as a result of the slaughter of animals.

This is not to say that practices that involve taking the lives of animals cannot possibly be justified. In some cases, perhaps, they can be, and the grounds on which we might rest such a justification would, I think, parallel those outlined in the preceding section in connection with the discussion of when we might be morally justified in approving a practice that caused animals nontrivial, undeserved pain. What we would have to show in the present case, I think, in order seriously to consider approving of such a practice, is (1) that such a practice would prevent, reduce, or eliminate a much greater amount of evil, including the evil that attaches to the taking of the life of a being who has as much claim as any other to an equal natural right to life; (2) that, realistically speaking, there is no other way to bring about these consequences; and (3) that we have very good reason to believe that these consequences will, in fact, obtain. Now, perhaps there are some cases in which these conditions are satisfied. For example, perhaps they are satisfied in the case of the Eskimo's killing of animals and in the case of having a restricted hunting season for such animals as deer. But to say that this is (or may be) true of *some* cases is not to say that it is true of all, and it will remain the task of the nonvegetarian to show that what is true in these cases, assuming that it is true, is also true of any practice that involves killing animals which, by his actions, he supports.

JAMES RACHELS

Do Animals Have
a Right to Liberty?

Philosophers used to talk about "natural" rights, but now we don't hear so much about that subject. Instead, books and articles are written about "human" rights. The change in terminology is thought to be a great improvement; first, because talk about human rights does not bring with it the ontological worries that often attended discussions of natural rights, and second, because the new terminology focuses more precisely on what we are trying to understand: the rights that all human beings have in common. One of my motives in raising the question in my title is to cast doubt on the importance of human rights. I will maintain that human rights are not nearly so interesting or important as philosophers and politicians have thought.

As Richard Wasserstrom puts it, "If any right is a *human* right, . . . it must be possessed by all human beings, as well as only by human beings."[1] What is usually emphasized is that such rights are possessed by *all* humans; thus the doctrine of human rights has been a formidable weapon against slavery, racism, sexism, and the like. But, as Wasserstrom correctly notes, if any right is a distinctively human right, it is also necessary that it be possessed *only* by humans.[2] It is this side of the

---

This essay has not been previously published.

[1] Richard Wasserstrom, "Rights, Human Rights, and Racial Discrimination," *The Journal of Philosophy*, vol. 61 (1964), p. 631.

[2] Joel Feinberg defines human rights as those belonging to all humans, but specifically denies that they must be possessed only by humans, "so that a human right held by animals is not excluded by definition." (*Social Philosophy*, Englewood Cliffs, N.J.: Prentice-Hall, 1973, p. 85.) I prefer Wasserstrom's definition because,

doctrine that I want to emphasize. If it can be made plausible that members of other species also have the rights that are most important to humans—such as the right to liberty—then the whole subject of *human* rights will come to have much less interest than before; and it will be seen that the differences between humans and other animals are not nearly so important, from a moral point of view, as we have usually assumed.

Some philosophers believe that nonhuman animals (I will sometimes follow the common practice and call them simply "animals," leaving off the qualifier) have no rights at all, because they are not the sorts of beings that *can* have rights. On their view, it is not logically possible for animals to have rights. Two things need to be done: first, their arguments must be refuted, and second, positive arguments must be advanced to show that animals *do* have specific rights. I take up the first task in an appendix to be found at the end of this paper. I have relegated this essentially negative material to an appendix so that I can go on here to the second, more positive task.

In arguing that animals do have rights—and in particular that they have a right to liberty—we may use the following method. First we select for discussion a right which we are confident that humans do have. Then we ask whether there is a relevant difference between humans and animals which would justify us in denying that right to animals while at the same time granting it to humans. If not, then the right in question is a right possessed by animals as well as by humans.

This method has a number of virtues. First, it has a clear rationale in the familiar principle of justice that we must treat like cases alike; or, to be more precise, that our moral judgments are unacceptably arbitrary if we judge one way in one case and differently in another case, without there being a relevant difference between the two cases which justifies the difference in our assessments. This principle has been used with great effect in arguing against racism. The assumption there has been that a person's race is not in itself a morally relevant consideration in determining how he is to be treated. Therefore, racist discrimination is unjustified unless some further differences between blacks and whites can be found which would be relevant to justifying the different modes of treatment. But, because there are no such further differences, such discrimination is unjustified. I am going to make the similar assumption that a mere difference in species is not enough, in itself, to justify any

---

if a right is shared by dogs and cows, there seems little reason to call it human rather than canine or bovine. And, by calling such rights "human," we are directing attention away from the fact that other beings have them, as though all that matters is whether we men have them.

difference in how beings are treated.[3] Thus if we want to grant a right to humans but deny it to members of other species, we must be able to point to some relevant difference between them other than the mere fact that the animals are members of another species. A second advantage of the method is that if we follow it closely we will avoid the trap of lumping all nonhuman animals together, as though what we say about one species we must say about all. For it may turn out that, with respect to some particular right, there is no relevant difference between man and one species of animal, but there are differences between man and other species. Finally, I should mention one limitation of this method. The use of this method does not guarantee that we will identify all the rights which animals have, for it is at least logically possible that they have some rights not possessed by humans. If so, then these rights could not be uncovered by my method. However, this is of no concern to me here, for I have no intention of trying to compile a complete list of animal rights.

Now let me give some illustrations of the kinds of results which may be obtained by this method. Article 5 of The United Nations Universal Declaration of Human Rights says that all men have a right not to be subjected to torture. But is this, in fact, a distinctively *human* right? If members of other species—say, rabbits or pigs or monkeys—are tortured, they also suffer. Of course, there are many impressive differences between men and these animals, but are they relevant here? A man can learn mathematics, and a rabbit can't; but what does that have to do with the business of being tortured? A man has an interest in not being tortured because he has the capacity to suffer pain, and not because he can do mathematics or anything of that sort. But rabbits, pigs, and monkeys also have the capacity to experience pain, and so they have the same basic interest in not being tortured. The right not to be tortured, then, is shared by all animals that suffer pain; it is not a distinctively human right at all. On the other hand, Article 18 of the same Declaration says that all men have the right to worship as they please. This, I think, *is* a right belonging only to humans, because only humans have religous beliefs and a capacity for worship.

The right not to be tortured, and to freedom of worship, are relatively clear and unproblematic. But what happens when we consider a more puzzling right, such as the right to property? Here we may proceed by asking why it is thought that men have this right—what is the basis of it?—and then, whether the same case can be made in behalf of animals.

[3]This point is brought out very powerfully by Peter Singer in "All Animals Are Equal," *Philosophic Exchange*, vol. 1, no. 5 (Summer 1974), pp. 103–16. [See selection included in this volume.]

Let us consider, for example, Locke's treatment of the right to property. Locke contends that a man has a natural right to his own labor and whatever he produces by it:

> The labor of his body and the work of his hands, we may say, are properly his. Whatsoever then he removes out of the state that nature has provided and left it in, he has mixed his labor with, and joined to it something that is his own, and thereby makes it his property.[4]

Locke then illustrates his view with this example:

> He that is nourished by the acorns he picked up under an oak, or the apples he gathered from the trees in the wood, has certainly appropriated them to himself. Nobody can deny but the nourishment is his. I ask, then, when did they begin to be his? When he digested or when he ate or when he boiled or when he brought them home? Or when he picked them up? And it is plain, if the first gathering made them not his, nothing else could. That labor put a distinction between them and common; that added something to them more than nature, the common mother of all, had done; and so they became his private right.

If Locke is right, then it follows that animals such as squirrels also have a right to property; for squirrels labor to gather nuts for their own nourishment in exactly the way Locke pictures the man laboring. There is no relevant difference between the man and the squirrel: they both pick up the nuts, take them home, store them away, and then eat them. Therefore there is no justification for saying that the man has a right to the nuts he gathers, but that the squirrel does not.

Now I turn to the right to liberty. The right to liberty has been counted among the most fundamental human rights in all the great liberal manifestos of modern history—the Declaration of Independence of the United States (1776), the French Declaration of the Rights of Man (1789), and the United Nations Universal Declaration of Human Rights 1948), to name three of the most important. Virtually every philosopher who has discussed the subject has followed suit; I have not been able to find any treatment of "human rights" which did not include liberty as a prime example. Considering this, and remembering that some philosophers doubt whether mere animals can have any rights at all, it may not be surprising to find liberty (or freedom, which for present purposes comes to the same thing) being *defined* by some in such a way that only humans could possibly *be* free. According to J. R. Lucas, for example,

---

[4]John Locke, *The Second Treatise of Government* (1690), chap. 5, par. 27. The next quotation is from the same chapter of the same work, par. 28.

The central sense of Freedom is that in which a rational agent is free when he is able to act as seems best to him without being subject to external constraints on his actions.[5]

If we start off by conceiving freedom in this way, then the question of whether animals have a right to be free will not even arise, since the notion of a "rational agent" who deliberates about which actions are best is so obviously formulated with only humans in mind. But, just as obviously, this definition won't do as a general definition of freedom, for that concept applies to animals as well as to men. A lion left alone in his natural habitat is free; a lion in a zoo is not. A chicken in a small wire cage is less free than one allowed to roam about a barnyard. And a bird who is released from a cage and allowed to fly away is "set free" in a perfectly plain sense. So, rewriting the definition to eliminate the prejudice in favor of men, we get:

The central sense of Freedom is that in which a being is free when he is able to do as he pleases without being subject to external constraints on his actions.

This expresses well enough the concept of liberty with which I shall be concerned. As before, we may proceed by asking why it is thought that men have this right—what is the basis of it?—and then, whether the same or a very similar case can be made on behalf of members of other species.

One possibility is to take liberty to be, simply and without need of any further justification, good in itself.[6] If we take this approach, then we might argue that men have a right to liberty simply because they have a right not to be deprived of any intrinsic goods which they are capable of enjoying. (And here the usual qualifications will be added, to the effect that the right will be only as extensive as is compatible with others having a similar right, that the right may be forfeited or overridden in certain circumstances, etc.) But this line of reasoning will apply equally well to other species of animals. It is parallel to the right not to be tortured, mentioned above. Any animal that has the capacity for suffering pain has a right not to be tortured; and the reason for this is connected with the fact that suffering pain is intrinsically bad. Similarly, if we grant to men a right to liberty simply because we regard liberty as

[5]J. R. Lucas, *The Principles of Politics* (Oxford: Oxford University Press, 1966), p. 144.

[6]For an account of this type, see Gregory Vlastos, "Justice and Equality," *Social Justice*, ed. Richard B. Brandt (Englewood Cliffs, N.J.: Prentice-Hall, 1962), p. 51.

something good in itself which men are capable of enjoying, then we must also grant a right to liberty to any other animal that is capable of desiring to act one way rather than another.

However, not many philosophers would be happy with this approach, because most believe it is possible to provide a rationale for the right to liberty that does not simply stop with calling it an intrinsic good. For example, it may be said that humans have a right to liberty because they have various *other* interests that will suffer if their freedom is unduly restricted. The right to liberty—the right to be free of external constraints on one's actions—may then be seen as derived from a more basic right not to have one's interests needlessly harmed.

But the interests of many other species are also harmed by a loss of freedom. It is a familiar fact that many wild animals do not fare at all well in captivity: taken from their natural habitats and put in zoos, they are at first frantic and frustrated because they cannot carry on their normal activities; then they become listless and inactive, shadows of their former selves. Some become vicious and destructive. They often will not reproduce in captivity, and when they do, their young often cannot survive; and finally, members of many species will die sooner in captivity than they would in their natural homes.

Dr. Herbert Ratcliffe, a pathologist, conducted a study of the animals in a Philadelphia zoo. He found that the animals were suffering from sharply increased rates of heart disease, cancer, and ulcers. The metabolism of some white-tailed deer had changed to such an extent that their horns became deformed. The zoo's breeding colony of nutria—small, beaverlike animals—had dwindled because the young animals were born dwarfed, failed to breed, and died early. Dr. Ratcliffe attributes all of this to the effects of the artificial, confined environment of the zoo.[7]

Another example is taken from a widely used psychology textbook, which tells the story of a baboon colony in the London zoo. Investigators

> observed many instances of bloody fighting, brutality, and apparently senseless violence. Some of the females were torn to pieces, and no infant survived to maturity. From these observations, it was concluded that such violence was typical of the "wild" baboons. . . . But later, when baboons were studied under natural conditions in Africa, in the "wild," it was discovered that they lived in well-organized, peaceful groups, in which the only aggressive behavior was directed at predators and intruders.[8]

---

[7]"The Shame of the Naked Cage," *Life*, November 8, 1968, p. 77.

[8]Floyd L. Ruch and Philip G. Zimbado, *Psychology and Life*, 8th ed. (Glenview, Ill.: Scott, Foresman and Company, 1967), p. 539.

Once it has been learned that animals can be made to suffer in a certain way, a new field is opened for scientific research. Experiments may then be performed to discover how they will behave when tormented, and exactly what forms their suffering will take. Numerous studies have been made of the effects of confinement on animals. One such series of experiments was reported in 1972.[9] One of the experimenters, Dr. Harry F. Harlow of the University of Wisconsin, is said to have "created" a vertical chamber, which "is basically a stainless steel trough with sides that slope inward to form a rounded bottom." The whole thing measures about four feet by one foot by a few inches. The idea behind the chamber is explained this way:

> Depression in humans has been characterized as embodying a state of "helplessness and hopelessness, sunken in a well of despair," and the device was designed on an intuitive basis to reproduce such a well both physically and psychologically for monkey subjects.

Rhesus monkeys were used for the experiments. These animals are often used in such experiments because they are intelligent, sociable creatures that resemble humans in a great many ways. The experiments were conducted by putting six-week-old monkeys into the "well of despair" for a period of *forty-five days*. The purpose of doing this was said to be to "investigate the chamber's effectiveness in production of psychopathology."

The chamber turned out to be very effective. While confined, the "subjects" were said to "typically spend most of their time huddled in a corner of the chamber." "Huddling" is defined as a "self-enclosed, fetal-like position incorporating any or all patterns of self-clasp, self-embrace, or lowered head." A nine-month period of observation following the confinement indicates that the effects on the animals are permanent:

> The results indicated that a 45-day period of vertical chamber confinement early in life produced severe and persistent psychopathological behavior of a depressive nature in the experimental subjects. These monkeys failed to show appreciable changes in home-cage behavioral levels during the 9-month period following removal from the vertical chamber. In comparison to control groups of cage- and peer-reared monkeys, the chambered subjects exhibited abnormally high levels of

[9]Stephen J. Suomi and Harry F. Harlow, "Depressive Behavior in Young Monkeys Subjected to Vertical Chamber Confinement," *Journal of Comparative and Physiological Psychology*, vol. 80 (1972), pp. 11–18. The quotations that follow are from pp. 11, 12, 13, and 14. For an account of this and related experiments, see Peter Singer, *Animal Liberation* (New York Review, 1975), chap. II.

self-clasp and huddle and abnormally low levels of locomotion and environmental exploration in both the home-cage and playroom situations. Most striking was the virtual absence of social activity among chambered subjects throughout the 8 months of playroom testing.

This new knowledge was obtained with financial assistance from the United States Public Health Service, the National Institutes of Health, and the National Institute of Mental Health.

Any creature that has interests has at least a *prima facie* right not to have those interests needlessly harmed. Animals that suffer in captivity have an interest in being free, and so at least a prima facie right to liberty. Lucas, immediately after giving the definition of "freedom" (restricted to "rational agents") quoted above, says that "not to be free is to be frustrated, impotent, futile." He is obviously thinking only of men; but the description applies equally well to animals in zoos, and certainly to the monkeys trapped in the well of despair.

Animals raised for food also suffer in confinement. Before being slaughtered cows spend their lives crowded into "feedlots" where they are deprived of any sort of herd life or even adequate exercise. Veal calves are kept in pens so small they cannot even turn around. Peter Singer points out that even the lowly chicken suffers from confinement in the sort of cages used by poultry-farmers:

> . . . hens are crowded four or five to a cage with a floor area of twenty inches by eighteen inches, or around the size of a single page of the *New York Times*. The cages have wire floors, since this reduces cleaning costs, though wire is unsuitable for the hens' feet; the floors slope, since this makes the eggs roll down for easy collection, although this makes it difficult for the hens to rest comfortably. In these conditions all the birds' natural instincts are thwarted: they cannot stretch their wings fully, walk freely, dust-bathe, scratch the ground, or build a nest. Although they have never known other conditions, observers have noticed that the birds vainly try to perform these actions. Frustrated at their inability to do so, they often develop what farmers call "vices," and peck each other to death. To prevent this, the beaks of young birds are often cut off.[10]

Some of these cruelties have to do with the *type* of confinement rather than with the bare fact that the birds are confined. So, if the cages had flat, solid floors, and perches for the hens, some of the grounds for complaint would be eliminated. But so long as the hens are confined to small cages, their natural desire to scratch the dirt, stretch their wings, build a nest, and so forth, will be frustrated. This is not to say that the interests of chickens can be satisfied only in a state of *total* freedom: I can

[10]Singer, "All Animals are Equal" *op. cit.*, p. 108.

see no harm that would be done to their interests if they were kept captive while being allowed freedom to roam a large area, where they could
do the things just mentioned. Thus many vegetarians who refuse to buy
eggs produced under the conditions described by Singer nevertheless will
buy eggs laid by "free-ranging" hens.

So, we need to distinguish two things: first, we need to distinguish
the *kinds* of animals whose interests are harmed by the denial of freedom; and second, we need to distinguish the *degree* of freedom that is
required if the animals' interests are not to be harmed. Lions, but not
chickens, may need to be set completely free in their natural habitats in
order to thrive; whereas the needs of most insects may be so limited that
they have no interest in freedom at all.

At this point the business about man's superior rationality must be
re-introduced. For, even if it is a mistake to *define* freedom in such a
way that only rational agents can be free, it may still be said that freedom has a special kind of importance for rational agents which it cannot
have for nonrational beings. In one form or another this thought is
found in the writings of almost all the philosophers who discuss the "human right" to liberty. I want to make two preliminary remarks about
this. The first has only to do with a certain sentiment that I have—so
you may want to discount it as an argument—but I will mention it anyway. It is that there is something very *sad* about a grand animal such as
a lion or an elephant being put on exhibit in a zoo, and being reduced to
nothing more than a spectacle for people's enjoyment. The reason I mention this here is that, in the past, humans who lacked "rationality" have
suffered the same fate. Salt notes that

> Two or three generations ago, pauper-lunatics used to be caged where
> passers-by—nurses perhaps with children in their charge—could see
> them as they passed, and the spectacle was sometimes enjoyed. (I re-
> member hearing from my mother that such was the case at Shrewsbury.
> The nurse would say, "Where shall we go to-day, children?" and the
> cry would be, "Oh, to see the madmen, please!")[11]

Most of us recoil at this, and many reasons may be given why such
practices are barbarous: perhaps because they teach children callous attitudes. But of course making a similar spectacle of animals may also
have that effect. However, it is hard to believe that our initial reaction
has much to do with such considerations. It has to do rather with the
sadness and indignity of the spectacle. And the fact that the being on
exhibit is not *rational* hardly matters, either in the case of the lunatic or
the lion. The second comment is to express a general doubt about the

[11]Henry Salt, *The Creed of Kinship* (New York: Dutton, 1935), pp. 60–61.

relevance of rationality to the value of freedom. It may be true, as philosophers have often stressed, that liberty is necessary if we humans are to develop and exercise our powers as rational agents, and to have the kinds of lives we want. But it is also true that liberty is necessary for many nonhuman animals if they are to live the sorts of lives, and thrive, in ways that are natural to them; or, to put things more plainly, if the interests they have, in virtue of the kinds of creatures *they* are, are to be realized.

So, just what relevance is rationality supposed to have? One very popular view, derived from the teachings of Kant, is that because of his rational powers man alone, among all the animals, is a *moral* agent, able to form a conception of right and wrong and guide his actions by it. It is even said that, because of this, there are two kinds of freedom that must be distinguished in discussions such as this: the natural freedom of any creature to do as he pleases, and the special, *moral* freedom of man to guide his actions by his sense of right and wrong.[12] The idea is that, when we talk of man's freedom, it is his moral freedom that is especially important and that must be protected. Thus man's right to liberty has a foundation and importance which the "liberty" of mere animals cannot have.

Although the idea of "moral freedom" is obscure, it is also very powerful, and it is easy to feel the force of it. Here, I do not want to quarrel with the notion, or even to analyze it very closely. Rather I want to suggest that some nonhuman animals have capacities which might very well be called "moral," so that, even if we do hold moral freedom to be an especially important type of liberty, there may still be no reason to deny that these animals have a claim to it. For even though these animals cannot form an intellectual conception of right and wrong, they are nevertheless capable of being motivated to act by desires which, in humans, we would take to be signs of moral goodness. For example, many nonhuman animals show devotion and love for their offspring, and self-sacrificial loyalty to the other members of their herd or pack or whatever. And if we think it especially important to allow humans the liberty to act on their conceptions of right and wrong, why should it not also be important to allow a nonhuman mother to act from love for her offspring? (Here again the differences between kinds of animals must be kept clearly in mind. Some animals are indifferent or cruel to their young; but others—for example, wild dogs—do show the type of protective love to which I am referring.)

But some animals have even more impressive virtues than these fa-

---

[12]See Edith Watson-Schipper, "Two Concepts of Human Freedom," *The Southern Journal of Philosophy*, vol. 11 (1973), pp. 309–15. Professor Watson-Schipper provides references to other thinkers who have held this distinction to be important.

miliar ones. Let me describe another series of experiments, this one conducted at the Northwestern University Medical School and reported in the psychological journals for 1964.[13] These experiments were designed to discover whether rhesus monkeys would be deterred from operating a device for securing food if doing so would cause pain to another monkey. One animal (called by the experimenters the "operator" or "O") would be placed in one side of a divided box and taught to secure food by pulling either of two chains. Food would be available only when a light signal was given (a different light for each chain), and the O would be trained to show no special preference for either chain.

Next, another monkey (called the "stimulus animal" or "SA") would be put into the other side of the box. The box was divided by a one-way mirror so that the O could see the SA but not the other way around. The floor on the SA's side of the box was covered by a grid attached to a shock source. The O was given three days to adapt to the presence of the SA, and then the circuit was completed so that whenever he pulled one of the chains to secure food the SA received a severe electrical shock. Pulling the other chain continued to give food, but produced no shock. Now, by turning on only one signal light at a time, in various sequences and at various intervals, the experimenters could determine the extent to which the perception of the SA's distress would influence the O's willingness to pull the shock-producing chain.

The experimenters concluded that "a majority of rhesus monkeys will consistently suffer hunger rather than secure food at the expense of electroshock to a conspecific." In particular, in one series of tests, 6 of 8 animals showed this type of sacrificial behavior; in a second series, 6 of 10; and in a third series, 13 of 15. One of the monkeys refrained from pulling *either* chain for 12 days, and another for 5 days, after witnessing shock to the SA—which means that they had no food at all and suffered really terrible hunger.

I believe that these experiments show that rhesus monkeys have a capacity for compassion, and by that I mean exactly the same moral virtue which we admire in humans.[14] Of course, these animals are not

[13]Stanley Wechkin, Jules H. Masserman, and William Terris, Jr., "Shock to a Conspecific as an Aversive Stimulus," *Psychonomic Science*, vol. 1 (1964), pp. 47–48; "'Altruistic' Behavior in Rhesus Monkeys," *The American Journal of Psychiatry*, vol. 121 (1964), pp. 584–85. Because each article is less than two pages long, and both concern the same series of experiments, I will not give page numbers for the quotations that follow.

[14]Wechkin et al. do not use the term *compassion* in describing the monkeys' behavior; they speak of 'altruism'. However, they always put the word in single quotes, apparently to indicate reservations about using it. I think that *compassion* is a slightly more accurate term—although it does not really matter much which word is used—but I see no reason for the single quotes.

able to form abstract moral conceptions. But, even for humans, *being compassionate* does not necessarily involve forming the idea that it is good to be compassionate, or that one is morally required to act compassionately. Being compassionate only requires desiring that others do not suffer, and acting on that desire.[15] Animals may not form abstract conceptions, but they do have desires, and apparently among the desires of the rhesus monkey is that he not cause suffering to others of his own kind. So I conclude that they have compassion. However, in order for this conclusion to be really plausible, we need more information. And the experimenters have provided what we need.

First, the experimenters tested to determine whether the O's reluctance to pull the shock chain was correlated to relative positions on a dominance-submissiveness hierarchy. Relative dominance was determined when the animals "were paired against each other in another apparatus and required to compete for 100 grapes presented one at a time. In most cases dominance was quickly established, the dominant animal getting 90 percent of the grapes." The experiments were then divided into those in which the dominant animal was the SA and the submissive animal was the O; those in which the roles were reversed; and so forth. And it was found that this made no difference to the O's willingness or reluctance to pull the shock chain.

Again, the experimenters were careful to observe whether differences in sex made any difference; that is, whether the O was male and the SA was female; whether they were both male; and so forth. This made no difference either.

These results are important because they are exactly what we would expect if the O's behavior is caused by a generalized compassion for other members of his own species rather than to fear of dominant animals or some sort of sexual conditioning. The experimenters also rule out "increased noise level" as a possible explanation because "the SA's vocalized infrequently"—although, even if the SA's had cried out often,

---

[15]Mrs. Foot has argued for a conception of morality according to which all moral behavior is governed by hypothetical imperatives; that is, imperatives which tell us what is to be done *if* we have certain desires. The desires which are important for morality are those associated with the moral virtues, such as the desire that others not suffer, associated with the virtue of compassion. This conception of morality is in contrast with others which place importance on acting from a sense of duty. (See Philippa Foot, "Morality as a System of Hypothetical Imperatives," *The Philosophical Review*, vol. 81 (1972), pp. 305–16.) If she is right about this, then perhaps even animals with no very great powers of abstract thought can be full moral agents. For, while having a "sense of duty" does require fairly sophisticated thinking, having desires such as the desire that others not suffer, and recognizing simple ways of acting on those desires, does not require any such sophisticated thinking.

this would not rule out compassion as the explanation because the cries would obviously be cries of pain. Moreover, the experimenters observe that "the rage and attack mimetics of large male or female SA's during shock proved to be no more effective than those of smaller animals in deterring the feeding responses of persistently indifferent O's or expediting 'altruism' in the others." So still another alternative explanation is ruled out.

Other aspects of the experiments support the hypothesis of compassion in a different way. The experimenters found that animals that had previously been SA's were significantly more reluctant to pull the shock chain when they were made O's than animals who had not been SA's themselves. "This behavior of the shocked O's was not attributable to an acquired aversion to the apparatus itself since they showed no decrement in chain-manipulation during the adaptation sessions immediately following their shock." The explanation suggested by the hypothesis of compassion is that these animals were more reluctant to pull the chain because, having suffered the shocks themselves, they had a more vivid comprehension of what it was like, and so a greater reluctance to see someone else in the same position.

It was also found that O's who had been cage-mates of their SA's were more reluctant to pull the shock chain than O's who had not been cage-mates of their SA's. Again, this is just what we would expect if we take our common knowledge of human beings as our model: we are less willing to harm someone we know than we are to harm strangers.

This, then, is the evidence that rhesus monkeys are compassionate. I can imagine several objections being made to this conclusion. I have already answered the most obvious objection, that animals cannot have moral characteristics because they are not capable of moral thinking. The answer was that having a virtue such as compassion does not require moral conceptions, but only acting on certain sorts of desires. The conclusion that these animals are compassionate is likely to be controversial, so let us consider three other possible objections:

First: "But the monkeys only showed an aversion to causing pain for others *of their own kind.* Would they do the same for *other* kinds of animals? The results here are much too limited to justify talk about a virtue of compassion." The answer to this complaint is that even if the compassion of the monkeys is limited to a feeling for others of their own kind, their compassion is no more limited than that of most humans. Most men—even those who have a fine respect for the interests of other humans—are fairly indifferent to the interests of beings not of their own kind. (For example, men give virtually no thought to arranging experiments in which severe electroshocks will be administered to members of other species, or in which they will be reduced to a lifetime of "huddling.") We would not say that a man was completely devoid of compassion merely because he limits his concern to the suffering of other men; and we should not judge other animals more harshly than we judge ourselves.

Second: "But only *some* of the animals tested showed 'compassionate' behavior. Many did not." Again, this is exactly the result we would get in the case of humans. Human compassion comes in varying degrees and strengths: some of us are quite compassionate; and some are relatively indifferent to the plights of others. When we find similar variations among the monkeys, why should we be surprised? Indeed, the remarkable thing is that, considering the superior ability for moral thinking of which we are so proud, the differences between us and them are not greater than they are.

Third: "This whole way of thinking about animals is unforgivably anthropomorphic. To speak of 'compassion' in nonhuman animals is simply to read human characteristics into their behavior when they are not really there." Now it is certainly true that we should be wary of overly anthropomorphic ways of thinking about animals. We should be careful to notice the differences between them and ourselves, as well as the similarities. But I have been as careful as I can—I hope that the foregoing discussion shows at least some signs of care—and I still think that the animals are compassionate.

We should notice that in many contexts the emphasis is the other way around: the similarities between ourselves and other animals is *under*-emphasized. Consider, for example, the language used by the experimenters whose work I have just been discussing. The monkeys being tormented are called "stimulus animals" and when they cry out in pain they are said to have "vocalized." The result of this is an "increased noise level"—the language suggests that the animal pulling the chain is not even able to perceive the cries for what they are. When the experimenters speculate as to the significance of the whole phenomenon, they conjecture that "aversion to the perceived pain of conspecifics may be an ethologically innate pattern that serves to preserve the species." Here the animals are pictured as something less than they are. Perhaps we run the risk of going too far in the opposite direction if we speculate that *compassion* is a quality that "serves to preserve the species"—but I see no reason to think so.

Now the point about "moral freedom" was that beings with moral capacities should be free to exercise those capacities. But why should the point be made by referring exclusively to beings that have intellectualized *conceptions* of right and wrong, rather than by referring simply to beings that have moral virtues? If it is objectionable to deny a man the right to act according to his moral judgments, it is also objectionable, for much the same reason, to place a compassionate animal in a position where he must either cause pain or starve.

The sum of all this is that, whatever rationale is provided for granting humans a right to liberty, it seems that a relevantly similar one is available in the case of at least some other species of animals. The right to liberty, then, is not a "human" right.

As I said at the outset, my motive in arguing the point is to cast doubt on the importance of the concept of human rights. It is not that I think there are no human rights. On the contrary, I think that there are. But they are *not* rights that we have *simply in virtue of being members of a certain species.* Rather, they are rights that we have in virtue of possessing other characteristics, which members of other species happen not to have: for example, the right to worship seems to be a distinctively human right, because only humans, among all the animals we know, have any interest in or capacity for worship. But once the reason for this is understood, and once it is seen that such important rights as the right to liberty are *not* distinctively human, then most of the interest of the notion of "human" rights is, I think, gone. It would be much better to talk about natural rights, or simply *rights*, and remain alert to the fact that we humans are not the only beings that have them.

Appendix

WHY SOME PHILOSOPHERS SAY THAT IT IS NOT EVEN LOGICALLY POSSIBLE FOR ANIMALS TO HAVE RIGHTS

In his paper "Rights," H. J. McCloskey says that "important conclusions follow from the question as to whether animals have rights. If they do, . . . it would seem an illegitimate invasion of animal rights to kill and eat them, if, as seems to be the case, we can sustain ourselves without killing animals. If animals have rights, the case for vegetarianism is *prima facie* very strong, and is comparable with the case against cannibalism."[16] However, McCloskey thinks that this unsettling conclusion can be avoided, because it can be shown that nonhuman animals are not even logically possible bearers of rights. He argues:

> A right cannot not be possessed by someone; hence, only beings which can possess things can possess rights. My right to life is mine, I possess

[16]H. J. McCloskey, "Rights," *Philosophical Quarterly*, vol. 15 (1965), p. 122. The next quotation is from p. 126.

it. It is as much mine as any of my possessions—indeed more so—for I possess them by virtue of my rights. . . . All these considerations seem to exclude the lower animals in a decisive way, and the higher animals in a less decisive but still fairly conclusive way as possible bearers of rights. (Consider "possess" in its literal use. Can a horse possess anything, e.g. its stable, its rug, in a literal sense of "possess"?)

But clearly this argument does not prove the point. Why can't animals possess things? When a bird gathers twigs and builds himself[17] a nest, isn't it *his*, and not mine or yours or any other bird's? Would we have the right to take the nest from him, to satisfy some trivial interest of ours, and leave him to build himself another? I think not. The bird's claim to the nest is not merely that he needs it; it is his because *he made it* by his own labor. (Remember our earlier discussion of the right to property—i.e., Locke's example of the man gathering nuts.) If a larger, stronger bird drives him out and takes over the nest by force, we can recognize an injustice here even though neither animal has or could have an intellectualized conception of justice. All of this presupposes that the bird possesses the nest as a matter of right, once the nest is built; and although saying this does clash with our usual amoral way of regarding animals, I find nothing *logically* odd about it.

Like McCloskey, D. G. Ritchie believed that if we recognize animal rights we will have to make drastic changes in our ways of treating them. But he also thought that such changes are not required because animals don't have rights. In his book *Natural Rights*,[18] Ritchie argued that absurd consequences follow from the assumption that they do: for example, if animals have rights, then cats who eat mice violate their rights—but this is absurd.

Now it does sound odd to speak of cats violating mice's rights, but this may be at least partly because we hardly ever think of the matter in this light, and this in turn may be due to the fact that we don't give much thought to the morality of how animals are treated. Some have thought that there is a deeper, conceptual reason for the oddity, but that, once this reason is understood, it provides no grounds for doubting

---

[17] I say "himself" rather than "itself" deliberately, although either choice may be thought prejudicial: "Words and names are not without their effect upon conduct; and to apply to intelligent beings such terms as *brute, beast, live-stock, dumb,* etc., or the neuter pronouns *it* and *which,* as if they had no sex, is a practical incitement to ill-usage, and certainly a proof of misunderstanding. For example, the *Morning Post* (September 26th, 1933) thus described a case of cruelty to a cow: "He (the culprit) struck the cow with a milking-stool. It fell to the ground and died." It! One's thoughts turn to the milking-stool, but the allusion was to the cow! Salt, *The Creed of Kinship,* p. 62.

[18] D. G. Ritchie, *Natural Rights* (London: Allen & Unwin, 1894), p. 109. [See extract reprinted in this volume.]

that animals have rights. Plamenatz,[19] for example, suggests that rights be understood as *rights against rational beings,* so that animals have rights against us but not against one another. Thus, even though the cat cannot violate the mouse's rights, we humans can do so. However, any such explanation as this, which absolutely excludes the possibility of any animal ever violating another's rights, seems questionable to me because I can think of at least some cases where it doesn't seem at all odd to speak of this happening. Consider again the case of the big bird driving the smaller bird out of the nest and taking it for his own use. Here I think that the smaller bird had a right to the nest—it is his, because he built it himself—and that it is not odd to say that the big bird violated his right to it.

There is, however, a somewhat deeper reason for doubting whether animals can have rights. It is plausible to think that moral requirements can exist only where certain conditions of reciprocity are satisfied. The basic idea here is that a person is obligated to respect the interests of others, and acknowledge that they have claims against him, only if the others are willing to respect his interests and acknowledge his claims. This may be thought of as a matter of fairness: if we are to accept inconvenient restrictions on our conduct, in the interests of benefiting or at least not harming others, then it is only fair that the others should accept similar restrictions on *their* conduct for the sake of *our* interests.

The requirement of reciprocity is central to contract theories of ethics. Hobbes, for example, conceived of moral rules as rules which rational, self-interested people will agree to obey on condition that others will obey them as well.[20] Each person can be motivated to accept such an arrangement by considering the benefits he will gain if others abide by the rules; and his own compliance with the rules is the fair price he pays to secure the compliance of others. That is the point of the "contract." It is a natural part of such theories that nonhuman animals are not covered by the same moral rules which govern the treatment of humans, for the animals cannot participate in the mutual agreement on which the whole set-up depends.

This implication is made explicit in the most outstanding recent contribution to contract theory, John Rawls's *A Theory of Justice.*[21] Rawls identifies the principles of justice as those which would be accepted by rational, self-interested people in what he calls "the original position"; that is, a position of ignorance with respect to particular facts about

---

[19]John Plamenatz, *Consent, Freedom, and Political Obligation,* 2nd ed. (Oxford: Oxford University Press, 1968), p. 83.

[20]Thomas Hobbes, *Leviathan* (1651), chaps. 13–16.

[21]John Rawls, *A Theory of Justice* (Cambridge, Mass.: Harvard University Press, 1971). The quotations that follow are from p. 505 of that work.

oneself and one's own position in society. The question then arises as to what sorts of beings are owed the guarantees of justice and Rawls's answer is:

> We use the characterization of the persons in the original position to single out the kinds of beings to whom the principles chosen apply. After all, the parties are thought of as adopting these criteria to regulate their common institutions and their conduct toward one another; and the description of their nature enters into the reasoning by which these principles are selected. Thus equal justice is owed to those who have the capacity to take part in and to act in accordance with the public understanding of the initial situation.

This, he says, explains why nonhuman animals do not have the "equal basic rights" possessed by humans; "they have some protection certainly but their status is not that of human beings." And of course this result is not surprising: for if rights are determined by agreements of mutual interest, and animals are not able to participate in the agreements, then how can *their* interests give rise to rights?

The requirement of reciprocity may seem plausible, and I think that it does contain the germ of a plausible idea—I will say more about this in a moment—but nevertheless there are good reasons to reject it. We need to distinguish the conditions necessary for *having* a moral obligation from the conditions necessary for being the *beneficiary* of a moral obligation.

For example: normal adult humans have the moral obligation not to torture one another. What characteristics make it possible for a person to have this obligation? For one thing, he must be able to understand what torture is, and he must be capable of recognizing that it is wrong. When someone (a severely retarded person, perhaps) lacks such capacities, we do not think he has such obligations and we do not hold him responsible for what he does. On the other hand, it is a very *different* question what characteristics qualify someone to be the beneficiary of this obligation. It is wrong to torture a man—he is the beneficiary of our obligation not to torture—not because of his capacity for understanding what torture is, or for recognizing that it is morally wrong, but simply because of his capacity for experiencing pain. Thus a person may lack the characteristics necessary for having a certain obligation, and yet may still possess the characteristics necessary to qualify him as the beneficiary of that obligation. A severely retarded person may not be able to understand what torture is, or see it as wrong, and yet still be able to suffer pain. So we who are not retarded have an obligation not to torture him, even though he cannot have a similar obligation not to torture us.

The requirement of reciprocity says that a person is morally required to accept restrictions on his conduct, in the interests of not harming others, only if the others reciprocate. The example of the retarded person shows this to be false. He is not capable of restricting his conduct in this way; nevertheless we have an obligation to restrict ours. We are in the same position with respect to nonhuman animals: like the retarded person, they lack characteristics necessary for having obligations; but they may still be proper beneficiaries of our obligations. The fact that they cannot reciprocate, then, does not affect our basic obligations to them.

I said that the requirement of reciprocity, although unacceptable, does contain the germ of a plausible idea. What I have in mind is the idea that if a person *is* capable of acting considerately of our interests, and *refuses* to do so, then we are released from any similar obligations we might have had to him. This may very well be right. But whether or not this point is accepted makes no difference to our duties to nonhuman animals, since they lack the capacity to "refuse" to recognize obligations to us, just as they are not able to accept such obligations.

These arguments are only concerned with whether it is *possible* for animals to have rights. My reasons for thinking that they *do* have rights, and what some of those rights are, are given in the main body of the paper.[22]

[22]A number of people have contributed in one way or another to my understanding of the topics discussed in this paper: E. M. Adams, Edward Erwin, David Marans, Howard Pospesel, Jack Glickman, Eduardo de Marchena, and Melanie Rabin. My greatest debt is to Peter Singer, who has influenced my whole way of thinking about the morality of how we treat nonhuman animals.

DONALD VANDEVEER

Defending Animals
by Appeal to Rights

In his essay "Do Animals Have a Right to Liberty?" James Rachels seeks to show that there are certain rights possessed by animals and that certain arguments purporting to show that it is not logically possible for animals to have rights are ineffective.[1] I shall primarily examine his constructive arguments designed to show that at least some animals have a right not to be tortured, a right to property, and a right to liberty. I do so in part I; in part II, I briefly consider his negative arguments concerning the possibility of animals having rights. It may well be the case that our common treatment of animals violates some important moral constraint; on this general point I am in agreement with Rachels. Still, it is philosophically desirable to correctly identify that constraint and provide something more than intuitive support of it. While Rachels's sentiments and general position are, I think, on the side of the angels, his arguments fail to show that animals have *rights* and that, for that reason, certain instances of imposing suffering or deprivation on them count as a violation of rights. Part of the difficulty he encounters, but insufficiently attends to, derives from the fact that we lack a clear grasp of basic notions such as *interests* and, more importantly, rights. Perhaps we can formulate a reasonable policy concerning the treatment of animals without possessing such perspicuity, but a certain caution seems to be in order.

This essay has not been previously published.
[1] See James Rachels, "Do Animals Have a Right to Liberty?" in this volume.

I

Rachels's first application of his proposed method concerns the right not to be tortured. His reason for thinking that humans have such a right, quite aside from its postulation by the United Nations Declaration, seems to be that a "man has an interest in not being tortured because he has the capacity to suffer pain." More explicitly, then, we have the following argument:

1. Human beings can suffer pain.

2. Hence, human beings have an interest in not being tortured. (from 1)

3. Hence, human beings have a right not to be tortured. (from 2)

His reconstructed parallel argument is, then:

a. Animals (some) can suffer pain.

b. Hence, animals have an interest in not being tortured. (from a)

c. Hence, animals (some) have a right not to be tortured. (from b)

But consider a third parallel argument.

A. Humans can suffer from sexual deprivation.

B. Hence, humans have an interest in not being sexually deprived. (from A)

C. Hence, humans have a right not to be sexually deprived. (from C)

It is not at all plausible to accept C, I submit, even though A and B are each plausible. For an equally dubious argument, substitute "be sick" (and cognates) in place of "sexual deprivation." For the sake of discussion let us treat the first inference in each of the arguments as unproblematic. There is undoubtedly a difficulty, however, in going from the second claim to the third. That is, it is not obviously correct to think a being's having an interest in something is a sufficient condition for concluding that it *has a right* to what is in its interest. So, I conclude that, in the absence of further argument, Rachels cannot justifiably infer that animals have a right not to be tortured (c) from his prior assumption (b). If there is any connection between a being's having interests (not, of course, the same as "being interested in")—and the concept of *interest* is one that needs fuller explication—and having rights, it may turn out that the former is only a necessary and not sufficient condition of the latter.

In Rachels's second attempt to show that animals have rights, he claims that if, as Locke urged, a man may acquire property by mixing his labor with something, so may the squirrel who gathers nuts to eat. Since, he alleges, "there is no relevant difference between the man and the squirrel," either both have a right or neither does. Rachels's argument may not be invalid; it is nonetheless inconclusive for the following reason. Locke's specification of the conditions in virtue of which a being (to be neutral) acquires a property right in something in the Second Treatise (see Sections 27 to 35) is more complicated and would read, more explicitly than Locke himself put it, something like this (where A is some agent and O is an object):

A owns (or comes to own) O if and only if

1. O was unowned (or, to avoid circularity, no one else has mixed his labor with O)

and 2. A mixed his labor with O

and 3. There is enough of O (or O-type stuff) left for others

and 4. What is left is as good as what A is taking.

Without broaching the difficulties with Locke's claims, it seems clear that "if Locke is right" quite a few conditions must be satisfied to acquire property, and it is not sure that squirrels could intentionally or wittingly satisfy these conditions. It is not clear, on the other hand, that one can unintentionally or unwittingly acquire property. Questions fly at us and our intuitions are diverse and shaky here. Does a squirrel's or a spider's energy expenditure count as Lockean *labor?* What of the energies of a Venus Fly Trap? Assuming that he (or she) mixed in the requisite labor, did the whale own Jonah? Perhaps Rachels is not wrong on this matter, but the argument is too sketchy to bear the weight he hopes to rest on it.

Rachels's effort to support the claim that animals have a third right concerns liberty. After considering the possibility that beings have a right to any intrinsic good they are capable of enjoying and liberty is an intrinsic good (to later conclude that animals have a right to liberty) Rachels, thinking few philosophers would agree that liberty is an *intrinsic* good, adopts another strategy and argues that limitations on their liberty, nonetheless, harm the interests of animals. The claim that animals are frequently and significantly harmed in serious ways by captivity, as in his zoo examples and in the case of factory-farming, is, I think, incontrovertible. Similarly, there is little doubt that many experiments on animals inflict extraordinary suffering, and are often done with little attempt to distinguish between cases where the research promises trivial or, alternatively, quite beneficial results. In the midst of documenting these points he proposes a principle similar to one previously considered, "Any creature that has interests has at least a prima facie right not to have those interests needlessly harmed." Let it be conceded that many animals have interests, that many are harmed and, in that sense, their "interests are harmed." Let it also be conceded that this harm often ocucurs needlessly. We still need an argument to *show* what Rachels *asserts:* that creatures with interests thereby have correlative prima facie rights of a sort.[2]

There is an evident alternative view to take here, and it is not merely a callous skepticism. It is simply that we have a duty not to impose suffering or serious deprivation on other sentient creatures and, hence, not on many animals, and we may have a strict obligation to so refrain in the absence of any countervailing moral considerations. Now it may be that the said claim of duty would be entailed by the claim that animals have rights or a prima facie right, say, not to be caused to suffer by rational beings, but the duty may exist without a correlative right. Rachels's arguments do support the claim that rational beings have certain duties toward animals of a certain sort, but he fails to argue the further assumption (if he indeed is implicitly making it) that such duties entail the mentioned rights. Alternatively, if he believes that the fact that a creature has interests entails that that being has rights of a sort, this needs to be argued, I think, and the type of objection to such a claim which I posed early on needs to be subverted. Perhaps it can be; my only point is that the task remains.

II

Partly for the reason of the difficulty just mentioned, I shall not remark at length on Rachels's substantial remarks on "moral freedom." His argument concerning such freedom and the related claim that some animals show compassion is, I submit, inessential to his basic contention

---

[2]This general assumption has been employed by Leonard Nelson in *A System of Ethics* (New Haven: Yale University Press, 1956) and by Joel Feinberg in "The Rights of Animals and Unborn Generations" in William Blackstone (ed.), *Philosophy and Environmental Crisis* (Athens, Georgia: University of Georgia Press, 1975).

about rights. He wishes to maintain that animals have interests and, therefore, prima facie rights. It is reasonable to assume that the set of animals exhibiting compassion constitutes a subset of the animals possessing interests; hence, if his prior argument based on interests were successful there would be no need to appeal to the particular further trait of exhibition of compassion as a basis for rights. Any animal showing a compassionate disposition which lost just that disposition (due, say, to alteration in glandular balance) would presumably still have interests and, hence, on Rachels's view, rights as well. Further, if he were to suggest that only animals exhibiting compassion have rights, the scope of animals possessing rights would surely be restricted in a way that he would disavow; we may assume, then, that he would reject such a move.

In making final remarks, I shall bypass the opportunity to fully explore Rachels's counterarguments in his Appendix, ones designed to show that it is possible for animals to have rights. However, I shall press the general theme; his objections to McCloskey and Ritchie are reasonable ones, but there are, I think, more tempting ways of arguing that animals are not the sort of entities that *can* have rights.[3] Rachels focuses on *similarities* between humans and animals and tends to deemphasize certain differences. This fact may be relevant, for one might argue, roughly along the lines of Michael Tooley or S. I. Benn (in another context), that it is analytic that only persons have rights, that only entities that can function as agents and, perhaps, can conceive of forwarding their projects by an exercising of rights could, in fact, have any rights at all; that animals *lack* this capacity, and hence, regardless of notable *similarities* to humans that have rights, animals are not the sorts of entities that can have rights.[4] I am not persuaded that this line of thought is compelling, but it strikes me as far more tempting than the objections which Rachels, in fact, considers. He cannot be faulted, of course, for not having explored all possible objections, and I offer the point only to advance the inquiry.

So far then I have tried to show that each of Rachels's attempts to show that animals have a right not to be tortured, a right to property if certain conditions are met, or a right to liberty is beset with one or

---

[3] I am not sure, however, whether the positions of Ritchie or Rawls must be or are properly posed as arguments to the effect that it is "not logically possible" for animals to have rights; for example, Ritchie argues only that since (1) if animals had rights, then cats who eat mice would violate the latter's rights, (2) the latter is absurd—so, (3) animals *do not* have rights.

[4] See S. I. Benn, "Abortion, Infanticide, and Respect for Persons" and Michael Tooley, "A Defense of Abortion and Infanticide" in Joel Feinberg (ed.), *The Problem of Abortion* (Belmont, Calif.: Wadsworth Publishing Company, 1973).

more difficulties. More generally the supposition that whatever creatures have interests have correlative rights needs defense, though many of the facts to which he legitimately and usefully calls our attention support a claim that we have certain specific duties to animals. Whether such duties correspond to rights needs investigation. That we have much neglected duties toward animals I have no doubt; the precise nature and extent of those duties is the more burdensome question. I have further suggested that on certain views about the grounds for having rights, even "natural rights," it may be that some humans (e.g., neonatal ones) as well as all animals do not possess rights; such an objection deserves examination.

As a final demurrer I note that at the outset Rachels states that one of his motives is to "cast doubt on the importance of human rights," but the body of his paper does not tend to do this at all. In fact, Rachels seems to seriously weaken the mentioned claim very quickly by defining "human rights" to mean "distinctively human rights" (rights possessed only by human beings if at all). Now even if many rights generally called human rights are not human rights in the sense of distinctively human rights (supposing that some are shared with animals), with the result that the *number* of distinctively human rights is fewer than previously thought, it is most difficult to see how this goes any distance toward the possible task of casting doubt on the importance of human rights, distinctively human ones or not. Nor is it clear why Rachels maintains "that human rights are not nearly so interesting or important as philosophers and politicians have thought."

JAMES RACHELS

A Reply to VanDeVeer

Suppose we believe that human beings have a right not to be tortured, and the question is raised whether other animals also have this right. How can this issue be investigated? One way is by asking whether there are any *differences* between humans and nonhumans that would justify us in thinking that humans have the right but that animals don't. If we cannot find any such differences, and if in fact humans and nonhumans are very much *alike* in the relevant respects—most obviously, in that both can suffer pain, and so both have the same basic interest in not being tortured—then we may conclude, provisionally at least, that nonhumans also have this right.

In the first part of his paper Donald VanDeVeer represents this argument as depending on the assumption that "a being's having an interest in something is a sufficient condition for concluding that it has a right to what is in its interest." But I don't think the argument requires any such assumption. That humans and nonhumans have the same sort of interest in not being tortured is simply an important fact that must be taken into account in assessing the similarities and differences between them. My argument only says that, if there are such important similarities, and there aren't any relevant differences, then human and nonhuman animals must be in the same boat.

I use the same strategy in arguing that animals have a right to liberty. Now it isn't clear exactly why *humans* have this right; therefore I consider several possibilities and argue in each case that there is no relevant difference between humans and (at least some) nonhumans. First I

This essay has not been previously published.

consider the view that humans have a right to liberty because liberty is intrinsically good, and individuals have a right not to be deprived of goods which they are capable of enjoying. If *that* is why humans have the right, then other animals must have it too, since they are also capable of enjoying this intrinsic good. Second, suppose it is thought that humans have a right to liberty because they have interests which are harmed by a loss of freedom, and individuals have a right that their interests not be needlessly harmed. Here I point out that other animals also have interests that suffer when they are deprived of liberty. Third, it has been suggested that liberty has a special importance for humans because humans are moral agents. Against this I argue that some other animals have moral capacities, too.

VanDeVeer objects that in order for my arguments to be successful it must be proved that "creatures with interests thereby have correlative prima facie rights of a sort." But I don't think so. All that is needed for my argument is to show that, for each plausible account of why humans have a right to liberty, a similar account may be provided in the case of other animals. The business about interests is one possible account of why humans have this right; and my point is just that there is no important difference between the human case and the animal case in this respect. As for the business about animals' moral capacities, I don't think there is anything in that argument which even slightly suggests that "*only* animals exhibiting compassion have rights." The point of that discussion was to show that we cannot cite the moral capacities of humans as a rational basis for ascribing to them rights which we deny to every other creature.

The strategy of argument that I employ is not absolutely conclusive, because it is always possible that with respect to some particular right there are relevant differences between humans and nonhumans that we have overlooked. But this only means that we must be careful. We must compare the characteristics of humans and other animals as carefully as possible, and we must be careful to distinguish the relevant characteristics from the irrelevant ones—bearing in mind that what is relevant in the case of one right may not be relevant in the case of other rights. If we are careful, then I think that the use of this method will bring us as close to the truth as we are likely to get in this area. At the very least, this method of investigating the issue of animal rights will produce more reliable results than arguments based on such dubious generalizations as "only entities that can function as agents and, perhaps, can conceive of forwarding their projects by an exercising of rights could, in fact, have any rights at all."

Nowhere in his paper does VanDeVeer try to show that there are differences between humans and nonhumans relevant to the question of whether animals possess the rights that I discuss. He does suggest that there *might* be such differences, and I concede that—I simply see no reason to think that there *are* any. And if there aren't, then we are wrong to deny these rights to animals while claiming them for ourselves.

Epílogue

JONATHAN SWIFT

A Modest Proposal

It is a melancholy object to those, who walk through this great town,[1] or travel in the country, when they see the streets, the roads, and cabin-doors, crowded with beggars of the female sex, followed by three, four, or six children, *all in rags*, and importuning every passenger for an alms. These mothers instead of being able to work for their honest livelihood, are forced to employ all their time in strolling, to beg sustenance for their helpless infants, who, as they grow up, either turn thieves for want of work, or leave their dear Native Country to fight for the Pretender in Spain, or sell themselves to the Barbadoes.

I think it is agreed by all parties, that this prodigious number of children, in the arms, or on the backs, or at the heels of their mothers, and frequently of their fathers, is in the present deplorable state of the kingdom, a very great additional grievance; and therefore whoever could find out a fair, cheap and easy method of making these children sound useful members of the commonwealth would deserve so well of the public, as to have his statue set up for a preserver of the nation.

But my intention is very far from being confined to provide only for the children of professed beggars, it is of a much greater extent, and shall take in the whole number of infants at a certain age, who are born of parents in effect as little able to support them, as those who demand our charity in the streets.

As to my own part, having turned my thoughts, for many years, upon

From Jonathan Swift, "A Modest Proposal for Preventing the Children of Poor People from Being a Burthen to Their Parents or Country, and for Making Them Beneficial to the Public" (1729).
[1] [Dublin].

this important subject, and maturely weighed the several schemes of other projectors, I have always found them grossly mistaken in their computation. It is true a child, just dropped from its dam, may be supported by her milk for a solar year with little other nourishment, at most not above the value of two shillings, which the mother may certainly get, or the value in scraps, by her lawful occupation of begging, and it is exactly at one year old that I propose to provide for them, in such a manner, as, instead of being a charge upon their parents, or the parish, or wanting food and raiment for the rest of their lives, they shall, on the contrary, contribute to the feeding and partly to the clothing of many thousands.

There is likewise another great advantage in my scheme, that it will prevent those voluntary abortions, and that horrid practice of women murdering their bastard children, alas, too frequent among us, sacrificing the poor innocent babes, I doubt, more to avoid the expense, than the shame, which would move tears and pity in the most savage and inhuman breast.

The number of souls in this kingdom being usually reckoned one million and a half, of these I calculate there may be about two hundred thousand couples whose wives are breeders, from which number I subtract thirty thousand couples, who are able to maintain their own children, although I apprehend there cannot be so many under the present distresses of the kingdom, but this being granted, there will remain an hundred and seventy thousand breeders. I again subtract fifty thousand for those women who miscarry, or whose children died by accident, or disease within the year. There only remain an hundred and twenty thousand children of poor parents annually born: The question therefore is, how this number shall be reared, and provided for, which, as I have already said, under the present situation of affairs, is utterly impossible by all the methods hitherto proposed, for we can neither employ them in handicraft, or agriculture; we neither build houses, (I mean in the country) nor cultivate land: they can very seldom pick up a livelihood by stealing till they arrive at six years old, except where they are of towardly parts, although, I confess they learn the rudiments much earlier, during which time, they can however be properly looked upon only as *probationers*, as I have been informed by a principal gentleman in the County of Cavan, who protested to me, that he never knew above one or two instances under the age of six, even in a part of the kingdom so renowned for the quickest proficiency in that art.

I am assured by our merchants, that a boy or a girl, before twelve years old, is no saleable commodity, and even when they come to this age, they will not yield above three pounds, or three pounds and half-acrown at most on the Exchange, which cannot turn to account either to the parents or the kingdom, the charge of nutriment and rags having been at least four times that value.

I shall now therefore humbly propose my own thoughts, which I hope will not be liable to the least objection.

I have been assured by a very knowing American of my acquaintance in London, that a young healthy child well nursed is at a year old a most delicious, nourishing, and wholesome food, whether stewed, roasted, baked, or boiled, and I make no doubt that it will equally serve in a fricassee, or a ragout.

I do therefore humbly offer it to public consideration, that of the hundred and twenty thousand children, already computed, twenty thousand may be reserved for breed, whereof only one fourth part to be males, which is more than we allow to sheep, black-cattle, or swine, and my reason is that these children are seldom the fruits of marriage, a circumstance not much regarded by our savages, therefore one male will be sufficient to serve four females. That the remaining hundred thousand may at a year old be offered in sale to the persons of quality, and fortune, through the kingdom, always advising the mother to let them suck plentifully in the last month, so as to render them plump, and fat for a good table. A child will make two dishes at an entertainment for friends, and when the family dines alone, the fore or hind quarter will make a reasonable dish, and seasoned with a little pepper or salt will be very good boiled on the fourth day, especially in winter.

I have reckoned upon a medium, that a child just born will weigh 12 pounds, and in a solar year if tolerably nursed increaseth to 28 pounds.

I grant this food will be somewhat dear, and therefore very proper for landlords, who, as they have already devoured most of the parents, seem to have the best title to the children.

Infants' flesh will be in season throughout the year, but more plentiful in March, and a little before and after, for we are told by a grave author, an eminent French physician, that fish being a prolific diet, there are more children born in Roman Catholic countries about nine months after Lent, than at any other season; therefore reckoning a year after Lent, the markets will be more glutted than usual, because the number of Popish infants, is at least three to one in this kingdom, and therefore it will have one other collateral advantage by lessening the number of Papists among us.

I have already computed the charge of nursing a beggar's child (in which list I reckon all cottagers, labourers, and four-fifths of the farmers) to be about two shillings *per annum*, rags included, and I believe no gentleman would repine to give ten shillings for the carcass of a good fat child, which, as I have said will make four dishes of excellent nutritive meat, when he hath only some particular friend, or his own family to dine with him. Thus the Squire will learn to be a good landlord, and grow popular among his tenants, the mother will have eight shillings net profit, and be fit for work till she produces another child.

Those who are more thrifty (as I must confess the times require) may flay the carcass; the skin of which, artificially dressed, will make admirable gloves for ladies, and summer boots for fine gentlemen. . . .

. . . I am not so violently bent upon my own opinion, as to reject any offer, proposed by wise men, which shall be found equally innocent, cheap, easy and effectual. But before something of that kind shall be advanced in contradiction to my scheme, and offering a better, I desire the author, or authors will be pleased maturely to consider two points. First, as things now stand, how they will be able to find food and raiment for an hundred thousand useless mouths and backs. And secondly, there being a round million of creatures in human figures, throughout this kingdom, whose whole subsistence put into a common stock, would leave them in debt two millions of pounds sterling adding those, who are beggars by profession, to the bulk of farmers, cottagers, and labourers with their wives and children, who are beggars in effect. I desire those politicians, who dislike my overture, and may perhaps be so bold to attempt an answer, that they will first ask the parents of these mortals, whether they would not at this day think it a great happiness to have been sold for food at a year old, in the manner I prescribe, and thereby have avoided such a perpetual scene of misfortunes, as they have since gone through, by the oppression of landlords, the impossibility of paying rent without money or trade, the want of common sustenance, with neither house nor clothes to cover them from the inclemencies of the weather, and the most inevitable prospect of entailing the like, or greater miseries upon their breed for ever.

I profess in the sincerity of my heart that I have not the least personal interest in endeavouring to promote this necessary work, having no other motive than the *public good of my country, by advancing our trade, providing for infants, relieving the poor, and giving some pleasure to the rich.* I have no children, by which I can propose to get a single penny; the youngest being nine years old, and my wife past childbearing.

DESMOND STEWART

The Limits of Trooghaft

The Troogs took one century to master the planet, then another three to restock it with men, its once dominant but now conquered species. Being hierarchical in temper, the Troogs segregated *homo insipiens* into four castes between which there was no traffic except that of bloodshed. The four castes derived from the Troog experience of human beings.

The planet's new masters had an intermittent sense of the absurd; Troog laughter could shake a forest. Young Troogs first captured some surviving children, then tamed them as "housemen," though to their new pets the draughty Troog structures seemed far from house-like. Pet-keeping spread. Whole zoos of children were reared on a bean diet. For housemen, Troogs preferred children with brown or yellow skins, finding them neater and cleaner than others; this preference soon settled into an arbitrary custom. Themselves hermaphrodite, the Troogs were fascinated by the spectacle of marital couplings. Once their pets reached adolescence, they were put in cages whose nesting boxes had glass walls. Troogs would gaze in by the hour. Captivity—and this was an important discovery—did not inhibit the little creatures from breeding, nor, as was feared, did the sense of being watched turn the nursing females to deeds of violence. Cannibalism was rare. Breeders, by selecting partners, could soon produce strains with certain comical features, such as cone-shaped breasts or cushion-shaped rumps.

The practice of keeping pets was fought by senior Troogs; the conservative disapproved of innovations while the fastidious found it objectionable when bean-fed humans passed malodorous wind. After the

Reprinted from *Encounter* (London, February 1972), by permission of Anthony Sheil Associates, agents for Desmond Stewart.

innovation became too general to suppress, the Troog elders hedged the practice with laws. No pet should be kept alive if it fell sick, and since bronchitis was endemic, pets had short lives. The young Troogs recognised the wisdom behind this rule for they too disliked the sound of coughing. But in some cases they tried to save an invalid favourite from the lethal chamber, or would surrender it only after assurances that the sick were happier dead.

Adaptability had enabled the Troogs to survive their travels through time and space; it helped them to a catholic approach to the food provided by the planet, different as this was from their previous nourishment. Within two generations they had become compulsive carnivores. The realisation, derived from pet-keeping, that captive men could breed, led to the establishment of batteries of capons, the second and largest human caste. Capons were naturally preferred when young, since their bones were supple; at this time they fetched, as "eat-alls," the highest price for the lowest weight. Those kept alive after childhood were lodged in small cages maintained at a steady 22 degrees; the cage floors were composed of rolling bars through which the filth fell into a sluice. Capons were not permitted to see the sky or smell unfiltered air. Experience proved that a warm pink glow kept them docile and conduced to weight-gain. Females were in general preferred to males and the eradication of the tongue (sold as a separate delicacy) quietened the batteries.

The third category—the ferocious hound-men—were treated even by the Troogs with a certain caution; the barracks in which they were kennelled were built as far as possible from the batteries lest the black predators escape, break in and massacre hundreds. Bred for speed, obedience and ruthlessness, they were underfed. Unleashed they sped like greyhounds. Their unreliable tempers doomed the few surreptitious efforts to employ them as pets. One night they kept their quarters keening in rhythmic sound; next day, they slumped in yellow-eyed sulks, stirring only to lunge at each other or at their keepers' tentacles. None were kept alive after the age of thirty. Those injured in the chase were slaughtered on the spot and minced for the mess bowl.

Paradoxically, the swift hound-men depended for survival on the quarry they despised and hunted: the fourth human caste, the caste most hedged with laws.

The persistence, long into the first Troog period, of lone nomadic rebels, men and women who resisted from remote valleys and caves, had perplexed the planet's rulers. Then they made an advantage out of the setback. The wits and endurance of the defeated showed that the Troogs had suppressed a menace of some mettle. This was a compliment and Troogs, like the gods of fable, found praise enjoyable. They decided to

preserve a caste of the uncorralled. This fourth caste, known as quarry-
men or game, were protected within limits and seasons. It was forbidden, for example, to hunt pre-adolescents or pregnant females. All
members of the caste enjoyed a respite during eight months of each
year. Only at the five-yearly Nova Feast—the joyous commemoration of
the greatest escape in Troog history—were all rules abandoned: then
the demand for protein became overpowering.

Quarry-men excited more interest in their masters than the three
other castes put together. On one level, gluttonous Troogs found their
flesh more appetising than that of capons. On another, academically
minded Troogs studied their behavior-patterns. Moralising Troogs ex-
tolled their courage against hopeless odds to a Troog generation inclined
to be complacent about its power. The ruins which spiked the planet
were testimony to the rudimentary but numerous civilisations which,
over ten millennia, men had produced, from the time when they first
cultivated grains and domesticated animals till their final achievement of
an environment without vegetation (except under glass) and with only
synthetic protein. Men, it was true, had never reached the stage where
they could rely on the telepathy that served the Troogs. But this was no
reason to despise them. Originally Troogs, too, had conversed through
sound hitting a tympanum; they had retained a hieroglyphic system deep
into their journey through time; indeed, their final abandonment of what
men called writing (and the Troogs "incising") had been an indirect
tribute to men: telepathic waves were harder to decipher than symbols.
It moved antiquarian Troogs to see that some men still frequented the
ruined repositories of written knowledge; and though men never re-
paired these ancient libraries, this did not argue that they had lost the
constructional talents of forbears who had built skyscrapers and pyra-
mids. It showed shrewd sense. To repair old buildings or build new ones
would attract the hound-men. Safety lay in dispersal. Libraries were a
place of danger for a quarry-man, known to the contemptuous hound-
men as a "book-roach." The courageous passion for the little volumes
in which great men had compressed their wisdom was admired by
Troogs. In their death throes quarry-men often clutched these talismans.

It was through a library that, in the fifth Troog century, the first attempt was made to communicate between the species, the conquerors
and the conquered.

Curiosity was a characteristic shared by both species. Quarry-men
still debated what the Troogs were and where they had come from. The
first generation had known them as Extra-Terrestrials, when Terra,
man's planet, was still the normative centre. Just as the natives of central America had welcomed the Spaniards as gods till the stake gave the

notion of the godlike a satanic quality, millions of the superstitious had identified the Troogs with angels. But Doomsday was simply Troog's Day. The planet continued spinning, the sun gave out its heat and the empty oceans rolled against their shores. Living on an earth no longer theirs, quarry-men gazed at the glittering laser beams and reflected light which made the Troog-Halls and speculated about their tenants. A tradition declared that the first space vehicles had glowed with strange pictures. The Troogs, it was correctly deduced, had originally conversed by means analogous to language but had discarded speech in order to remain opaque, untappable. This encouraged some would-be rebels. They saw in precaution signs of caution and in caution proof of fallibility. A counter-attack might one day be possible, through science or magic. Some cynics pretended to find the Troogs a blessing. They quoted a long-dead writer who had believed it was better for a man to die on his feet when not too old. This was now the common human lot. Few quarry-men lived past thirty and the diseases of the past, such as cardiac failure and carcinoma, were all but unknown. But most men dreamed simply of a longer and easier existence.

The first human to be approached by a Troog was a short, stocky youth who had survived his 'teens thanks to strong legs, a good wind and the discovery of a cellar underneath one of the world's largest libraries. Because of his enthusiasm for a poet of that name, this book-roach was known to his group as "Blake." He had also studied other idealists such as the Egyptian Akhenaten and the Russian Tolstoy. These inspired him to speculate along the most hazardous paths, in the direction, for example, of the precipice-question: might not the Troogs have something akin to human consciousness, or even conscience? If so, might man perhaps address his conqueror? Against the backspace of an insentient universe one consciousness should greet another. His friends, his woman, laughed at the notion. They had seen what the Troogs had done to their species. Some men were bred to have protuberant eyes or elongated necks; others were kept in kennels on insufficient rations, and then, at the time of the Nova Feast or in the year's open season, unleashed through urban ruins or surrounding savannah to howl after their quarry—those related by blood and experience to Blake and his fellows. "I shall never trust a Troog," said his woman's brother, "even if he gives me a gold safe-conduct."

One Troog, as much an exception among his species as Blake among his, read this hopeful brain. It was still the closed season and some four months before the quinquennial Nova Feast. Quarry-men still relaxed in safety; the hounds sang or sulked; the Troogs had yet to prepare the lights and sounds for their tumultuous celebrations. Each morning Blake climbed to the Library. It was a long, rubbish-encumbered place with aisles still occupied by books, once arranged according to subject, but now higgledy-piggledy in dust and dereliction, thrown down by earthquake or scattered in the hunt. Each aisle had its attendant bust—Plato, Shakespeare, Darwin, Marx—testifying to a regretted time when men, divided by nationality, class or colour, suffered only from their fellows.

In the corner watched by Shakespeare, Blake had his reading place. He had restored the shelves to some order; he had dusted the table. This May morning a Troog's fading odour made him tremble. A new object stood on his table: a large rusty typewriter of the most ancient model. In it was a sheet of paper.

Blake bent to read.

Are you ready to communicate question.

Blake typed the single word: *yes.*

He did not linger but retreated in mental confusion to the unintellectual huddle round babies and potatoes which was his cellar. He half feared that he had begun to go mad, or that some acquaintance was playing him a trick. But few of his group read and no man could duplicate the distinctive Troog smell.

The days that followed constituted a continual seance between "his" Troog and himself. Blake contributed little to the dialogue. His Troog seemed anxious for a listener but little interested in what that listener thought. Blake was an earphone, an admiring confessor. Try as he feebly did, he got no response when he tried to evoke his woman, his children.

"Trooghaft, you are right," wrote the unseen communicator, attested each time by his no longer frightening scent, "was noble once." Blake had made no such suggestion. "The quality of being a Troog was unfrictional as space and as tolerant as time. It has become—almost human."

Then next morning: "To copy the habits of lower creatures is to sink below them. What is natural to carnivores is unnatural to us. We never ate flesh before the Nova; nor on our journey. We adopted the practice from reading the minds of lower creatures, then copying them. Our corruption shows in new diseases; earlier than in the past, older Troogs decompose. It shows in our characters. We quarrel like our quarry. Our forms are not apt for ingesting so much protein. Protein is what alcohol was to humans. It maddens; it corrupts. Protein, not earth's climate, is paling our. . . ."

Here there was a day's gap before the typewriter produced, next morning, the word *complexion.* And after it, *metaphor.* Blake had learnt that the old Troog hieroglyphs were followed by determinants, symbols showing, for example, whether the concept *rule* meant tyranny or order. Complexion could only be used metaphorically of faceless and largely gaseous creatures.

To one direct question Blake obtained a direct answer: "How," he had typed, "did you first turn against the idea of eating us?"

"My first insight flashed at our last Nova Feast. Like everyone, I had been programmed to revel. Stench of flesh filled every Troog-Hall. Amid the spurt of music, the ancient greetings with which we flare still, the coruscations, I passed a meat-shop where lights pirouetted. I looked. I saw. Hanging from iron hooks—each pierced a foot-palm—were twenty she-capons, what you call women. Each neck was surrounded by a ruffle to hide the knife-cut; a tomato shut each anus. I suddenly shuddered. Nearby, on a slab of marble, smiled a row of jellied heads. Someone had dressed their sugar-hair in the manner of your Roman empresses: 'Flavian Heads.' A mass of piled up, tong-curled hair in front, behind a bun encoiled by a marzipan fillet. I lowered myself and saw as though for the first time great blocks of neutral-looking matter: 'Paté of Burst Liver.' The owner of the shop was glad to explain. They hold the woman down, then stuff nutriment through a V-shaped funnel. The merchant was pleased by my close attention. He displayed his Sucking Capons and Little Loves, as they call the reproductive organs which half of you split creatures wear outside your bodies."

"Was this," I asked in sudden repugnance, "Trooghaft?"

Encouraged by evidence of soul, Blake brought to the Troog's notice, from the miscellaneous volumes on the shelves, quotations from his favourite writers and narrative accounts of such actions as the death of Socrates, the crucifixion of Jesus and the murder of Che Guevara. Now in the mornings he found books and encyclopaedias open on his table as well as typed pages. Sometimes Blake fancied that there was more than one Troog smell; so perhaps his Troog was converting others.

Each evening Blake told Janine, his partner, of his exploits. She was at first sceptical, then half-persuaded. This year she was not pregnant and therefore could be hunted. For love of her children, the dangers of the Nova season weighed on her spirits. Only her daughter was Blake's; her son had been sired by Blake's friend, a fast-runner who had sprained his ankle and fallen easy victim to the hounds two years before. As the Nova Feast approached, the majority of the quarry-men in the city began to leave for the mountains. Not that valleys and caves were secure; but the mountains were vast and the valleys remote one from another. The hound-men preferred to hunt in the cities; concentrations of people made their game easier.

Blake refused to join them. Out of loyalty Janine stayed with him.

"I shall build," the Troog had written, "a bridge between Trooghaft and Humanity. The universe calls me to revive true Trooghaft. My Troog-Hall shall become a sanctuary, not a shed of butchers."

Blake asked: "Are you powerful? Can you make other Troogs follow your example?"

The Troog answered: "I can at least do as your Akhenaten did."

Blake flushed at the mention of his hero. Then added: "But Akhenaten's experiment lasted briefly. Men relapsed. May not Troogs do likewise?" He longed for reassurance that his Troog was more than a moral dilettante.

Instead of an answer came a statement:

"We can never be equals with *homo insipiens*. But we can accept our two species as unequal productions of one universe. Men are small, but that does not mean they cannot suffer. Not one tongueless woman moves, upside-down, towards the throat-knife, without trembling. I have seen this. I felt pity, *metaphor*. Our young Troogs argue that fear gives flesh a quivering tenderness. I reject such arguments. Why should a complex, if lowly, life—birth, youth, growth to awareness—be sacrificed for one mealtime's pleasure?"

Although Blake recognised that his Troog was soliloquising, the arguments pleased him. Convinced of their sincerity, Blake decided to trust his Troog and remain where he was, not hide or run as on previous occasions. There was a sewer leading from his refuge whose remembered stench was horrible. He would stay in the cellar. On the first day of the Nova Feast he climbed as usual to his corner of the library. But today there was no paper in the typewriter. Instead, books and encyclopaedias had been pulled from the shelves and left open; they had nothing to do with poetry or the philosophers and the stench was not that of his Troog. Sudden unease seized him. Janine was alone with the children, her brother having left to join the others in the mountains. He returned to his cellar and, as his fear already predicted, found the children alone, wailing in one corner. The elder, the boy, told the doleful tale. Two hound-men had broken in and their mother had fled down the disused sewer.

Blake searched the sewer. It was empty. His one hope, as he too hid there, lay in his Troog's intervention. But neither the next day nor the day after, when he stole to the library, watching every shadow lest it turn to a hound-man, was there any message. This silence was atoned for on the third morning.

"If we still had a written language, I should publish a volume of confessions." The message was remote, almost unrelated to Blake's anguish.

He read, "A few fat-fumes blow away a resolution. It was thus, the evening of the Nova Feast's beginning. Three Troog friends, *metaphor*, came to my Hall where no flesh was burning, where instead I was pondering these puny creatures to whom we cause such suffering. 'You cannot exile yourself from your group; Trooghaft is what Troogs do together.' I resisted such blandishments. The lights and sounds of the Nova were enough. I felt no craving for protein. Their laughter at this caused the laser beams to buckle and the lights to quiver. There entered four black hound-men dragging a quarry-female, filthy from the chase, her hands bound behind her. I was impassive. Housemen staggered under a great cauldron; they fetched logs. They placed the cauldron on a tripod and filled it with water; the logs were under it."

Blake shook as he read. This was the moment for his Troog to incarnate pity and save his woman.

"They now unbound and stripped the female, then set her in the water. It was cold and covered her skin with pimples.

"Again laughter, again the trembling lights and the buckling lasers.

"We, too, have been reading, brother. We have studied one of their ways of cooking. *Place the lobster*—their name for a long extinct sea-thing—*in warm water. Bring the water gently to the boil. The lobster will be lulled to sleep, not knowing it is to be killed. Most experts account this the humane way of treating lobster.*

"The logs under the cauldron gave a pleasant aroma as they started to splutter. The female was not lulled. She tried to clamber out: perhaps a reflex action. The hound-men placed an iron mesh over the cauldron."

Blake saw what he could not bear to see, heard the unhearable. The Troog's confession was humble.

"The scent was so persuasive. 'Try this piece,' they flashed, 'it is so tender. It will harden your scruples.' I hesitated. Outside came the noise of young Troogs whirling in the joy of satiety. A Nova Feast comes only once in five years. I dipped my hand, *metaphor*"—(even now the Troog pedantry was present)—"in the cauldron. If one must eat protein, it is better to do so in a civilised fashion. And as for the humanity, *metaphor*, of eating protein—I should write Trooghaft—if we ate no capons, who would bother to feed them? If we hunted no quarry, who would make the game-laws or keep the hound-men? At least now they live, as we do, for a season. And while they live, they are healthy. I must stop. My stomach, *metaphor*, sits heavy as a mountain."

As Blake turned in horror from the ancient typewriter, up from his line of retreat, keening their happiest music, their white teeth flashing, loped three lithe and ruthless hound-men. All around was the squid-like odour of their master.

FURTHER READING

This is not a complete list of sources but a select list of especially valuable books in the field. Many of the earlier works are out of print, but may be found in a major reference library.

AMORY, CLEVELAND. *Man Kind?* New York: Harper & Row, 1974. This book is worth reading for its account of what humans have done to wild animals.

GODLOVITCH, S. and R. and HARRIS, J., eds. *Animals, Men and Morals.* New York: Taplinger, 1972. A collection of thirteen contributions detailing the facts of our treatment of animals, placing these facts within a critical moral framework, and suggesting sociological perspectives from which to understand our attitudes to animals. The most radical book about animals to be published since *Animals' Rights.*

GOMPERTZ, LEWIS. *Moral Inquiries on the Situation of Man and of Brutes.* London, 1824. One of the first carefully argued proposals for a radically different attitude to animals, with a discussion of the effect this would have on our lives. The author, who was a driving force in the early animal welfare movement, later published another work, *Fragments in Defence of Animals* (1852), but the earlier book is more thorough.

HARRISON, RUTH. *Animal Machines.* London: Stuart, 1964. The first book to reveal the effects of factory farm techniques on animal welfare. Still the best source of information on many aspects of modern farming.

Report of the Technical Committee to Enquire into the Welfare of Animals Kept under Intensive Livestock Husbandry Systems ("The Brambell Report"), Command Paper 2836. London: Her Majesty's Stationery Office, 1965. The full report of the most authoritative impartial study of animal welfare under modern farming conditions.

RYDER, RICHARD. *Victims of Science*. London: Davis-Poynter, 1975. The most complete and up-to-date account of the use of animals in experimentation, by a psychologist who was once himself an experimenter.

SALT, HENRY S. *Animals' Rights*. London, 1892; revised eds. until 1915. The first chapter, partially reprinted in this volume, contains an argument for granting rights to anmals if we grant them to humans. Later chapters discuss cruelties to domestic and wild animals. There are many valuable references to earlier works on the subject.

SINGER, PETER. *Animal Liberation*. New York: New York Review, 1975. A radical attack on our present attitudes and practices toward other animals.

TURNER, E. S. *All Heaven in a Rage*. London: Michael Joseph, 1964. A history of the fight in Britain against cruelty to animals, which manages to be both informative and entertaining.

WILLIAMS, HOWARD. *The Ethics of Diet*. London, 1896. A compilation of extracts from writers advocating vegetarianism, from the ancient Greeks to the nineteenth century. An invaluable reference for anyone interested in the history of vegetarianism.

BIOGRAPHICAL NOTES

AQUINAS, SAINT THOMAS (c. 1224–1274), was a Catholic theologian and philosopher. His writings have had an enormous influence on subsequent Catholic thought.

ARISTOTLE (384–322 B. C.), one of the greatest of Greek philosophers. Wrote extensively in all the major areas of philosophy, and has had a lasting influence.

BENTHAM, JEREMY (1748–1832), an English philosopher and one of the most famous spokesmen for the view called "utilitarianism"; also made important contributions in the field of jurisprudence.

DARWIN, CHARLES (1809–1882) was an English biologist whose theory of evolution had a profound impact on ideas in science, theology, and philosophy.

DESCARTES, RENÉ (1596–1650), sometimes called "the father of modern philosophy," was one of philosohy's most original and influential thinkers. His *Meditations* remains a philosophical classic.

FEINBERG, JOEL is a professor of philosophy and chairman of the Department of Philosophy at The Rockefeller University, New York. He has written many books and articles, including *Doing and Deserving, Essays in the Theory of Responsibility* (Princeton University Press, 1970) and *Social Philosophy* (Prentice-Hall, 1973).

HUME, DAVID (1711–1776) was born in Edinburgh, Scotland. He wrote extensively in philosophy, history, and economics. His major philosophical works include *A Treatise of Human Nature* and *An Inquiry Concerning the Principles of Morals.*

JENKINS, PETER is political columnist of *The Guardian*, London. He broadcasts on political and international questions and is the author of *The Battle of Downing Street* (Charles Knight, 1970).

KANT, IMMANUEL (1724–1804) was a German philosopher who credited the work of David Hume with "waking him from (his) dogmatic slumber." Kant's important works in ethics include *Groundwork for the Metaphysic of Morals* and *Lectures on Ethics*.

MIDGLEY, MARY is a lecturer in philosophy at the University of Newcastle upon Tyne, England. Her publications include "Is Moral a Dirty Word?" (*Philosophy*, 1972), "The Game Game" (*Philosophy*, 1974), and "The Neutrality of the Moral Philosopher" (*Proceedings of the Aristotelian Society*, 1974).

MILL, JOHN STUART (1806–1873), English philosopher and economist, was perhaps the most influential spokesman for the liberal view of man during his lifetime. His *Utilitarianism* is a classic text in ethics.

MONTAIGNE (1533–1592), French philosopher and essayist, was an important spokesman for skepticism. His most important philosophical work is "Apology for Raimond Sebond."

PLUTARCH (c. 46–120), Greek biographer and moralist, is most famous for his *Lives*.

RACHELS, JAMES is a member of the philosophy department at the University of Miami. He is the editor of the popular anthology *Moral Problems* (Harper and Row, 1971, 1975) and the author of articles on ethics in various philosophical journals, as well as being chairman of the Society for Philosophy and Public Affairs.

REGAN, TOM teaches philosophy at North Carolina State University, Raleigh, where he has twice received recognition as an Outstanding Teacher. He is the author of a number of articles as well as an introductory text, *Understanding Philosophy* (Dickenson, 1974).

RICKABY, JOSEPH, S. J. (1845–1932), was a nineteenth-century Jesuit philosopher whose *Moral Philosophy* had a wide circulation in Roman Catholic colleges and institutions.

RITCHIE, D. G. (1853–1903) was a British philosopher who wrote mainly on ethics and political philosophy. His most important work was *Natural Rights*.

RYDER, RICHARD a clinical psychologist who gave up experimental psychology, in part because of his opposition to experiments using animals, is now vice-chairman of the R.S.P.C.A.'s Animal Experimentation Advisory Committee. He is the author of *Victims of Science* (David-Poynter, 1975) as well as several articles on aspects of animal welfare.

SALT, HENRY S. (1851–1939), English humanitarian, wrote many books and essays on topics ranging from flogging to wildflowers. An active reformer, he campaigned against the death penalty, and for improved prison conditions, as well as in behalf of animals. His best known works about animals are *Animals' Rights, The Logic of Vegetarianism,* and *The Humanities of Diet.* Although now little read, he was friendly with and had considerable influence on such figures as George Bernard Shaw and Gandhi.

SCHOPENHAUER, ARTHUR (1788–1860), a German philosopher, is the author of writings that are famous both for their pessimism and for the importance attached to the will. His major work in ethics is *The Basis of Morality.*

SCHWEITZER, ALBERT (1875–1965), renowned missionary and winner of the Nobel Peace Prize of 1952, was active in philosophy, theology, and music.

SINGER, PETER has taught philosophy at University College, Oxford, and New York University. He is now a member of the Department of Philosophy at La Trobe University, Victoria, Australia. His publications include *Democracy and Disobedience* (Oxford University Press, 1973) and *Animal Liberation* (New York Review/Random House, 1975).

STEWART, DESMOND describes himself as "educated in England, re-educated in Iraq." He has lived largely in the Middle East since 1948, and has been a vegetarian since 1970. His novels include the trilogy *A Sequence of Roles* (Chapman and Hall, 1965, 1966, 1968), and among his factual works is the recently published *Theodor Herzl, Artist and Politician* (Doubleday and Hamish Hamilton, 1974).

SWIFT, JONATHAN (1667–1745) was born in Dublin and served as Dean of St. Patricks, Dublin. He is famous for essays both humorous and satirical.

VANDEVEER, DONALD is a member of the philosophy department at North Carolina State University, Raleigh. He teaches in the areas of political and moral philosophy, and medical ethics. His publications have appeared in the *American Political Science Review, Philosophy & Phenomenological Research,* and the *Canadian Journal of Philosophy.*

VOLTAIRE (1694–1778), French philosopher and essayist, is the author of the *Philosophical Dictionary* and, among other moral tales, *Candide.*

WHITE, ROBERT J., M. D. is currently Director of the Neurological and Brain Research Laboratory at Cleveland's Metropolitan General Hospital. He is a leading figure in brain transplant research.